Kid Stuff

PUBLISHING FOR THE WORLD
125 Years
THE JOHNS HOPKINS UNIVERSITY PRESS

. . . . Kid Stuff

Marketing Sex and Violence to America's Children

Edited by

Diane Ravitch *&* Joseph P. Viteritti

THE JOHNS HOPKINS UNIVERSITY PRESS
Baltimore & London

The Johns Hopkins University Press
2715 North Charles Street
Baltimore, Maryland 21218-4363
www.press.jhu.edu

Library of Congress Cataloging-in-Publication Data

Kid stuff : marketing sex and violence to America's children / edited by
Diane Ravitch and Joseph P. Viteritti.
    p.   cm.
Includes bibliographical references and index.
    ISBN 0-8018-7327-4 (hardcover : alk. paper)
    1. Violence in popular culture—United States.   2. Vulgarity in
popular culture—United States.   3. Violence in mass media—United
States.   4. Children and violence—United States.   5. Youth and
violence—United States.   6. United States—Social conditions—1980—   7.
Violence—Psychological aspects.   I. Ravitch, Diane.   II. Viteritti,
Joseph P., 1946–
    HN90.V5 K5 2003
    303.6'0973—dc21

                                                        2002011066

A catalog record for this book is available from the British Library.

Illustrations by Adrienne Brook Gruver.

Contents

Contributors

Diane Ravitch (Editor) is a research professor in the Steinhardt School of Education at New York University and holds the Brown Chair in Education Policy at the Brookings Institution. She served as assistant secretary in the U.S. Department of Education from 1991 to 1993. Her most recent book is *The Language Police: How Pressure Groups Restrict What Students Learn.*

Joseph P. Viteritti (Editor) is a research professor of public policy in the Wagner Graduate School of Public Service at New York University. He has served as a senior advisor to the heads of the New York, Boston, and San Francisco public school systems. His most recent book is *Choosing Equality: School Choice, the Constitution and Civil Society.*

Professors Ravitch and Viteritti co-chair the Program on Education and Civil Society at New York University. They have previously co-edited *Making Good Citizens: Education and Civil Society; City Schools: Lessons From New York;* and *New Schools For a New Century: The Redesign of Urban Education.*

Craig A. Anderson is a professor and chair in the Psychology Department at Iowa State University. He served as a consultant to the National Institute of Mental Health for the preparation of the Report of the Surgeon General on Youth Violence. He recently testified before the U.S. Senate on the impact of interactive violence on children.

Jeffrey Jensen Arnett is affiliated with the Department of Human Development at the University of Maryland. He is the author of *Metalheads: Heavy Metal Music and Adolescent Alienation* and *Adolescence and Emerging Adulthood: A Cultural Approach.*

Peter G. Christenson is a professor of communication at Lewis and Clark College in Oregon. He is the co-author of *It's Not Only Rock & Roll: Popular Music in the Lives of Adolescents* and two recent reports on substance abuse in entertainment media.

Ed Donnerstein is a professor of communications and dean of the College of Social and Behavioral Sciences at the University of Arizona. His major research interests are in mass-media violence, as well as mass-media policy. He has published over two hundred scientific articles in these areas and serves on the editorial boards of a number of academic journals in both psychology and communication.

Jeanne B. Funk is a professor of psychology and director of the clinical psychology training program at the University of Toledo. She has published several studies examining the relationship between playing violent video games and aspects of children's personality and behavior. She gave testimony on her research to the U.S. Senate Committee on Commerce, Science, and Transportation in March 2000.

Todd Gitlin is a professor of journalism and sociology at Columbia University. His books include *Media Unlimited: How the Torrent of Images and Words Overwhelms Our Lives* and *The Twilight of Common Dreams: Why America is Wracked by Culture Wars*.

Kay S. Hymowitz is a contributing editor to *The City Journal*, a quarterly publication of the Manhattan Institute, and an affiliate scholar at the Institute for American Values. She is the author of *Ready or Not: What Happens When We Treat Children as Small Adults.*

Elisabeth Lasch-Quinn is a professor of history in the Maxwell School at Syracuse University. Among her books are *Black Neighbors* and *Race Experts*. She also edited *Women and the Common Life.*

Nell Minow is the author of *The Movie Mom's Guide to Family Movies* and has operated the Movie Mom's Web site since 1995.

Newton Minow, counsel to the Chicago law firm of Sidley, Austin, Brown, and Wood, served as chair of the Federal Communications Commission by appointment of President John F. Kennedy. He is the co-author of *Abandoned in the Wasteland: Children, Television and the First Amendment.*

Thomas N. Robinson is an assistant professor of pediatrics and of medicine in the Division of General Pediatrics and the Center for Research for Disease Prevention at Stanford University. He has performed a number of studies of the effects of media exposure and experimental reduction of media exposure on children's health and behaviors.

Stacy L. Smith is an assistant professor in the Department of Communications at Michigan State University. She has written extensively on how exposure to media violence influences the socio-emotional development of children.

Acknowledgments

This book is the fourth in a series of edited volumes published under the auspices of the Program on Education and Civil Society at New York University. General funding for the Program and this project has been generously provided by the John M. Olin Foundation. We take this occasion to especially thank Peter Flanigan, James Piereson, and Janice Riddel for their warm support and encouragement over the last eight years.

This book has given us another opportunity to collaborate with our friends at the John Hopkins University Press. As usual, our editor Jacqueline Wehmueller was a great source of ideas and energy, and Carol Zimmerman was a delight to work with through the final stages of production.

We also received valuable assistance from two of our graduate students. Kevin Kosar helped with the research for our introductory chapter; Hannah Meira Richman worked with the other authors to help assemble the various chapters into a book.

The views expressed in the chapters are solely attributable to their authors. We appreciate their cooperation and high standards of scholarship.

Kid Stuff

Toxic Lessons

Children and Popular Culture

Diane Ravitch and Joseph P. Viteritti

Raising children has never been more difficult in the United States than it is today. Families, religious institutions, and communities have been weakened by a variety of forces associated with modernization and technology. The social consensus that once supported parents in projecting the values they wish to teach their children has faltered. Some parents are confused about their own values, about what they should teach their children, or whether they should try to project any values at all. Even as such bedrock institutions as the family appear shaky, the mass media grow stronger and more assertive in the lives of most people. Television, movies, and the Internet have become our primary sources of information and, in some cases, of our judgments and values. Since the mass media usually project elite values or conflicting messages, the result has been a mixed bag of opportunities and risks. Although there is great social benefit in the rapid distribution of information through our populace, there is a potential danger when key institutions of civil society lose their influence and abdicate their most important functions to distant and unaccountable institutions.

In the past generation, several trends have coincided to create problems for families raising children. First, many children have a significant amount of disposable income, making them attractive as consumers to commercial enterprises and giving them a degree of independence from parental control that is unprecedented. Second, many parents of these children came of age in an era when they learned not to be judgmental about the values and behavior of others. Third, during this same period of time, the entertainment industry developed sophisticated means of targeting young people with music, video games, and other media that contain pernicious messages. This book aims to examine these trends and the mass marketing of popular entertainment that merchandises hatred, violence, and pornography.

In our society, the courts consider virtually all forms of communication to be protected by the First Amendment of the Constitution. In a seven to two decision handed down in May 2002, the United States Supreme Court struck down a federal law that made it a crime to create, distribute, or process "virtual" child pornography that used computer images rather than actual children, finding that the production of such material creates no real victims.[1] In the same month, a federal appeals court in Philadelphia struck down the Children's Internet Protection Act of 2001, which required public libraries to install filtering technology to prevent access to Internet material that could be harmful to minors.[2] Here the court found the filtering technology used under the legislation to be a "blunt instrument" that excluded unobjectionable as well as objectionable material and violated the First Amendment rights of other library patrons. The Children's Internet Protection Act of 2001 was the third attempt by Congress since 1996 to pass a law to protect children from pornography on the Internet. Each of these laws was overturned in the courts.

We count ourselves among those who are devoted to a generous interpretation of the First Amendment and to the fullest protection by law for speech and expression. We have no desire to see the government censor what we read, hear, and view. We think, however, it is time to look closely at the question of whether families have a responsibility to supervise their children's exposure to certain forms of the popular culture and, when appropriate, shield them from certain media that may actually be harmful to their development. One purpose of this collection, therefore, is to present the existing research evidence on the observed effects of media that glorify and exalt hatred, violence, racism, sexism, homophobia, and other extreme forms of antisocial behavior. Another is to open a dialogue among thoughtful scholars about whether and how a democratic society should protect children from harmful messages without compromising the basic rights granted by its Constitution.

Certainly there is much that is available to young people through the mass media that is beneficial. A reasonable amount of time devoted to watching television can increase children's knowledge of the world, especially if parents are involved in monitoring their selections. Television offers a broad range of programs that teach about history, literature, music, science, the arts, current affairs, and world cultures; as a result, children today have greater opportunities to learn about the world than any generation before them. Similarly, children today can gain access to treasure lodes of information through wise use of the Internet. Every form of media offers a wide array of experiences for children, from enlightening to horrible. It is the job of parents to encourage the former and exclude the latter.

The authors of the chapters that follow explore the effects of a toxic version of the popular culture: the video games that enable children to kill and maim with impunity, the music and videos that celebrate hatred and violence, and other media that attack the norms of responsible behavior. The merchandising of this popular culture—which is created in the studios of media giants—has become an important and incredibly lucrative aspect of the entertainment industry. We distinguish this phenomenon from a genuine popular culture that emanates from ordinary people as *vox populi*.

There are several important issues we seek to address in this volume. First, how pervasive is popular culture in the lives of young people? Second, what effect does it have on impressionable young people? Third, which young people are most influenced—and how—by the most egregious forms of popular culture? Fourth, is it possible, without diluting, jeopardizing, or violating the requirements of our constitutional system, to restrict children's access to the most toxic versions of these media? Can our democracy encourage discretion without encouraging censorship? That is the dilemma presented to us today by the growing availability of extreme media and the absence of any reasonable standards by which to judge its effects.

American Adolescents

In 2002 psychologist Lawrence Steinberg summarized disturbing new data about the condition of our nation's youth, drawn from the National Longitudinal Study of Adolescent Health (known among social scientists as Addhealth).[3] Steinberg, an expert on adolescence, presented a troubling array of new findings about American students in grades 7 through 12. Approximately 40 percent of the twelve thousand adolescents surveyed indicated having feelings of depression. Nearly half had begun smoking regularly by the age of 14. Half drank alcohol at least monthly. Nearly 30 percent had tried marijuana by the age of 14, and one-third of them had come to school intoxicated. One-third had had sexual intercourse by the end of the 9th grade, over two-thirds by the time they graduate from high school, and 20 percent of the girls had become pregnant at least once. Nearly 20 percent of urban students had seen someone shot or stabbed during the year prior to the Addhealth survey.

Professor Steinberg cited this data in the context of other behavioral patterns he had observed in his research, which show the extent to which today's young people are psychologically and emotionally disengaged.[4] He and his colleagues have found that between 30 and 40 percent of the adolescents they interviewed describe themselves as "just going through the motions" with regard to school and say that neither they nor most of their peers take school very seriously or believe that it is an important influence in their lives. Even more distressing, many are also disengaged from their parents. Steinberg discovered that between one-fourth and one-third of American parents are not even minimally involved in their children's lives, including what goes on in their schools. When neither schools nor parents exert a serious influence on the lives of young people, others will fill the void. This is where the media comes in. Media influence, for good and ill, becomes far greater when parents abstain from responsibility for their children.

When young people, for example, are exposed to the homophobic and misogynist lyrics of Eminem, the sexual adventurism of Madonna, or the violent, drug-infested life styles of "gangsta" rappers, they are exposed to values that undermine good character. Each of these performers in his or her own way, is teaching lessons in life, lessons about how people are supposed to interact. Each is teaching behavior, attitudes, and ideals that most parents would reject. Several of the chapters in this book explore how this version of the popular culture affects children whose values and character are still developing. Do parents know what their children are doing? One point that emerges from these chapters is that they do not; apparently, many parents knowingly or unknowingly allow their children to spend hours each day with these performers, listening to, watching, and perhaps absorbing antisocial messages.

In Loco Parentis

There was a time, not so long ago, when parents expected to exert a definitive influence in shaping their children's attitudes and behavior, when churches played an important role in developing a sense of moral responsibility, when community institutions helped inform and engage civic commitment, and when schools instilled ideals of correct behavior that supported strong citizenship and responsible personal behavior. These institutions still exist, but their role in cultivating the character and behavior of young people has been compromised and neglected in the past generation. In many cases, these institutions have relinquished to the popular culture, as defined by the mass media, their responsibilities for shaping the minds, hearts, and souls of the younger generation. The information kids receive daily influences their attitudes and ideals, not just those concerning sex and violence, but also their views about institutions, material wealth, consumerism, their peers, and themselves. These messages help shape individual character, but not always in positive ways.

Eyes shut, many parents in this media age hand off their children as if they were cars at a car wash. They send them to school and then neglect their ongoing responsibility to meet with teachers and to remain involved with what happens to their children, not only during school hours but also after school. As children grow older, parents grow less involved in their daily lives. They relinquish their children unthinkingly to anyone who comes along over the airwaves. The process of parental acquiescence happens so gradually that it is hardly detectable without some appreciation of history.

The emotional bond between parents and their children has for many centuries been considered one of the most fundamental instincts of human nature. Most parents, like most other living beings, are inclined to protect their offspring and do what is best for them. Aristotle observed long ago that the family is the primary unit upon which all other social institutions are built.[5] In ancient Greece the family also served as an economic unit. Family farms produced food; and various artisans—be they coopers or blacksmiths, weavers or millers—provided other necessities with the help of their children. This kind of social arrangement existed in most of Europe through the Middle Ages.[6] As various crafts developed into guilds, the family remained the key unit for social development and interaction. Fathers would initiate their sons into a trade, and mothers would teach their daughters how to run a household. One of the more striking aspects of this feudal structure was the level of control that parents had over the upbringing of their children, integrating within the family the physical, social, moral, and occupational development of the child. Even apprentice relationships outside the family structure were highly personal, often based on a strong sense of mutual obligation between the master and his charge.

A similar pattern existed in the United States until well into the nineteenth century. Even when colonial Americans assigned the education of their children to someone outside the household, it was usually a teacher or clergyman who reinforced values that were initially learned at home.[7] The industrial revolution changed much of this. Parents—first the father and then also the mother—left home to work in factories. Before child labor laws, children too entered the workforce. No longer under the tutelage of caring adults, children who became factory workers were now valued solely as objects of economic production, better understood as a form of exploitation. While children were expected to work hard under the apprenticeship arrangement, attention was also given to their personal development and the acquisition of skills. In the factory, they merely functioned as unskilled laborers.

The creation of the public schools provided by the government transferred responsibility for children's education from the household to a governmental institution. The well-documented religious controversies that took place in the United States during the nineteenth century between Catholics and Protestants over what was taught in public schools were the first sign of a tension between values inculcated in the home and values taught by the government.[8] Many leaders of the common school movement saw schools as a mechanism to replace the traditions and customs of their immigrant parents, which school reformers considered inadequate, immoral, or backwards.[9] Throughout the twentieth century, schools have served as battlegrounds over values that adults could not resolve among themselves.[10] Despite these episodic political outbursts among the "grown ups," one could generally assume that by the end of the twentieth century, children, now removed from the factories and attending school, were spending their days with caring adults who were focused on their healthy upbringing.

When the late sociologist James Coleman completed his landmark study of adolescents in the late 1950s, he found that most teenagers lived in self-created autonomous communities, a teen world situated in the high school.[11] Most, especially those in cities, attended school in large institutions that were created to process large numbers of students and where close interactions with adults were difficult and haphazard. The resulting adolescent subcultures, set apart from adult influence, were built around a desire to win the respect and admiration of one's peers. In many ways, the adolescent society was a mirror of the adult society.

Adolescent autonomy was encouraged by the belief, prevalent among many educators, that young people were independent beings capable of forming their own opinions about important life issues, especially the difference between right and wrong. An ascending legal culture, focused on children's rights, drew boundaries between educators and children that made it increasingly difficult for the former to set rules and norms for the latter.[12] With the rise of student rebellions in the late 1960s, schools became targets for litigation, and many educators simply backed off from asserting adult authority rather than risk not only conflict and lawsuits but also being perceived as authoritarian. Some educators have even displayed a reluctance to enforce the basic standard of honesty on school examinations, compromising the fundamental integrity of the educational process. In a national survey taken by the Josephson Institute on Ethics in the year 2000, seven out of ten of the 8,600 high school students interviewed admitted cheating on a test at least once in the previous year.[13]

When adults are reluctant to set norms concerning the difference between right and wrong, youngsters get the message that there is no difference. This reluctance on the part of adults to become involved with young people is an abdication of responsibility. Psychological research dating back nearly a century has portrayed adolescence as a troublesome period characterized by "storm and stress."[14] Today, far too many teenagers are expected to weather the storm without a rudder. Worse, they are left to make their own way to adulthood with the popular media as their guide.

In 1982 James Coleman published a series of lectures he had delivered at Syracuse University in a book aptly titled *The Asymmetric Society*.[15] In it Coleman described a new social order, which, unlike that of a previous age, did not grow out of the household as the manor and the estate once did. In this new order, the family was depleted as a locus of production and socialization, with both adults and children spending more time outside the home. Evacuation of the home left certain people vulnerable, especially those who were dependent, including children and the elderly. Children became vulnerable because the corporate structure that defined the outside world did not, for the most part, have their interests in mind. The messages children got on the outside were often in conflict with the values taught in the home. In order to develop a moral sense that allows them to distinguish between right and wrong, Coleman explained, children need consistency and reinforcement. When children who move between one setting and another are barraged with conflicting messages, the dissonance hampers their ability to grow into well-balanced adults.

Coleman put his finger on the one powerful influence that would define the potential and the hazards of child rearing at the turn of the new century. He predicted that the instructional role once played by the school would be shared with the popular media. Unfortunately, the captains of the media industries are no more inclined to act in the best interests of the child than the factory masters of yesteryear. Contrasting the current situation with a time when the formation of social norms took place in institutions that were an extension of the family, Coleman explained: "The genesis of norms in a society with extensive mass media controlled by corporate actors . . . is a by-product, sometimes even an accidental one, of the interests of the corporate actor in gaining an audience or in changing attitudes to favor its interests. Part of this occurs through advertising, part through movies, television, and music. The extensive use of sex in both these areas exemplifies this well: the use of sex attracts attention and is important both to advertisers and to purveyors of entertainment generally."[16]

Coleman made that observation in the early 1980s. Even he, however, could not have anticipated the immense power that the media command today. The average American child spends 5.5 hours a day interacting with some form of electronic entertainment.[17] For those between the ages of 8 and 18, the time devoted to the popular media climbs to 7 hours, meaning that exposure increases with age. This exceeds the time adolescents spend with their parents or teachers. The enchantment begins at a very early age, before children even learn to walk or talk, and continues through adulthood.

It is difficult to assess the full impact that the media have on the quality of our individual and communal lives because some effects are more subtle than others. For example, in his groundbreaking work on the decline of civic involvement among Americans, political scientist Robert Putnam identified television as one of the major causes of people's detachment from their neighbors. The more time people spend in front of a television, the less time they spend with each other or involved in the kinds of social activities that once animated civic life. According to Putnam, television absorbed 40 percent of Americans' free time in 1995, an increase of one-third since 1965.[18] One wonders how many hours of study or other productive activity might be lost by the average child sitting in front of a screen. What effect does the negative portrayal of political leaders on television and in movies have on the level of cynicism that young people exhibit? Who are the heroes today that our young people are encouraged to emulate?[19] Are they the valiant police officers and firefighters who braved the flames at the World Trade Center? Or are they the popular performers that Hollywood produces for mass consumption?

Other influences are less subtle. A recent study by the Henry J. Kaiser Family Foundation found that the amount of sexually explicit material shown on television significantly increased in only three years in the late 1990s.[20] The study found that the probability that a television character engaging in sexual intercourse was a teenager had tripled. Research reported in the *Journal of the American Medical Association* revealed a high level of violence in cartoons and animated movies regularly viewed by young children.[21] Once popular scenes of Tom and Jerry whacking each other have given way to *anime*, a more sophisticated genre of head-smashing combat among superheroes and exotic warriors produced in Japan. At the same time, the *Journal of the Academy of Child and Adolescent Psychiatry* reported growing evidence that violent presentations in the media may have a negative influence on children and adolescents.[22] The lessons children learn from the media can be as toxic to their psychological development as tobacco smoke is to their physical development. Yet, while merchants are prohibited from selling cigarettes to minors, material that is inappropriate for young audiences is easily accessible to all.

Several years ago, a dispute broke out in Harlem when a local minister protested a billboard advertisement that he claimed was marketing tobacco products to children. He said that the familiar cartoon figure of a camel smoking a cigarette gave children the false impression that smoking is fun and harmless. When the minister's protests drew the attention of local news stations, the tobacco company took the sign down. Joe Camel is now an extinct species in the world of marketing. At the same time, however, young people remain exposed to role models in the entertainment media who regularly indulge in all forms of substance abuse, including drinking alcohol and taking dangerous drugs.

To be sure, the analogy between tobacco and toxic media is not perfect. The relationship between what kids see and how they behave is not measurable in the same way as the effect of smoke on the lungs. The link between smoking and cancer can be scientifically proven with laboratory experiments, but conclusions about the effects of interacting regularly with violent and obscene images must rely on the softer evidence of social science research. Some social scientists assert that there is no verifiable connection.[23] Given the ambiguous nature of much behavioral research, there may never be unanimity on this question within the scholarly community. Nonetheless, evidence for the negative effects of such interaction is growing, suggesting that very young children and at-risk adolescents are especially vulnerable to the influence of the media. And children are increasingly the targets of sophisticated marketing campaigns to promote media products.

An investigation released by the Federal Trade Commission in 2000 found that movie, music, and video game producers aggressively market violent entertainment products to young people.[24] Today the 32 million adolescents who live in the United States have more disposable income than ever before. In the year 2000, they spent a total of $100 billion.[25] It is no mystery why big media have exploited this lucrative market.

Cool Heads Prevail

When violence occurs in a school—as it did in 1999 at Columbine High School in Littleton, Colorado, where two students killed thirteen of their classmates—a shocked nation turns its attention to the possible role that the media play in fostering such a tragedy.[26] Media violence and other forms of inappropriate entertainment have been the subject of Congressional hearings and emerged as widely discussed topics in the 2000 presidential campaign. Following the tragedy at Columbine High School, the American Medical Association, the American Academy of Pediatrics, the American Psychological Association, and the American Academy of Child and Adolescent Psychology issued a joint statement warning that depictions of violence in television, music, and video games are linked to an increase in violence among young people.[27] The statement explained that prolonged exposure to violence causes emotional desensitization and eventually leads to aggressive attitudes, values, and behavior. A more recent study performed by researchers from Columbia University and the New York State Psychiatric Institute found a significant association between the amount of time spent watching television during adolescence and early adulthood and aggressive acts in later years.[28]

Video games intensify the power of the media in the lives of children. Now violence is no longer just a spectator sport; interactive media like video and computer games allow children to simulate violence while perpetuating the illusion that it is harmless and has no consequences. The Internet presents its own unique risks. Through it young people have access to products once restricted to adults-only establishments, and child pornographers sell lurid and exploitative photographs.[29] The existence of anonymous chat rooms and other forms of personal communication makes children vulnerable to adults who pursue them as sexual prey.[30] From time to time, we learn of a child who was abducted by a stranger whom she or he initially encountered in an Internet chat room.[31] Kids no longer need to leave their homes, or even their rooms, to consort with unsavory, dangerous, or predatory characters.

Parents frequently express alarm about the violent or vulgar merchandise that is targeted on their children. In a report prepared by Public Agenda, a survey research organization, 63 percent of the parents interviewed said that they worried about the amount of sex and violence their children see on television.[32] More than 90 percent indicated that they supported a rating system. Despite their expressions of concern, however, parents let their children stay tuned, like chain smokers switching from one brand to another without ever breaking the habit. Although the V-chip, which excludes inappropriate material, has been installed as standard equipment on every television manufactured since 1999 and is widely available, only 7 percent of parents utilize it to monitor what their children watch.[33] Part of the problem with the V-chip is supposedly technical, with many parents claiming ignorance of how to use it. This is a generation of parents who have mastered a wide range of electronic equipment, including personal computers, cell phones, VCRs, and palm-corders. Why are they so intimidated by the V-chip? Could the problem be motivational? Are parents reluctant to exercise their responsibilities as adults?

The same Public Agenda survey documenting parental concerns showed a wide gap between the attitudes of younger and older adults. Twenty-five percent of the 18–30 cohort "are worried" about sex and violence on TV, compared to 49 percent in the 31–44 cohort, 57 percent in the 45–60 cohort, and 69 percent in the 61+ cohort. Ironically, men and women in their primary childbearing years are less concerned than older adults.

Perhaps the 18–30 age group will change its views as it becomes older and its children become adolescents. Many American parents seem to be fearful of being considered prudes by their peers. They are prudophobic. Prudophobia is a condition that first afflicts people when they reach adolescence. Like nearsightedness, it usually abates with age. Like most mental conditions, however, its cure is affected by other psychological needs evident among the afflicted. Since the condition is associated with youth, many aging parents have an especially difficult time overcoming it. They don't want to seem like old fogies. They want to appear youthful and open-minded to each other, their children, and, most of all, themselves. Some convince themselves that the condition allows them to get along better with their children, who are also experiencing adolescent anxieties. They want to be their children's friends, which may not be in the best interest of their children.

A Matter of Upbringing

Parents have an immediate stake in the popular media that envelop their children. They are the only individuals in the world who can be expected to put the interests of their children before anything else. They don't need to justify the actions they take to protect their own children. They do not need to wait for definitive evidence that the material their children see and hear is harmful in order to act. Parents are constantly required to calculate the risks their children are exposed to, and many are sanguine about setting firm boundaries for their protection when it comes to other matters. While others might argue that the uncertainty of risk is a justification for inaction, parents should be more inclined to think that uncertain consequences are a reason to act prudently.

Setting standards for young people, however, is not just a matter of avoiding risk. The upbringing of children involves a conscious commitment to elevation of the mind, body, and spirit, not their degradation. That means cultivating sound civic and personal values. It means cultivating the capacity to distinguish between entertainment that is enriching and entertainment that degrades and diminishes human life. It means cultivating an appreciation for good literature, music, film, and art in its many wonderful manifestations. When government sets the standards, it is censorship; when parents set standards, it is an affirmation that they are ready and able to be responsible adults and take charge of their children's formative process.

The marketing of noxious products to children is one aspect of a general degradation of the culture that affects everyone. In our society, there are certain social norms that are widely shared: we do not have public executions; we do not torture people or animals; we do not tolerate cock fighting or dog fighting; we do not laud suicide bombers; we respect human life and celebrate the dignity of the individual. These are not values and attitudes that spring from the air. They are carefully cultivated in our houses of worship; they are respected by our secular public officials. They pervade our culture, but they are not self-taught. They must be consistently taught by parents, teachers, and responsible adults to growing children.

Although the social environment offers them meager support, mothers and fathers are powerful influences on their children. They can serve as role models for their children; they can determine what materials are welcome in their homes; they can restrict spending on undesirable products; and they can enforce standards for their children's behavior.

Our objective in this book is to raise the level of public awareness concerning the nature of the messages conveyed by certain elements of the popular media and the way in which these messages affect our children. The book is directed to parents, media executives, educators, scholars, and anyone else who cares about children. Books seldom change individual behavior, but they can launch public discussions that do. Our hope is that the ensuing discussion will help develop a better symmetry between those who care about our children, especially parents, and those who take charge of their upbringing.

About This Book

Incorporating the observations and research of scholars from a variety of backgrounds, the essays in this book are of two types: Some are thoughtful commentaries on how popular media shape the environment for child rearing in our time; others examine the existing empirical evidence on what we know and what we don't know about the effects of exposure to these media. Since expertise on the subject tends to be dispersed among researchers who focus on particular forms of media, we have chosen contributors who are experts in each of these forms, including television, movies, the Internet, music, and video games.

In the next chapter, Todd Gitlin explains how the lessons children learn through the popular culture function as the unacknowledged curriculum that they bring to school. He warns that this curriculum creates an expectation of sensation and interruption that has a negative effect on a young person's ability to be a disciplined student. He notes how this curriculum works against the best efforts of good teachers. He urges educators to resist the use of dumbed-down programs in media literacy and to stick with good writing, good film, and the historical fundamentals in a manner commensurate with their professional and civic responsibilities.

Elisabeth Lasch-Quinn (chapter 3) writes that exposing children to the imagery of explicit sex and violence is part of a larger problem with the American culture, which she finds obscene in both style and substance. She describes a ubiquitous obscenity marked by a fundamental indecency, moral relativism, and offensiveness. Drawing on the work of historians, political theorists, and cultural critics, she explores four characteristics that contribute to this culture: the absence of social boundaries, an instrumental view of people, a lack of proportion in human endeavors, and an overall incoherence.

Stacy L. Smith and Ed Donnerstein (chapter 4) investigate the effects that exposure to different types of content in television and film has on the social and emotional development of young viewers. They review the research on how much time youngsters spend with mass media, what depictions they are routinely exposed to, and the possible negative effects of such exposure. They discuss how the Internet—the newest mass medium—may be influencing children.

Peter G. Christenson (chapter 5) asserts that music is the medium that adolescents take most seriously and on which they depend most to establish their personal and social identities. He summarizes thirty years of research on the effects of popular music, focusing on the nature of many problematic messages that now prevail, especially those concerning sexual relationships, violence, and substance abuse. He concludes that popular music can exert a number of influences, some benign, but others more troubling for particular youths.

Jeffrey Jensen Arnett (chapter 6) concentrates on music "on the edge" that has widely been viewed by adults as offensive, outrageous, and dangerous. Providing an overview of music in the twentieth century he looks at jazz, rock 'n' roll, rock, heavy metal, and rap. He explains why such music has appealed to so many young people. Considering whether such music is a problem, he concludes that edge music such as heavy metal and rap should not be dismissed as "just music" because it can have a cumulative effect on the character, worldview, and behavior of some listeners.

Craig A. Anderson (chapter 7) begins his essay with a brief history of video games, their changing content, and the rising level of exposure to them. He reviews the research evidence on how they affect thoughts, feelings, and behavior. He presents recent findings showing that exposure to violent video games increases aggressive thoughts and behavior among youngsters while decreasing positive social affects and behavior.

Jeanne B. Funk (chapter 8) has developed a psychological model for identifying children who are most vulnerable to the influence of violent video and computer games. She finds that the most at-risk children are those whose moral development is a "work in progress" or already impaired—for example, younger children, bullies, those who have problems regulating their emotions, those easily frustrated, and those who constantly seek stimulation. Her profile is relevant to other forms of media exposure.

Thomas N. Robinson (chapter 9) analyzes the effects that reduced exposure to television and video games has on behavior. Drawing on a series of his own empirical studies, he finds that reduced exposure decreases the incidence of aggressive behavior as well as the level of consumerism children exhibit.

Kay S. Hymowitz (chapter 10) challenges the common assumption that most parents are inclined to control their children's exposure to violent and sexually explicit media. Citing research, she explains that many parents are the product of a revolution in thinking about child rearing — shared by educators, judges, and entertainment executives — that redefines children as competent, independent and autonomous decision-makers. Caught between their distaste for a coarse and degraded popular culture and their belief in a free flow of information, parents, she finds, are in a bind that makes them ill-equipped to deal with the new realities of contemporary childhood.

Newton Minow and Nell Minow (chapter 11) consider how the fear of censorship has curtailed government action in protecting children from inappropriate material. They provide a historical overview of the role that government has played in regulating television and other media. They discuss how the government and the public can assume a more positive role protecting children without undermining cherished constitutional principles.

NOTES

1. *Ashcroft v Free Speech Coalition*, 122 Sup.Ct. 1389 (2002).

2. *American Library Association v United States* (Civil Action #011303); *Multnomah County Public Library v United States* (Civil Action #011322).

3. Laurence Steinberg, "The State of Adolescence," paper presented at the Brookings Institution May 14, 2002.

4. Laurence Steinberg, B. Bradford Brown, and Sanford M. Dornbusch, *Beyond the Classroom: Why School Reform Has Failed and What Parents Need to Do* (New York: Touchstone Books, 1997).

5. *The Politics of Aristotle*, Ernest Barker, ed. (New York: Oxford University Press, 1962), pp. 1–38.

6. Philippe Ariés, *Centuries of Childhood: A Social History of Family Life* (New York: Alfred A. Knopf, 1962).

7. Barry Alan Shain, *The Myth of American Individualism: The Origins of American Political Thought* (Princeton: Princeton University Press, 1994), pp. 48–83.

8. Diane Ravitch, *The Great School Wars: A History of the New York City Public Schools* (Baltimore: Johns Hopkins University Press, 2000); Lloyd P. Jorgenson, *The State and the Non-Public School, 1825–1925* (Columbia: University of Missouri Press, 1987).

9. Christopher Lasch, *Children in a Heartless World: The Family Besieged* (New York: Basic Books, 1977).

10. Rosemary C. Salomone, *Visions of Schooling: Conscience, Community, and Common Education* (New Haven: Yale University Press, 2000).

11. James S. Coleman, *The Adolescent Society* (New York: Free Press, 1961). See also James S. Coleman, *Adolescents and Schools* (New York: Basic Books, 1965).

12. Gerald Grant, *The World We Created at Hamilton High* (Cambridge: Harvard University Press, 1988).

13. Giselle Durham, "Many Teen-Agers Lie, Cheat," Associated Press, 16 October 2000.

14. G. Stanley Hall, *Life and Confessions of a Psychologist* (New York: Appleton, 1922).

15. James S. Coleman, *The Asymmetric Society* (Syracuse: Syracuse University Press, 1992).

16. Ibid., p. 136.

17. Donald F. Roberts, Ulla G. Foehr, Victoria J. Rideout, and Mollyann Brodie, *Kids & Media @ the New Millennium: A Comprehensive National Analysis of Children's Media Use* (Menlo Park, Calif.: The Henry J. Kaiser Family Foundation, 1999).

18. Robert D. Putnam, *Bowling Alone: The Collapse and Revival of American Community* (New York: Simon and Schuster, 2000), p. 223.

19. William Damon, "To Not Fade Away: Restoring Civil Identity Among the Young," in *Making Good Citizens: Education and Civil Society*, ed. Diane Ravitch and Joseph P. Viteritti (New Haven: Yale University Press, 2001).

20. "Sex on TV: A Biennial Report," Kaiser Family Foundation, 2001.

21. Fumie Yakota and Kimberly Thompson, "Violence in G-rated Animated Films," *Journal of the American Medical Association*, vol. 283 (May 2000).

22. Susan Villani, "Impact of Media on Children and Adolescents," *Journal of the Academy of Child and Adolescent Psychiatry*, vol. 40 (April 2001).

23. Henry Jenkins, Testimony Before the United States Senate Committee on Commerce, Science, and Transportation, 4 May 1999. *Congressional Record*, 106th Cong., 2nd sess., pp. 1–18.

24. Federal Trade Commission, *Marketing Violent Entertainment to Children: A Review of Self-Regulation and Industry Practices in the Motion Picture, Music Recording and Electronic Game Industries* (Washington, D.C., September 2000).

25. *Frontline*, "The Merchants of Cool," Public Broadcasting System, 2000.

26. Such violence is not a uniquely American phenomenon. In spring 2002, a student who had been suspended from the Gutenberg School in Erfurt, Germany opened fire with an automatic weapon, killing sixteen people and himself.

27. Jesse J. Holland, "Groups Link Media to Child Violence," Associated Press, 26 July 2000.

28. Jeffrey G. Johnson et al., "Television Viewing and Aggressive Behavior During Adolescence and Adulthood," *Science*, vol. 295 (29 March 2002).

29. Philip Jenkins, *Beyond Tolerance: Child Pornography on Line* (New York: New York University Press, 2001).

30. David Finkelhor, Kimberly J. Mitchell, and Janis Wolak, "Online Victimization: A Report on the Nation's Youth" (Alexandria, Va.: National Center for Missing and Exploited Children, June 2000).

31. See, for example, Cory Kilgannon, "Slain Girl Used Internet to Seek Sex, Police Say," *New York Times*, 22 May 2002.

32. Public Agenda Online, www.publicagenda.org/issues/nation_divided_detail.cfm?issue_type=family&list=

33. Jim Rutenberg, "Survey Shows Few Parents Use TV V-Chip to Limit Children's Viewing," *New York Times*, 25 July 2001.

. . . 2

Teaching amid the
Torrent of Popular Culture

Todd Gitlin

L et us start with the obvious—so obvious, in a way, it is commonly taken for granted. You are a teacher, you are supposed to teach the young, meaning that when you are done with them, they are supposed to know things they did not know when they walked into your classroom, including how to know still more and how to assess what they know. You are supposed to leave them knowing what (theories, facts, methods) and knowing how (procedures for learning what they have not yet learned and for sorting wheat from chaff). At best, you are to leave them not only more knowledgeable but also more curious about the world. You are to start with their potential for knowledge and understanding and ex- tract—educe—from them some of their unrealized powers, in particular the powers of reason, imagination, and character. You are to do this in part through your command of the curriculum, the (in principle) orderly structure in which knowledge arrives. Your professional skill lies in your ability to deliver that curriculum, which consists both of specific facts and procedures (names, dates, mathematical methods, and so on) and of demonstrations of what it is like to think.

Of course, your students do not arrive in class as tabulae rasae. Your curriculum, the official one approved and passed down by school authorities, inscribed in textbooks, tested, graded, and succeeded by other curricula, contends with an informal curriculum, the one that the students bring with them to school—a huge and interwoven set of songs, stories, gestures, terms, tones, slogans, icons, cartoon and celebrity names and gossip which they have derived from a virtually lifelong immersion in television, recorded music, radio, billboards, video games, and the other media that penetrate their everyday lives. I am not saying that this unacknowledged curriculum is all that your students experience or know. A great deal of thought and imagination is bound up in their lives elsewhere, in the play that they undertake beyond media, their sports, reading, informal home lessons, family contact, and religious activities; but to a large and probably growing degree, their sense of the world is bound up with media. It is from media that much of their shared vocabulary is drawn. The heroes that bind them are likely to be media celebrities, drawn mainly from the worlds of entertainment and sports.

Not that media channels supply a formal curriculum in the strict sense of an ordered sequence of knowledge. On the contrary, the curriculum of popular culture is not sequential. No authorities test knowledge of popular culture in a rigorous way that leads to promotion, failure, and mental improvement or the lack of it. Still, the informal curriculum of popular culture takes up much of your students' mental attention. Equally important, it contributes mightily to the web of social associations that bind them to one another. A welter of items, associations, and fascinations circulate through all the media of our time and through peer groups, making jingles, themes, names, styles, logos, and the like familiar to them—and not only familiar, but interesting.

Youngsters' *interest* is what interests me. Interest is not only an intellectual but an emotional state. Popular culture absorbs a great deal of young people's attention and does so in a fashion that commands feeling. It is not just that information about stars, sneakers, and teams circulates. What these fascinations deliver to your students is more than facts. They deliver emotions—indeed, they are expected to do so—and sometimes the much more protracted moods, which are, in the words of the psychologist Dylan Evans, "background states that raise or lower our susceptibility to emotional stimuli."[1] (If media fail to deliver emotions or moods, they are boring—boredom being an emotional state to be avoided, but an emotional state nevertheless.) Your students not only know popular culture, they feel it. The feeling supports the knowledge.

They love, like, hate, disdain, fear, and otherwise experience emotions triggered by popular culture and in circulation there. (If "hate" has become synonymous with "dislike," and "great" or "incredible" synonymous with "good," the preference for such extreme, one-dimensional expression in soap operas, popular music, and so forth is surely not irrelevant.) At peak moments of enthusiasm, your students may be obsessed with the products, styles and celebrities popular culture throws up. At these heights of intensity, students become fans, whether of musicians, athletes, or others, meaning that they focus on the objects of their fascination not only during their performances but during the rest of life, in the penumbra of magazines, Web sites, and paraphernalia devoted to the celebrities of their choice.

Media offer emotional payoffs—and expectations of payoffs. The rewards are immediate: fun, pleasure, excitement. Images and sounds register in the here and now. Media consumers are supposed to feel good; this is the expectation. Media make a cardinal promise: You have a right not to be bored. Yet the media must not feel too good for too long, because part of their goodness is that they change. One stimulus yields to the next, and this, too, is expected. Accordingly, your students have become accustomed to feel feelings with a particular quality: feelings that are relatively disposable, fast-rising, and fast-fading—excitements and expectations that readily give way (and are expected to give way) to other fast-rising and fast-fading feelings, excitements, and expectations. Young people expect their images and soundtracks not only to cause enjoyment but also to change. They expect jolts of sensation, surges of unexpected (yet, paradoxically, predictably unexpected) feelings. Besides the changes provided by the media, they expect to change the channel—or fast-forward the tape, or search out a different song on the CD—if the current one does not please them.

Thus, the unacknowledged curriculum readies your students not only for sensation but for interruption. Interruption is a phenomenon unto itself, a premise of contemporary perception. It is no small part of young people's experience of media. Besides the interruption of one medium by another, deliberately or not, interruption is also built into content. In the spelling lessons of *Sesame Street* as in the commercials after which it was patterned, in action movies as in video games, in music videos as in disk jockey chit-chat, in sportscasting as in news, children expect split screens, moving logos, and quick cuts, even if some continuity may be supplied by the soundtrack. The acceleration of editing during the past generation is striking, with images jump-cutting to other images in a split second. The contrast with the past is plain whenever one sees a movie more than twenty years old: how static it looks! Finally, within the unedited footage, there is the now-normal glide or zoom or other movement of the image itself, the product of a handheld camera or one on a dolly or Steadicam. In media, the "story line" turns out to be a jagged line. The experience of a story or song, frequently interrupted, is connected with feelings, but the feelings are often lightweight, readily yielding to the next in a sequence of feelings, and expected to dissolve. The expectation of immediate but disposable rewards has become normal.

In this light, the curious obsessions of fandom can be seen as something more than irrational idiosyncrasies. They are, among other things, means of navigating the media torrent. Insofar as they are dissatisfied with the relative weightlessness of the media experience on which they mainly rely, the young still hope to find occasions for passion within the stream of their experience. Occasions for passion are one thing they seek, and sometimes find, in a craze. They seek to find themselves in brief shining moments, in reflected light from their stars. In the Taiwanese director Edward Yang's wonderful movie, Yi Yi (A One and a Two), a teenage character exclaims that movies don't just look like the actual world, they expand it. "We live three times. Two times as much life at the movies!" The intensity frequently lacking in everyday life may be had through the media. In the presence of media, feelings that must be suppressed in the course of normal activity can be released. But the rewards of experience as a fan are not easily found in the rest of life—including the classroom. So much the worse for the classroom.

The young have also become accustomed to dividing their attention. Two or more media messages frequently come to them simultaneously or nearly simultaneously—and they expect them to come that way, likely maintaining that their attention does not suffer in the process. The habit of switching channels or devices is partly a function of the convenience of switching. Thanks to the remote control device, one of the most underestimated of contemporary technologies, the young may conveniently graze between two or three television channels in rapid alternation or they may switch between a video game and a soap opera or sports event.

For this reason, among others, I do not want to argue that when children attend to the media of popular culture they are necessarily deeply focused on them. On the contrary, they are frequently paying attention to more than one medium at once, and even more frequently, shift edgily from one stimulus to another or anticipate the next. There is much evidence that children, like adults, tune out much of the time. They select what they attend to. They retain unevenly. Sometimes they focus and sometimes not. Those who approve of the habit of simultaneous media viewing and listening refer to the cognition this practice demands as "parallel processing." Those who disapprove consider it distraction. But however one evaluates this common condition of half-attention, it is not the focus that is required for intellectual mastery—learning a language, performing complex computations, grasping the contours of history. It is not the educational mood.

Then, too, there can be no doubt that the time that children spend relating to media is time they are not spending at other pursuits. Nor can it be doubted that, whatever the precise quality of attention, to a tremendous degree, popular culture is supplying a great many items that students are talking about (positively or negatively) when they arrive at school, the ones they take with them into the playgrounds and gyms, the ones they leave with, the ones they chat about with friends on the phone or over the Internet. Among peers, they provide a sort of social cement. Their likes and dislikes in popular culture are badges of membership, measures for in-groups and out-groups. Scorn is a cement of another kind, for the group is bound together by the way its members demarcate their tastes from the tastes of nonmembers, and scorn is convenient for demarcation. There will be some students who bring with them a more or less cogent ideological repertoire—religious, most likely—but even many of these will be connecting to religious symbols and stories, many of them received via the media, where their style of attention may not differ much from their secular equivalents.

Some recent statistics will suggest the magnitude of the place and flow of popular culture in the United States. According to a thorough survey organized by Professor Donald F. Roberts of Stanford University, the average American household with children aged 2 to 18 contains 2.9 television sets, 1.8 VCRs, 3.1 radios, 2.6 tape players, 2.1 CD players, 1.4 video game players, and 1.0 computers. A child's daily media exposure lasts, on average, 6 hours and 32 minutes. Of this time, 44 minutes are spent with "print media," including illustrated books and magazines, while 2 hours 46 minutes are spent with television, an additional 39 minutes with videotapes (including taped TV shows), and 20 minutes with video games, so that the total spent with image-based media is more than five times the time spent reading.[2] Among 8- to 13-year-olds, 40 percent said they did not read books the previous day; among 14- to 18-year-olds, that figure rose to 70 percent (table 11-B, p. 30). Around one-sixth of the time, children use two or more media simultaneously—not including times when they were zapping between two or more television programs (p. 18).

The level of household media use is not uniform. At ages 2 to 4, it is already over 4 hours a day, increasing to over 8 hours at ages 8 to 13, then slackening somewhat during the high school years. Boys watch 20 minutes a day more than girls (p. 18). There is some variation by race and ethnicity, with white children averaging about one hour less media exposure than blacks and Hispanics (table 7, p. 19). Blacks and whites average 45 minutes a day of reading, Hispanics only 37 minutes. Class differences are smaller than one might expect: In communities where average income is under $25,000 per year, the total exposure is 6 hours and 8 minutes; where average income is between $25,000 and $40,000, the total is 5 hours and 32 minutes; where the average is over $40,000, the total is 5 hours and 13 minutes (table 7, p. 19). These figures are adjusted for times when the child is exposed to more than one medium). Sixty-five percent of children 8–18 have a TV set in their bedrooms; 86 percent, a radio; 81 percent, a tape player; 75 percent, a CD player; 45 percent, a video game player (table 4, p. 13). Forty-two percent of all the children 2–18 (and 56 percent of black children, as opposed to 39 percent of white children) live in households where the television is on most of the time, sometimes as an object of attention, sometimes as background noise; 58 percent live in households where the television is on during meals (table 6, p. 5).

There remains the question of whether the Internet significantly varies these patterns of use and attention. It is of course hazardous to make predictions about the future of a technology growing so fast from zero. Still, it is noteworthy that in 1999, among children who used computers at all, 60 percent, or 52 minutes, of average daily computer use (1 hour 26 minutes) was classified by the researcher as "recreational," including games and Web sites, although just which Web sites the children were visiting and what they were doing there is more difficult to know (p. 34). It is a safe assumption that the interruptions, playfulness, kinetic emphasis, divided attention, emotional stimulus, and sheer pleasure in movement that are prominent in relations with visual and sound media also prevail online. The case that online experience fundamentally changes the overall relation to media remains decidedly unproved.

None of the survey statistics that I have cited speak to the experience of media outside one's household—at the homes of friends, on the street, at theme parks, in video game arcades. Plainly the sum is an embracing environment, although one that is (like a biological ecology) unevenly experienced. If a civilization can be described by how people live their lives, the media are central features of our civilization, a civilization that young people are well on the way to entering by the time they arrive at school. Their connections with media—including their connections with each other through their relations with media—do not add up to total immersion, but they are of an unprecedented scale. The pervasiveness of media is in part a function of opulence. It is a function, too, of available time, one consequence of the sequestering of the young away from the rigors of work. It is a function of the deep shift in national character characterized in 1950 by David Riesman as a turn from "inner-direction" to "other-direction," in which the source of authority shifts from an internalized hierarchy to peer groups and mass media.[3] Whatever the complexity of the causes, the sheer profusion of children's time spent in relation to the media cornucopia poses a set of problems for education that need to be forthrightly addressed.[4]

The Unacknowledged Curriculum: Content and Values

When I speak of students' attention, I mean two qualities of attention. First, there is the real-time ability to concentrate in the classroom. The question naturally arises of whether the immersion in fast-moving popular culture, from *Sesame Street* to video games, is responsible for the mushrooming of attention deficit and hyperactivity disorders (or at least the diagnosis of them). Second, there is the question of students' ability to concentrate on their homework—to learn how to reason, how to order their work, how to reread and revise.

Again, the cardinal expectation in media is immediate gratification. Boredom is anathema. The media of preference must be speedy and sensational, full of surprises and rapid shifts. Sense gratification in media is always within reach. In the visual media, edits come quickly—in music videos and commercials, frequently several per second. Sports are sped up by simultaneous stats, animations, and instant replays streaming across and punctuating the screen, so that even such a viscous spectacle as baseball becomes an explosion of dazzling bits. While human bodies have limits to their capacity to race, bend, and otherwise delight, animation does not. Music will be percussive, dominated by rhythmic pulsation. Electronic rumbles and drums bring up emotional effects, bass notes producing an aura of menace, strings a whiff of cheer. Stories are full of conflict, images kinetic. Many media tales have morals and may kindle a certain order of moral reflection, but usually the morals of the tale emerge quickly and demand rapid resolution.

Much of what streams through the media is funny—often self-consciously so. Jokes come thick and fast, or are supposed to, pitched at the average level of early teens. Physical humor, pratfalls, and goofiness are plenteous. Popular culture itself serves as the repertory on which popular culture draws, so that there is little or no recognition that any other, perhaps more demanding, more difficult, worthier culture might exist. In recent decades, a recognition of the omnipresence of popular culture, as well as its foolishness, has been built into popular culture in the form of sarcasm and tongue-in-cheek attitudes, commonly known as "irony." Cartoons that mock the rest of popular culture (most brilliantly *The Simpsons*, the exception that proves the rule), ads that smirk at other ads, soap-opera characters who selectively disparage popular culture, magazines and Web sites that mercilessly unmask others—these are the common currency. Stupidity is subject to mockery, too, but in a way that suggests that what is wrong with stupidity is that it isn't hip and that those who rise above stupidity are, more than likely, snobs.

Despite the occasional thoughtful or beautiful exception, shallowness is the condition of the bulk of popular culture and remains so even if the observer does not sink into a chiding voice. There are of course exceptions, media products that do not insult intelligence, judgment, or good taste. The best to be said for the mainstream is that it brings a certain diversity into parochial households and recommends tolerance. Whatever the merits of nonstop popular culture, the question that faces us here is its spillover into the classroom and homework. A caution is due: Truly, for all the marketing of educational toys and programs, children do understand that the prime purpose of media is enjoyment and that life offers, and demands, other pursuits with varying purposes. For all the contemporary emphasis on succeeding, getting ahead, and getting high scores on tests, they know that a sphere of pleasure exists—a sphere in which media feature prominently—for which little justification is needed other than its immediate rewards. At some level, they understand that the classroom and homework have a different—even contrary—purpose. Still, to expect that students' expectations of popular culture are tidily put away the moment they walk into the classroom or open a textbook is naive—insupportably so.

Aside from the value of limited-liability feelings and sensations—especially jolts of excitement—and the speed with which they loom up and change, which values are commended in and through the media torrent? The value of material acquisition is taken for granted as the backdrop to the dramas of everyday media. Even the morals commended by American serial drama, daytime and nighttime, are usually played out against backdrops of prosperous lives. Enclosure by commercials puts quandaries in their place. The anguish of moral ambiguity and unresolved conflict in the end yields to the slickness and glibness of advertising, whose presence, promise, and invocation of fun are felt to be normal features of life. The easy glamour of music videos is yet more schooling in the tangibility of the good life. Sensations within reach, emotions on demand, ease of access and rapid rewards: these are the hallmarks of the prevailing media experience. Given that media take up so much of a child's life, the nub of the matter is plain: Media values are not strong training in the disciplines of schoolwork.

What, then, of the violence that is frequently held to be the worst effect of the media? It is lost on no one that throughout the popular media casual violence is an awfully common value. On this score, video games considerably compound the effects of network television, and video games are compounded by videocassettes, heavy metal, and rap music. The deeper significance of all the casual violence is not, however, self-evident. Throughout the past century, reformers have maintained that media violence causes violence in the real world, but of this causal link—first attributed to movies, then to comic books—there is little serious evidence and much counterevidence.[5] This is not to say that media violence is unimportant. Any routine of everyday life is significant if only because so much of human time is taken up with it. Its importance, however, lies largely in the sensory experience that it generates, not in the dire behavioral effects popularly attributed to it. The evidence from laboratory studies, limited as it is as a predictor of effects in the outside world, suggests that violent images cultivate both anger and indifference, neither of which is conducive to the intellectual receptivity, disciplined competence, and methodical deliberation that schoolwork requires.

In other words, violence in the media is best addressed as a commonplace feature of children's experience with media, that is, a feature of the lives they actually live, not a trigger for violence in the actual world. Media violence is experience. It is itself a reality, a part of the life that young people live, a part that registers as cognitive and emotional. It is not an intimation of violence to be performed at some other time or place. It is already here in experience, carried into the child's everyday life through the deep reach of popular culture. It may or may not teach the lesson that force pays or that human life is expendable, but even if it doesn't, it teaches that violence is a routine recourse. Even when violence in the media pours forth without a corresponding uptick in the violence of the actual world, media's violent message makes the world—at least the world of human connection with the media themselves, a world that young people live in during many hours a day—appear casually cruel. In these everyday adventures, aggressiveness is the common currency of life.

Violence is only one of the regular crudities of everyday media. They are soaked in coarseness of many sorts. Primitive jeers, double entendres, easy jokes about body functions feature regularly in many programs radiated to young people through network sitcoms, MTV, the Comedy Channel, and other commercial sources, as well as video games (which now outgross movies, in both senses of "outgross") and Internet entertainments.[6] The sexual innuendo of music videos is hard to miss, whence its huge adolescent appeal. Overall, though, probably more prevalent than sexual suggestiveness is the crude style evident in vocabulary, look, gestures—the whole expressive repertory of popular culture. The full range of human emotions is collapsed into the rudimentary alternatives of "love" and "hate," "cool" and "gross." Of one over-17 video game, Nintendo's *Conker's Bad Fur Day*, a critical aficionado, Seth Stevenson, writes: "Conker's is great fun to play. The animation's gorgeous, and the manic wackiness grows on you. You can't help but giggle a bit while herding screaming, motile pieces of cheese, so you can slam them with a frying pan, so you can feed them to a flatulent mouse, so he will explode, so you can drop a giant ball of poop on a dung beetle's head."[7]

Such are the cultural contributions brought to market by large corporations hiring technically talented people who were reared on previous achievements in the same vein. As today's brain-dead movies are written by admirers of previous brain-dead movies, so do today's video games, pop songs, and music videos derive from their own "traditions." As Seth Stevenson writes, "Current designers come from programming backgrounds, so millions of dollars in development costs produce a beautifully rendered world full of farting scarecrows."[8]

Through such productions, the media take the side of the simple over the complex, the id over the superego, the pleasure principle over the reality principle, the popular over the unpopular. These fundamental commitments of media are often mistaken for cultural subversion, the "transgression" equally beloved of the cultural left and despised by the cultural right, each of which is selective, seizing upon the object of its discontent in order to feel embattled and justified. Left-wing antiauthoritarianism often seizes on easy transgression as a sign of hope—as if brute disrespect might undermine an oppressive social order—but the conservative embattlement is better known. In recent decades, facing widespread assaults on patriarchal authority, conservatives have frequently challenged the social values of popular culture, operating on the dubious premise that such programs translate directly into personal action. Vice President Dan Quayle's attack on the *Murphy Brown* sit-com during the presidential campaign of 1992, when he chastised the producers for endorsing single motherhood, is a good example. During most of the past century, in the eyes of anti-modernizing forces in American life, *Hollywood* has been code for *permissiveness*.[9]

The truth in the conservative charge is that Hollywood cultivates youthful rambunctiousness over adult-enforced order. Its desire for profit dovetails with the unruly and profligate desires of adolescence. The multiplication of media offers vast opportunities to capitalize upon segmented youth markets. It defies intuition to think that Hollywood has no effect on the spirit and expectations of children. But the exaggeration is that Hollywood imposes an unwanted culture. Hollywood stokes the fires of an all-consuming culture that observes what the psychologist Martha Wolfenstein memorably called "fun-morality": Thou

Must Have Fun.[10] This all-consuming culture did not burst fully-formed from the head of Rupert Murdoch any more than from that of Louis B. Mayer or, for that matter, P.T. Barnum. It is not the unwelcome product of Madison Avenue hipsters or of Hollywood liberals. It is the spirit commended by a whole civilization. It is the ideal toward which the culture of modern capitalism has been tending for centuries—not unopposed, not irresistibly, but with the tremendous force and momentum of modern individualism.[11]

Media Accommodation and Media Literacy

It would be astounding if the expectations of ease, speed, simplicity, disposable feeling, and crudeness set out in the media did not enter deeply into the expectations that students bring to school.[12] Yet the onrush of popular culture has been only sporadically or indifferently acknowledged as an important force shaping the educational situation—perhaps because popular culture is so prevalent that it appears to be an unstoppable force of nature. Informally, however, in corridor talk and occasional lamentations heard in the media themselves, teachers, parents, and school administrators do sense that popular culture matters for—and against—education. Teachers and administrators have developed two approaches to address the phenomenon.

Accommodation

The accommodationist strategy says, in effect, "If you can't beat 'em, join 'em." The premise is that linear, disciplined teaching approaches are obsolete. Children, heavily influenced by popular culture, must be taken as they are. The saturation of everyday life by popular culture may not be desirable, but it is a fixture that cannot be repealed, it can only be worked with. Hence, accommodationists welcome Channel One (and similar commercial programs) and the computerized classroom. They support the dumbing down of textbooks and build assignments on popular culture knowledge.

Channel One is a private enterprise that delivers a daily twelve-minute news broadcast to some eight million students in twelve thousand public schools, including one in four middle and high schools in the United States. Each school accepts the free loan of a 19-inch television set, along with two VCRs and a fixed satellite dish that receives only the Channel One signal, in return for delivering captive audiences to the advertisers who fill two of the twelve minutes with their commercials. Although New York State bans the broadcast, some 40 percent of American high school students watch Channel One daily—are required to watch it, in fact, for the condition of the corporate gift to schools is that the viewing be mandatory. (Two students at Perrysburg Junior High School in Ohio spent a day in Wood County Juvenile Detention Center for refusing to watch Channel One.) The news, most of it high-velocity weather, sports, disasters, features, and promotions, is packaged in modules comparable to the out-of-school media torrent, replete with entertainment recommendations, contests, quizzes, and self-promotion.[13] Advertising is a mélange including snack food and violent movies. Channel One's proprietors, the Primedia Corporation, who made $346 million on advertising in 1999, maintain that their hosts know how to speak children's language. What they are capable of saying in it is another matter. The educational outcome is doubtful.[14]

The glamour of computer connections to the Internet reaches even deeper into the classroom, though again with undemonstrated educational results. The premise of this technological fix is that Internet access is the sine qua non of learning. President Clinton was only the most prominent public figure to champion "closing the digital divide." But computerization is only the most easily remedied discrepancy between rich and poor classrooms. What the streaming of entertainment and information (much of it of dubious provenance) into the classroom has to do with deepening knowledge, improving reading or writing skills, learning to reason, or distinguishing between worthy and unworthy authorities is not clear. The indiscriminate choice celebrated in the ideal of consumer sovereignty is not consistent with the authority of the school. Multimedia programs, including sound, certainly boost enjoyment, but the connection between immediate enjoyment and either intellectual or aesthetic mastery remains unclear. The rule-bound nature of computer use—one mouse-click produces one result—does not translate into forms of learning that are not mechanical. Yet, as with all propaganda in behalf of technological improvements, there is, behind the advocacy of computers in every classroom, a presumption operating to the effect that no one learned well before the invention of computers. While it may turn out that some uses of computers do expedite certain forms of learning by converting drills into fun, the major payoff of widespread computerization in school, especially in the lower grades, may be familiarity with computers themselves—a most restricted educational objective. The fulsome rhetoric in favor of computerization leaves modest expectations behind. Meanwhile, at least one Internet company, ZapMe!, donates to schools computers that will also conduct market research.[15]

The education-industrial complex has also seen to the dumbing down of textbooks, where a diminished vocabulary and simplistic exercises are accompanied by the equivalent of split-screen capability. The proliferation of gaudy designs featuring snippets and marginal "factoids" like ubiquitous trivia quizzes would seem more likely to equate knowledge with the skimming of marginalia rather than understanding. The fun increment is considerable. Children probably like glitzed-up textbooks more than the grayer ones they replace, but whether liking translates into learning is another matter.

Accommodationists also use popular culture as a teaching device—peppering classes with references to popular music, movies, and celebrities, and hanging assignments upon such pegs. A mild ingratiation is surely a harmless expedient. Popular culture can offer examples for any number of points. Teachers must find some common ground with their students. Equivalent techniques have been used in curricula since time immemorial, for instance, teaching arithmetic and algebra using shopping-related problems. But this common ground can be muddy. Students can usually tell when they're being condescended to. The trick is to avoid being mired.

In any event, this tactic, like other accommodations, fails to address the central features of the torrent of popular culture: first, its quantity, and second, the quality of its kinetic experience, the sensational and emotional pleasures to be found there, its penchant for speed and interruption. Accommodations may offer useful contrivances, at most and on occasion, but no comprehensive remedy.

Media Literacy

After decades of popular campaigning, media literacy has become the dominant strategy for teaching students to see through the tactics of media, especially those of advertising. The general principle was enunciated in the 1980s by Ernest L. Boyer, then the president of the Carnegie

Foundation for the Advancement of Teaching: "It is no longer enough simply to read and write. Students must also become literate in the understanding of visual images. Our children must learn how to spot a stereotype, isolate a social cliché, and distinguish facts from propaganda, analysis from banter, and important news from coverage."[16] That some such program ought to be in place in schools is no longer controversial. After a recent state-by-state survey, Professor Robert Kubey of Rutgers and public television broadcaster Frank Baker concluded that "at least forty-eight state curricular frameworks now contain one or more elements calling for some form of media education."[17]

On paper, at least, some state requirements fully lay claim to Boyer's ambitious objectives. For example, North Carolina's language/communication-arts guidelines state:

It is an important goal of education for learners to be able to critique and use the dominant media of today. Visual literacy is essential for survival as consumers and citizens in our technologically intensive world. Learners will appreciate various visual forms and compositions, compare and contrast visual and print information, formulate and clarify personal response to visual messages, evaluate the form and content of various visual communications, identify and interpret main ideas and relevant details in visual representations, apply insights and strategies to become more aware and active viewers in their leisure time, relate what is seen to past experience, convey and interpret ideas through nonprint media, recognize the persuasive power of visual representations.

California's history/social sciences research framework for grades 9–12 stipulates:

Students evaluate, take, and defend positions on the influence of the media on American political life, in terms of: (1) the meaning and importance of a free and responsible press, (2) the role of electronic, broadcast, print media, and the Internet as means of communication in American politics, (3) how public officials use the media to communicate with the citizenry and to shape public opinion.

How well these goals are achieved in the classroom is hard to know. These programs are usually elective. Moreover, several different concepts are bound together under the general heading of media literacy. Taking advantage of the semantic ambiguity of the term *media literacy*— "literacy" in the strict sense refers to the generalized ability to produce and judge language as well as to read it, while "media literacy" can be construed to emphasize the production more than the critical side— some may be satisfied to instruct students in the nuts and bolts of television production. Note this excerpt from a 2001 book by John Merrow prominently posted on the *Media Literacy Clearinghouse* Web site of the Alliance for a Media Literature America: "Children should be given access to information about how television is made *and to the TV-making equipment itself* [italics mine]."[18] Time spent teaching how to make television must be subtracted from time otherwise spent. Technological education is worthy, but to demonstrate production techniques, which part of the curriculum will be sacrificed? Writing? Grammar? Athletics? History? Science? How easily the line between teaching about television and teaching television is crossed!

The value of training in media literacy stems from its specificity. Looking critically at media, image by image, ad by ad, reveals that far from being marvelous gifts inexplicably bestowed by a benign universe, media are human contrivances produced by human beings in institutions with human motives, ulterior and otherwise. The weakness of the media literacy approach, however, also lies in its specificity. It makes the images stand still in order to teach how they work one at a time. This is constructive. It helps students fend off those who casually take advantage of their gullibility. But images do not arrive one at a time. They arrive in a torrent. The texture of the overall media experience is what is inimical to the steady discipline of serious learning.

At the very least, a media literacy program should point the finger at the built-in features of the media torrent: its immensity, its speed, its impact on the attention span. It must be acknowledged that sugar tastes sweet, but it must also be pointed out that it rots the teeth. Three generations into the history of television, one generation into video games and the Walkman, the verdict on media literacy programs in schools must be: fine as far as they go and better than nothing, but by themselves, too little, too late.

An Approach Commensurate with the Problem

Media literacy is a critique, but a critique is not a curriculum. In the end, teaching stands and falls on whether or not it offers alternatives to a junk culture: ways of thinking, forms of intellectual and aesthetic experience, with their own rewards. "Teach me to fish and I can fish for a lifetime," as the saying goes. Teachers must go about their work with an eye to defending the good—clear thinking, fine prose, analytical care, beauty—regardless of whether the market pays heed.

It ought to go without saying, but any defense of the good rests on acquaintanceship with the good. A curriculum that dumbs down to the humdrum standards of mainstream popular culture is a curriculum unworthy of its name. First, good literature is a sine qua non of an education that will stay with students throughout their lives. The pleasures of serious literature will come as a surprise to students who grow up—as the vast majority do—in homes with parents who themselves lack acquaintance with serious literature. Given the lack of such literature in their homes and the steep decline in library funding, students will only systematically come into contact with serious writing in school. Teachers should resist any tendency to trim the reading curriculum to suit the trends of the moment. The emphasis should not be on the symbol-sniffing that literary criticism foists upon readers and not strictly on narrative paraphrase and plot-tracking. It should be on the beauties of good writing. Most students have little knowledge of how to read—how to savor a sentence, how to attend to its rhythm, how to distinguish between one word and an apparent synonym. Most have not heard anyone read well aloud. In a nonstop, fast-food culture, they do not have the experience of the pleasures of slowing down. The classroom can give them at least a taste of that pleasure.

Second, media literacy deserves positives as well as negatives. The realm of the image should not be forfeited to the mediocrity of conventional taste. Almost all students will have been to the movies and looked at television, but few will have seen the best work—either contemporary films or their foregoers. They may not even know that movies have a history outside the multiplex of the mall, or television a history beyond commercial hits. Moving pictures deserve a place in the curriculum. Their pleasures should be pointed out with the affection that literature also deserves. Beyond the criticism that points a finger at the propagandistic uses of media, students need to see what film and video are capable of.

Third, training in civics simply cannot be reduced to the banalities of talk shows or the joys of corrosive humor without undercutting democracy. The great warm bath of popular culture is full of acid for civil society, and schooling is one place where this acid may, in part, be neutralized. Therefore the teaching of historical fundamentals—for example, the Declaration of Independence and the Constitution, the elements of the Civil War and the World Wars—needs to be coupled with civic reasoning. The powers of explanation need to be made available. Students ought to understand historic disputes as something more than the byplay of heroes or the clichés of patriotism. The teaching of history should not be consigned to commercial enterprises like The History Channel, which tend toward spectacular presentations, which must compete with prime time network offerings, and which, in any event, are unavailable to those without cable or satellite access. The necessity of civic reasoning—reasoning about the public good, apart from private interest—can only be taught live, as it were, in the classroom. The overriding point to be taught is that democracy requires commitments that are different in kind and tempo from the easy style of popular culture.

Finally, educators should not end their responsibilities when they walk out of the classroom. They should be reformers. Much of the torrent of popular culture is the product of public decisions—the awarding of the publicly owned broadcast spectrum gratis to private corporations with only the most meager provision for the public good; the subsidy of advertising through tax deductions; permission to pepper children's programs with nonstop commercials. Citizens who care about the health of civil society should embrace a serious reform program for media. Tax deductions for corporate advertising should be curtailed. Public service requirements should be restored and enforced as a condition for holding broadcast licenses. A user fee for broadcasters should be used to boost subsidies for public television and radio. The profitability of political commercials during election campaigns—the prime source of the corruption of party politics—should be curbed. These are minimal steps if, as a society, we are to find some purchase for deep values amid the churning flow of popular culture. The torrent of popular culture is the huge unacknowledged feature of our civilization. It stands in the way of education and civic improvement. If educators do not take it seriously as a social problem, who will?

NOTES

1. Dylan Evans, *Emotion: The Science of Sentiment* (London: Oxford University Press, 2001), p. 68.

2. Donald F. Roberts, Ulla G. Foehr, Victoria J. Rideout, and Mollyann Brodie, *Kids & Media @ the New Millennium: A Comprehensive National Analysis of Children's Media Use* (Menlo Park, Calif.: The Henry J. Kaiser Family Foundation, 1999), table 8-A, p. 20.

3. David Riesman with Nathan Glazer and Reuel Denney, *The Lonely Crowd* (New Haven: Yale University Press, 1950).

4. I explore the origins of torrential media and popular dependency on it in chapter 1 of Todd Gitlin, *Media Unlimited: How the Torrent of Images and Sounds Overwhelms Our Lives* (New York: Metropolitan Books/Henry Holt, 2002), from which many of the following arguments are drawn.

5. I make this argument in "Imagebusters: The Hollow Crusade Against TV Violence," *The American Prospect* (winter 1994), www.prospect.org/print/v5/16/gitlin-t.html. See also my response to critics, "Imagebusters: The Sequel," *The American Prospect* (spring 1994), www.prospect.org/print/v5/17/rowe-j.html. See also the summary in Marjorie Heins, *Not in Front of the Children: Indecency, Censorship and the Innocence of Youth* (New York: Hill and Wang, 2001).

6. See Mark Crispin Miller's analysis of the television jeer, "Deride and Conquer," in *Watching Television*, ed. Todd Gitlin (New York: Pantheon, 1987), pp. 183–228.

7. Seth Stevenson, "Why Are Video Games For Adults So Juvenile?" *Slate.com*, 19 April 2001.

8. Ibid.

9. On the Legion of Decency, the Hollywood Production Code, and other such regulatory regimes, see Gregory D. Black, *Hollywood Censored: Morality Codes, Catholics, and the Movies* (Cambridge, Eng.: Cambridge University Press, 1994). On the evangelical campaign against television sex, see Todd Gitlin, *Inside Prime Time* (Berkeley: University of California Press, 2000 [1983]), chapter 12.

10. Martha Wolfenstein, "The Emergence of Fun Morality" in *Mass Leisure*, ed. Eric Larrabee (Glenco, Ill.: Free Press, 1958), p. 86.

11. In the vast and burgeoning literature on modern consumption, the following books are especially important: John Brewer and Roy Porter, eds., *Consumption and the World of Goods* (London: Routledge, 1993); Gary Cross, *Time and Money: The Making of Consumer Culture* (London and New York: Routledge, 1993); and Gary Cross, *An All-Consuming Century: Why Commercialism Won in Modern America* (New York: Columbia University Press, 2000).

12. Or the arts, for that matter. David Denby offers a damning appraisal of his children's engagement with popular culture in *Great Books: My Adventures with Homer, Rousseau, Woolf, and Other Indestructible Writers of the Western World* (New York: Simon and Schuster, 1996), pp. 70–75.

13. Russ Baker, "Stealth TV," *The American Prospect* 12, no. 3 (2001): 28.

14. Gary Ruskin, *National Affiliate School Board News*, 18 April 2000, available at www.nsba.org/sbn/oo-apr/041800-8.htm

15. Quoted in Robert Kubey and Frank Baker, "Has Media Literacy Found a Curricular Foothold?" *Education Week*, 19, no. 9 (1999): p. 56.

16. Kubey and Baker, "Has Media Literacy?" *Education Week*, 27 October 1999, www.edweek.org/ew/ewstory.cfm?slug=09ubey2.h19

17. John Merrow, *Choosing Excellence: "Good Enough" Schools Are Not Good Enough* (Lanhan, Md.: Scarecrow Press, 2001).

3

Socializing Children in
a Culture of Obscenity

Elisabeth Lasch-Quinn

The rearing of children entails not just the ensuring of their physical survival, but their induction into the social order. This involves the daunting task of helping them to make sense of the world around them. How can they accomplish this task when the social order itself does not make sense?

This is no small dilemma. It is a frightening reality that socialization is becoming an increasingly fraught task in the Western world today. This is certainly not the first time parents have faced difficulties in their primary task, and one might argue that the general peace and prosperity of contemporary life in the United States until very recently rendered any worries about children's socialization relatively insignificant. Such a dismissal, however, fails to explain why more and more parents find that raising their children in the dominant culture is no longer viable.

The status of our culture is, by any measure of taste and morality, appalling. Many parents and other observers have made known their horror. They have voiced their concern over the issues of explicit sex and violence in everything from daytime and prime-time television to movies, music lyrics, and video games. This chapter seeks to show that this kind of content is only a small symptom of a much larger set of problems that our culture poses and to join those who suggest that we need a drastic strategy for battling these problems.

The Inescapability of Popular Culture

A recent *Washington Post* article captured the desperation many parents now feel about their children's socialization—a desperation with much deeper roots than a slight uneasiness about inappropriate language or imagery in music or movies. Journalist Don Oldenberg told of a mother named Loretta Pleasant-Jones who sneaked into the back of a movie theater where her 15-year-old and her friends were watching a movie. She wanted to keep tabs on what they were viewing. An exemplar of engaged parenthood, Pleasant-Jones had stayed home to raise her children and took great pains to monitor and control what her children were exposed to. She found, however, that it was nearly impossible, given the ubiquity of the media and the extremity of the gap between how she wanted to raise her children and how mainstream society sought to do it. She characterized that gap in strong terms: "I honestly feel that there is a war going on out there. It's my values against this whole group of advertisers, marketers—everybody who is trying to sell my child something. And it offends me enormously."[1] Knowing that it is no longer enough to monitor what comes into the home, Pleasant-Jones felt it necessary to get acquainted with what her teenager was experiencing outside the home as well.

Another mother, Enola Aird, is director of the Motherhood Project, an organization that has formed precisely to engage what its members and supporters see as the battle for their children's futures. This group seeks to provide a critique of and a counter-offensive to the messages being purveyed in advertising, as well as the exploitation and manipulation of children through marketing more broadly and the frustration of parents' best laid plans to raise healthy children. About the advertising industry, Aird writes: "We've got this incredible external force out there that has some of the smartest people in the world working for it, using the greatest technology, and telling my children things that are diametrically opposed to what I've been telling them since I brought them into this world." She continues: "Somebody else is trying to raise my children and being pretty successful at it. They aren't evil; they are just trying to make a buck—but by competing with me to raise my child."[2]

One response to those who have raised specific concerns about sexual or violent content in the popular culture has been that it is the responsibility of the parents—not the advertisers, television or film executives, or marketers—to oversee their children's upbringing. The notion of parental responsibility is widely accepted even by those appalled by popular culture. Critics of this culture have used tactics resting on the ways parents can take responsibility over what their children hear and see: the V-chip, ratings systems, magazines that guide parents through the thicket of the popular culture, and even home-schooling. Those parents most cognizant of their own responsibilities, however, are often the ones who also recognize the limits of their ability to monitor a whole culture.

One parent, an editorial writer for the *Hartford Courant*, worried about the "sexually suggestive—and sometimes explicit—dialogue or gestures" on children's television cartoons. Okey Ndibe acknowledged that the standard response to a parent's objections to such material would be, "It's up to you to monitor what your kids watch," and she conceded that, "Of course, only a foolish parent would shirk his responsibility to ensure that children see or listen to wholesome fare on television or radio." She expressed frustration, however, about an aspect of the popular culture that solutions like the V-chip or ratings simply cannot address: its inescapability. "Sex has become so ubiquitous and blatant a part of society that parental vigilance, finally, is inadequate. Indeed, wherever kids turn these days, there is some sex symbol, image, or idea inviting their attention."

Ndibe makes the crucial point that it is not just advertisers and marketers who promote these inappropriate symbols, images, or ideas—but often parents themselves. She describes "theme" birthday parties for very young children, for instance. Parents ask party-goers to dress up like particular entertainers, calling on them "to assume provocative sexual identities," with "the saucier, raunchier, or plain sexier the model" the "more attractive" it is considered to be. One party had the children dress up like skimpily, suggestively clad members of a group of singers, the Spice Girls. When a mother of a kindergartner invited to the party expressed gentle reservations, the mother hosting the party replied that the Spice Girls "represented 'female power.'" She defended her choice of this group to Ndibe by insisting that the "girls just love them." Ndibe also encountered images of a partially clad singer, Christina Aguilera, on

T-shirts in the children's section of Sears. The clerk informed her that the shirts were highly popular.

Comments by parents concerned about the inescapability of the popular culture get at something beyond occasional lyrics or scenes that contain age-inappropriate material. They depict a whole culture with its own internal logic, values, and rationale: those of personal liberationism and the advanced market culture combined. Even when vigilantly controlling what their children witness, parents often face the reality that their fellow parents are not nearly as concerned as they are—if they are even concerned at all. Instead of isolated cases of obscenity—inappropriate language, explicit sexuality, brutal or meaningless violence—we confront a larger culture that at its very core has taken on elements of the obscene. Traits of this culture include an absence of social boundaries, an instrumental view of human beings, a lack of a sense of proportion in human endeavors, and incoherence.

The Culture of Obscenity

No rating system, parental diligence, or even outright censorship, could address the sheer obscenity of what passes for culture in America. By obscenity here, I mean not only what is considered adult-rated sexual material or pornography, but also a kind of fundamental offensiveness, vulgarity, indecency, perversity, and vacuity on our part as a nation, generation, or civilization. Often having little to do with sexuality itself, this kind of obscenity bears on nearly all realms of society. It is rooted in a radically antisocial ethos premised on the right to individual fulfillment at all costs and is fed by the belief that appeals to morality have no standing because they are all relative and subjective. To try to understand it is a difficult and imposing task, but it is one that we must undertake if we are to grasp the full dangers of the culture we are passing on to our children.

Social observers from communitarian Amitai Etzioni to historian Gertrude Himmelfarb have pointed to our growing confusion about morality and ethics. An illustration of this confusion is found in a recent article by Frank Rich in the *New York Times Magazine*, which gives an in-depth account of the businesses involved in producing and distributing pornographic videos. These businesses haul in approximately $4 billion (in video rentals and purchases) of the annual $10 billion to $14 billion earnings of the pornography industry (including "porn networks and pay-per-view movies on cable and satellite, Internet Web sites, in-room hotel movies, phone sex, sex toys and . . . magazines"), signaling that "an unseemly large percentage of Americans" indulge in pornography "as daily entertainment fare." In an attempt to explore the business as a business, Rich listened at length to various participants in the production of this material, letting them speak for themselves in lengthy quotes in the article. While they seemed proud of their work, they operated within a general climate of "secrecy." Staff members for the primary adult video magazine, for instance, write under pseudonyms and receptionists at pornography companies "answer the phone generically: 'Production company' or 'Corporate office.'"[3]

Rich's interviewees said they had difficulty with the question of whether or not they should identify the nature of their occupation to people they met, say, through their children's schools. One company owner said, "Being in the business you walk that line all the time—do you say what you do or not? . . . I'm comfortable with what I do, but I don't want parents of our child's friends saying their kids can't play with her because of it." Worried about his nine-year-old stepdaughter, he and his wife consulted a therapist, who advised them to put off informing her of their line of work, saying "don't overexplain." Further showing his lack of clarity on this issue, this executive wears a T-shirt with the logo of his video company in front of his child, saying "She knows I make something only adults can see." At the same time, however, he wonders about a scene she witnessed in a prime-time CBS sitcom: "The guy's rolling off his wife, and my 9-year-old asks, 'What do they mean by that?'" At a loss, the pornography executive asks, "Should I be letting her watch it?"

A female executive and former pornography star has a similar difficulty, on the one hand reminiscing fondly about the "golden age of porn cinema" and casting pornography as merely part of the entertainment business, a humbler and "more down to earth" Hollywood, and, on the other hand, admitting that her occupation has ramifications for the lives of her two teenage sons. While she states her career choice "is horrible for them," she seems unaware of any difference between sex and a career of selling sex; she assumes their feelings to be akin to a natural embarrassment at the thought of a parent having sex at all. She goes on: "I'm not ashamed of what I do. I take responsibility for who I am. I chose. From the time they were kids, my stripping gear was washed and hanging in the bathroom tub. At the same time, I apologize to my kids for how the choices in my life have affected them. They're well adjusted and can joke with me about it: 'I know I'm going to spend the rest of my life on the couch.'"[4] While these comments suggest that even successful executives proud of their careers in pornography can harbor lingering doubts about their ability to reconcile their activities with the rearing of children, they seem most concerned with the pressures their children might feel from the outside world. Remarkably absent from their remarks is a sense of anything inherently wrong or damaging to their children about their engagement in making adult "product."

Despite the vastness of the pornography empire, individuals actually engaged in the pornography business are still, of course, atypical. Their perfunctory confrontation with the nature of their enterprise, however, sheds light on a dilemma our culture faces more broadly. These executives feel the double standard of a career that is fostered behind the scenes but formally proscribed — at least this is how they interpret their parenting dilemma. They cannot seem to resolve their lives of contradiction precisely because they cannot see any clear contradiction. They know it exists only because of the disapproval they sense lurking vaguely in some antipornographic public.

While there is no doubt a reserve of social disapproval for those actually engaging in the production of pornography, however, disapproval of the materials themselves has eroded drastically. In fact, there is now so much pornographic content in the more mainstream media — and in everyday public life — that the boundary between informal and formal institutions of pornography is increasingly blurred.

Another executive said he draws a strict boundary between work and home, deliberately keeping all materials and reference to his company outside of domestic confines. Still another made clear the industry's general condemnation of child pornography when he said that "No one in this business will complain" if Attorney General John Ashcroft steps up controls over the "kid angle." The line between a career in pornography and one's own home life or between child pornography and every other form is welcome and vital. However, to focus solely on the age of pornography consumers or performers ignores deeper questions about pornography and its popularity and reflects a severely impoverished version of propriety. What is worse, this version is increasingly the one that dominates.

Propriety, in its fullest sense, entails a sense of legitimate and appropriate boundaries that help structure our shared social world as well as a sense of decorum, or basic guidelines, that should prevail in given social situations. It relies on the exercise of taste and judgment, which are rooted in traditions, community standards, and common sense. Of course, history gives many examples of the misuse of notions of propriety in political regimes that were elitist, discriminatory, and cruel. In battling such regimes, however, we have lost solid grounding for an understanding of propriety that fits with democratic aspirations.

The Absence of Boundaries

Historian Rochelle Gurstein has written eloquently of the wholesale breakdown of any principled defense of propriety in the transition in American life from a reticent sensibility, which prevailed in the nineteenth century, and the cult of exposure, which came to dominate the twentieth. Her examination of this shift suggests that attention to the line dividing childhood from adulthood is an incomplete way of addressing the problem of obscenity in contemporary life. While the absence of proper and legitimate boundaries in social life has everything to do with the ubiquity of various forms of obscenity, the boundary she has in mind is the fundamental division of the social world for people of all ages between private and public arenas.

Gurstein writes that the middle and upper classes in the nineteenth century possessed a social disposition based on "such then-current terms as common sense, taste, judgment, refinement, politeness, reserve, propriety, tact, discretion, and decency." The key to this reticence was a firm differentiation between—and a specific rendering of the qualities of—public and private experience: "Knowing which things were capable of flourishing in public and which things were so fragile that they required the shade of privacy if they were to retain their meaning depended on a highly modulated sense of the sacred and the desecrated, of honor and shame." Gurstein takes great pains to show that this distinction predated the obsessive concern with individual rights and prerogatives and the use of privacy as a basis for buttressing an overly individualistic ethos. Instead, she describes an ideology of intimacy, which posited that the quality of both intimate relations and public life depended, in part, on the separation between them.[5]

Critics of exposure, Gurstein shows, "believed that open or casual discussion about intimate experiences would erode their meaning and vitality, and give rise to a world that was shameless in the literal sense that nothing was considered sacred or worthy of awe and reverence." Just as the intimate sphere risked losing its integrity in its shameless display in public, the public sphere risked losing its distinctiveness to "public pollution" from the onslaught of inappropriate private images, which numbed the mind and the senses. But the reticent sensibility increasingly troubled twentieth-century reformers dedicated to a number of causes from free love to social realism. This "party of exposure" drew on pop-Freudianism to argue that public silence about those details of life formerly deemed private amounted to pathological repression and constituted restraint on avant garde artistic expression. Committed to an undifferentiated view of individual liberation, which lumped together all quests and definitions of freedom, these self-professed progressives saw their critics as reactionary and puritanical. In attendant legal changes, obscenity was reconsidered. No longer taking into account obscenity's affect on the quality of the public realm, legal debate revolved around the question of whether a particular person was harmed. In the absence of a clear victim, notions of obscenity lost their "broad view," which considered community well-being, and were recast as a narrow issue of consenting adults' right to harmless exercise of personal preferences.[6]

Gurstein's work goes beyond helping us recover the public/private distinction itself, which has often been commandeered to support individual rights at all costs. Her work points to the decline in the *quality* of both spheres that results from their convergence. This convergence and decline help explain the sense critics have that obscenity is all-pervasive. Because the debates over obscenity usually center narrowly on the question of censorship, they sidestep the deeper issue of the effects of obscenity on "the tone, texture, and substance of our public life and culture" and on intimacy.[7]

Gurstein drew in part on Harry Clor, whose book *Obscenity and Public Morality* attempted to carve out a middle ground between the libertarian position, which regarded any form of censorship as a violation of free speech, and a camp of moralizers, who sought to legislate their own notion of propriety. In so doing, he articulated a definition of obscenity that pointed to its transgression of the private/public boundary. He observed: "(1) obscenity consists in making public that which is private; it consists in an intrusion upon intimate physical processes and acts or physical-emotional states; and (2) it consists in a degradation of the human dimensions of life to a sub-human or merely physical level."[8]

Clor's definition presupposes that there exists a distinction between public and private life and that the uninhibited expression of thoughts deemed obscene leads to violations of privacy. Yet, both Clor and Gurstein clearly resist casting the issue solely as one of individual rights—the right not to encounter obscenity. Instead, they are more concerned with the cumulative effect on the populace—as a collective body and as individuals. Both authors warn us about the dehumanizing effect of obscenity, which "makes a public exhibition" of parts of life properly confined to an immediate, personal level of experience and wrests them out of that human context. Clor quotes a critic's attempt to pinpoint what is so undesirable about an inappropriate proximity to private details:

> We have a certain sense of specialness about those voluntary bodily functions each must perform for himself—bathing, eating, defecating, urinating, copulating . . . Take eating, for example. There are few strong taboos around the act of eating, yet most people feel uneasy about being the only one at table who is, or who is not, eating, and there is an absolute difference between eating a rare steak washed down by plenty of red wine and watching a close-up movie of someone doing so. One wishes to draw back when one is actually or imaginatively too close to the mouth of a man enjoying his dinner; in exactly the same way one wishes to remove himself from the presence of a man and a woman enjoying sexual intercourse.[9]

Thus, what is disturbing about the ubiquity of sexual images in the popular culture consumed by children is not just that those images are inappropriate for people under a certain age. Granted, the appearance of these images results from poor judgment on the part of a particular author, producer, or media executive. But even further, it results from a larger erosion of any sense of propriety at all.

Furthermore, the nature of these images betrays *particular* conceptions of sexuality—ones marred by crassness and publicity, surely, but also by uniformity. In their mass production and distribution, they betray one of the main gifts sexuality brings: its uniqueness. Sexual expression, like all truly intimate experience, defies duplication. What gives it its intensity, complexity, and meaning cannot be reproduced. Attempts at commodification trivialize and distort it by severing some part from the whole, by interpreting it through an outsider's limited vision, and by wrenching it from its context in the sacred precincts created by the union of individuals. The result—a degraded version of intimacy—is not the one that has inspired great works of art, music, literature, poetry, let alone daily acts of love and devotion. Humans are certainly capable of degrading intimacy without the help of the marketplace, however the current view of sexuality, shorn of any romantic or spiritual dimension, is now the dominant one to which children are introduced publicly by those eager to make money by any means possible.

Instrumentalism

In his book, Clor expressly noted that his notion of obscenity referred not only to sexual matters: "There can also be obscene views of death, of birth, of illness, and of acts such as that of eating or defecating." According to his definition, obscene treatments of all of these matters are those that objectify human beings, stripping them of their very humanity. In proposing tentative standards for legal regulation, he defined obscene materials as those that have the following tendencies:

1. Arouse lust or appeal to prurient interests.
2. Arouse sexual passion in connection with scenes of extreme violence, cruelty, or brutality.
3. Visually portray in detail or graphically describe in lurid detail the violent physical destruction, torture, or dismemberment of a human being, provided that this is done to exploit morbid or shameful interest in these matters and not for genuine scientific, educational, or artistic purposes.[10]

Since Clor wrote this definition at the end of the 1960s, there has been a dramatic increase not just in the explicitness and prevalence of commodified images of sexuality aimed at all age levels in our culture, but also of violence. In their survey of dehumanizing images in what they call our "poisonous popular culture," Sylvia Ann Hewlett and Cornel West summarize the shocking (if now familiar) statistics:

- Children who watch an average amount of TV see 8,000 murders and more than 100,000 other acts of violence during their elementary school years.
- By renting just four videos—*Total Recall, Robocop 2, Rambo III,* and *Die Hard III*—a child would witness 525 deaths.
- MTV music videos average twenty acts of violence per hour. Indeed, 60 percent of programming on MTV links violence to degrading sexual portrayals.
- Saturday morning children's programs average twenty to twenty-five violent acts per hour.[11]

Hewlett and West point to the numerous studies since 1960 of television's clear role as a factor in children's aggressive behavior. In one revealing example, a mother is quoted as saying that after viewing just one violent children's show, "Power Rangers," "my four-year-old ran off to her room to 'pow, bam, bang,' her dolls." News stories have now made us familiar with the trend of "copycat violence," in which killers—including children—are inspired by particular movies to carry out acts of violence in the same manner.[12] One of the most disturbing aspects of these accounts is the way the killers see their victims as mere objects whose destruction serves the killers' quest for fame, image, or other gruesome gain.

This is not to say that television shows, movies, and music lyrics alone cause crime. It is eminently clear that many factors such as the availability of guns and the breakdown of the family—to cite only two obvious factors—are involved in actually causing a particular person to commit a violent criminal act. What is important to realize is how a culture that daily bombards its citizens with violent imagery desensitizes or numbs them.

In July 2000, the American Academy of Pediatrics, the American Medical Association, and the American Academy of Child and Adolescent Psychology issued a joint statement along precisely these lines. As a result of three decades of research, these organizations concluded that "viewing entertainment violence can lead to increases in aggressive attitudes, values, and behavior, particularly in children." Viewing such matter, they asserted, has "measurable and long-lasting effects," and can cause "emotional desensitization toward violence in real life." The report stated that children exposed to violence are more prone to consider violence an acceptable solution to everyday conflicts and to adopt a view of the world as a "violent and mean place." This cynicism in turn fosters a disproportionate fear of becoming a victim and a reluctance to help real victims of violence, as well as a cultivation of "self-protective behaviors and a mistrust of others."[13]

One of the glaring effects of this desensitization to violence is a tendency to objectify human beings—to see them not as living, breathing, persons endowed with unique characters and souls, but as replaceable objects or instruments. This instrumental view of humankind casts the individual in a role of supreme importance and portrays others as mere objects either standing in the way or serving the individual's needs and desires. This objectification of people goes far beyond the one-dimensionality that can appear in any expressive form from drama to painting, especially when it is poorly executed. Instead, it is a result of the accumulation of vast numbers of a certain kind of such renderings. The primarily visual media of our day have combined with market imperatives to create a toxic mixture. Video depictions have a unique capacity to create an imaginary world that can actually appear to be the real world. This version of the world, immersed as it is in commodity-oriented market imperatives, makes objects and commodities out of everything. Objectification is found as much in music videos and advertisements as in scenes of senseless violence. It has a cumulative effect on how we view other people. Psychologists agree that the basic minimum requirement for the formation of moral conscience in children is the early development of a sense of empathy for others.[14] Thus, it is possible that the objectification of human beings in much of popular culture acts directly against basic requirements for moral development.

Media critics have established that one of the primary techniques used in advertising is the objectification of the human body. In his seminal *Captains of Consciousness*, the historian Stuart Ewen showed that, beginning in the 1920s, advertisers drew on social psychology in order to get customers to make purchases. An article in the main advertising journal of the time actually declared that "the future of business lay in its ability to manufacture customers as well as products." Advertisers provided a critique of contemporary industrial life, "playing upon the fears and frustrations evoked by mass society"—the loneliness, cutthroat competition, and unhealthy conditions of cities and factories—at the same time they provided a solution: consumerism. They learned to capitalize on the uneasiness already present in the new urban populations by getting customers to scrutinize themselves ruthlessly and measure themselves against a manufactured image of how they assumed others saw them.[15]

Advertisers drew on such psychological theories as the idea of the "social self" put forth by Floyd Henry Allport, who argued that "our consciousness of ourselves is largely a reflection of the consciousness which others have of us" (p. 34). Another theory was that material goods fulfilled profound human instincts, such as the drive for "prestige," "beauty," "acquisition," "self-adornment," or "play." Ewen showed how the marriage of these psychological theories and the desire to create "fancied need" resulted in a "self-conscious change in the psychic economy." This change entailed a new "critical self-consciousness" (p. 35).

According to Ewen, advertisers deliberately decided to follow this policy. One advertiser, Frederick Parker Anderson, told about the "industry's conscious attempt to direct man's critical faculties against himself or his environment, to make him self-conscious about matter of course things such as enlarged nose pores, bad breath." Another, Roy Dickinson, said that "advertising helps to keep the masses dissatisfied with their mode of life, discontented with the ugly things around them. Satisfied customers are not as profitable as discontented ones" (p. 39).

Ewen wrote that this new self-consciousness combined, on the one hand, a "self-denigrating paranoia" and, on the other, a "self-fetishization"—an antidote to self-criticism that had "auto-erotic" undertones: "Though the victorious heroines of cosmetic advertisements always got their man, they did so out of a commodity defined self-fetishization which made that man and themselves almost irrelevant to the quality of their victory" (p. 48). The self here was defined as a set of problems, and the body was seen part by part, with each part held up to close examination. The role of other people was increasingly that of a faceless audience, a mere backdrop to the self's main endeavor: presentation.

The flip-side of self-fetishization was paranoia—an uncontrollable anxiety about how society perceived one. Depictions of the world as naturally inimical to one's interests not only made the self a central preoccupation, but it also made that preoccupation take the form of fear and doubt. The head of one major New York advertising agency quoted by Ewen spoke of the usefulness of fear in getting Americans to consume.

Advertisements then (as now) delivered an antisocial, atomistic vision of society in which each individual had to go it alone against a hostile world. One ad for soap depicted a "mountain of men, each climbing over one another to reach the summit." Naturally, just one man prevailed, reaching his arms up to the sun, the rays of which said "Heart's Desire." Consumerism thus appeared to provide the solution to the anonymity, overcrowding, and homogeneity of mass society in the ostensible individuality of consumer choice. In the process, other people appeared increasingly as objects, mere obstacles in the way of the fulfillment of one's dreams. Ewen wrote that the world created by advertising was one "in which there was the total absence of positive bonds between people" (pp. 45, 98–99). Advertisements now take this logic to its most brutal extreme. One ad for the soft drink 7-Up cited by Enola Aird shows a young black man walking toward the camera with a T-shirt that reads "Make 7." As he turns and walks away the back of his T-shirt reads "Up Yours."[16]

In recent years, advertisers have stepped up their targeting of children, raising their direct expenditures (excluding appeals to parents to spend on behalf of their children) from $100 million in 1990 to $2 billion in 2001. "Overall," reports one article, "direct spending by minors has tripled since 1990," with children under age twelve spending approximately $28.4 billion in 1998 alone. Children as young as three years old recognize on the average "as many as 100 brand names," and children in general witness an average of 40,000 ads per year. While shocking to the average citizen, this is just business for the advertisers and merchants involved. Market-research is now conducted wherever children are found, "from daycare centers to schools to camps." Professional conferences unabashedly examine the theme of marketing to preschoolers or even the age 0–3 market. Together with an advocacy group called Commercial Alert, founded by Ralph Nader, sixty psychologists recently reported to the American Psychological Association their alarm at the use of psychology "to manipulate" and "exploit" youngsters "for commercial purposes." They consider "the use of psychological insight and methodology to bypass parents and influence the behavior and desires of children" to be a "crisis for the profession of psychology."[17]

Media critic Jean Kilbourne has specifically pointed to the portrayal of women and girls as objects, positing a link between the unrealistic thinness of models in fashion magazines and on television and the high incidence of girls' and women's dissatisfaction with their bodies, their embrace of dieting fads, and even the prevalence of eating disorders such as anorexia and bulimia.[18] In support of this connection, a recent article in the *New York Times* stated that until recently the Pacific Island nation of Fiji was a place where eating disorders were "virtually unheard of." Curvaceousness and a healthy appetite were actually considered positive goods. A study presented at the American Psychiatric Association meetings in 1999, however, showed that a rise in eating disorders has accompanied the recent introduction of television into a Fiji province, Viti Levu. The study drew a correlation between hours spent viewing television and increased incidences of and risk for this illness.[19] The proliferation of men's magazines and beauty aids has also accompanied a rise in eating disorders among men. The obsession with body image cited by patients with these disorders clearly results from a complicated set of psychological factors, yet it is impossible to ignore the barrage of images objectifying the body as an aggravating factor.[20]

Beyond images in magazines and advertisements, an entire industry has arisen to engineer and manipulate the body. Mainstream businesses are now engaged in everything from body piercing to tattooing, and the beauty industry's hair and skin dyes, permanent wave and hair removal solutions, and other chemical applications enjoy skyrocketing popularity. Moreover, the medical profession and scientific community have become involved in the manipulation of the body through plastic surgery, sex-change operations, and even exploration of the possibility of human cloning.[21] Most alarming here is the lack of any sense of the integrity of the body as a creation of nature or God. This objectification is strikingly different from the traditional medical model of healing, which presumed this integrity.

Other writers have pointed to more blatant antisocial messages in popular culture, ones that directly condemn other people and even call for their extermination—the logical consequence of objectification and instrumentalism when taken to their extremes. Hewlett and West trace one such theme—antiparent sentiment—through television talk shows, movies, and best-selling self-help or therapy books. In numerous examples, they show parents being depicted as inept and unintelligent— "ineffectual fools" is how they put it—or else as severely dysfunctional and vicious. A band called Body Count sold 500,000 copies of an album that contained the gruesome and abhorrent song "Momma's Gotta Die

Tonight." The singer Marilyn Manson, whose lyrics are also reprehensible, sells concert-goers T-shirts that read "Kill Your Parents." Hewlett and West pointed out that this same hateful spirit is actually buttressed by movements in pop psychology and therapy that justify self-obsession and target parents for disproportionate blame and invective.[22]

Loss of Proportion

One need only tune in to mainstream television or radio at any time during the day to glimpse the world to which most American children and teenagers are exposed. As the Motherhood Project's report, "Watch Out for Children," puts it, the "driving messages" of advertising alone "are 'You deserve a break today,' 'Follow your instincts. Obey your thirst,' 'Just Do It,' 'No Boundaries,' 'Got the Urge?'" The overriding point here is "that life is about selfishness, instant gratification, and materialism." According to one advertising company president quoted in the report, the media actively promotes a "got-to-have-it or gimme attitude."[23]

Unfortunately, this attitude goes well beyond advertisements. The idea that there are no legitimate limits on individual needs and freedoms is reinforced on talk shows, game shows, soap operas, and other programs. Indeed, political theorists and social critics have observed that radical, atomistic individualism is a fundamental aspect of American political life and culture more broadly. One critical voice in this chorus is that of the political theorist Jean Bethke Elshtain, who has written extensively on the breakdown of any sense of separation between public and private life. She posits that this breakdown is so complete that private needs have become reinterpreted as public rights. The role of a citizen—someone who puts on a public persona in order to consider issues affecting community well-being and places private concerns temporarily to the side—has vanished. In its place is "a world of triumphalist I's." In this world, writes Elshtain, "everything I 'want' gets defined politically as a 'right.' Thus, for example, my desire, now a right, to have easy access to a pornography channel on cable television is conflated with my right to be safe from arrest or torture for my political views."[24]

One of the most jarring aspects of this ethos of hyperindividualism is its complete lack of any sense of proportion and perspective. Any and all needs, however fleeting or trifling, have equal standing, and the self is assumed to be the legitimate subject of nearly any conversation or pursuit.

Self-aggrandizement is considered valid and desirable. Individual preferences are subsumed into one vast force of want or need and treated with the utmost seriousness.

This disproportionate emphasis on the more trivial aspects of the self defines the way Americans now approach being in the world. For example, the number of possessions many Americans acquire far surpasses any measure of reasonable need or, for that matter, luxury—as it was defined by all those (except the very rich) in preceding generations. The time spent contemplating or making purchases edges out nearly all other endeavors except work, which is recast as a necessary prelude to consumption. The amount of time spent on superficial aspects of self-presentation precludes more profound forms of self-development, the cultivation of artistic or other capacities, intellectual pursuits, civic engagement, spiritual observance, and family or social life. Entertainment has taken on such massive proportions, invading such realms as education and news reportage, that media critic Neil Postman validly warned nearly twenty years ago that we were "amusing ourselves to death."[25] Americans' infatuation with celebrities and celebrity culture suggests how entertainment has been reconstrued to comprise the very purpose of social existence, setting the everyday aspirations of Americans, however unrealistic. Addicted to a numbing level of comfort and luxury beyond what we can appreciate, we use natural resources at unprecedented rates without any relation to need or impact on the planet. The list of examples of our lack of balance and proportion is endless.

This loss of proportion about our endeavors as humans—which has proceeded to the point where it threatens not only the quality of our own daily lives but also our very existence on Earth—is deeply rooted in our history. Historian Christopher Lasch traced this attitude to the doctrine of progress as it emerged in the eighteenth century and increasingly gained purchase in the twentieth century as a rationale for continually expanding commercial exploitation. In *The Culture of Narcissism*, he described how, by the late twentieth century, the denial of limits on human mastery created such dire social conditions—the threat of nuclear annihilation, the impending exhaustion of the earth's resources, the anomie of large bureaucracies, the erosion of any sense of legitimate controls—that it produced a new American personality type. Far from an overly confident, selfish individual, the narcissist exhibited anxiety and self-doubt. Narcissists are characterized by the lack of a solid, stable conception of the self and its boundaries. They view the world as a projection of their own desires for gratification and look to others only for a reflection of the self. Lacking any sense of the limits of their desires and the existence of other selves apart from their own, they are unable to develop natural bonds with other people and experience the normal, bounded pleasures of everyday life. At the mercy of unrealistic cravings they can never satisfy, they feel intense dissatisfaction and loneliness.[26]

Incoherence

When each individual believes that his or her needs are unlimited and supreme, the result is obviously a brutal social life. Even further, this social life is chaotic. Among many other shortcomings, it lacks any sense of the point of its own existence, any fundamental coherence. For instance, at the same time that life becomes increasingly artificial and removed from nature, marketers advertise everything from cigarettes to cosmetics as a way to make oneself appear more natural. In everyday life, images of commodities jarringly appear in places hitherto understood to be non-commercial. The particular content of these images disturbs older aesthetic expectations, creating further nonsensical juxtapositions, such as an oversized picture of a reclining bikini-clad woman with seductive gaze or head thrown back in ecstasy, taking up the whole side of a city bus.

Much of the incoherence of the world we are passing on to our children derives from a fundamental clash between the regnant market culture and any version of a moral culture. Elshtain quotes Pope John Paul II's criticism of the current stage of modern capitalism for its "superdevelopment," which is based on the frantic production and distribution "of every kind of material good." This market orientation "makes people slaves of 'possession' and of immediate gratification, with no other horizon than the multiplication or continual replacement of the things already owned with others still better."[27] The upshot, in Elshtain's words, is "materialism and restless dissatisfaction."[28]

The consumer culture is fundamentally contradictory. On the one hand, it holds out a promise of total self-fulfillment through extreme pleasure and satisfaction. On the other, it relies on its ability to create or tap into profound feelings of dissatisfaction. Still further, it proposes that a deep sense of personal satisfaction, a sense of identity, and happiness can all be obtained through purchases that help one project a superficial image aimed at manipulating other people, thus actually paving the way for a feeling of emptiness and pointlessness.

The Motherhood report speaks of a divide between the "money world" and the "motherworld," which it casts as a fundamental "conflict of values" between "the values of commerce and the values required to raise healthy children": "The difference between the money world and the motherworld is the difference between means and ends. In the motherworld, children are ends in themselves. They are priceless gifts. We love them. We care for their dignity and for their character. We are concerned for their souls. In the money world, our children are primarily means to other ends. You [corporations] want to maximize sales. For you, our children are customers, and childhood is a 'market segment' to be exploited, a 'demographic' for which you are competing." The report does not take issue with the marketplace itself, or "economic freedom," which it calls "one of the foundations of democracy." But it does zero in on the "value system" pushed by the current market. This system of values "promotes self-indulgence, assaults the idea of restraint, degrades human sexuality, promotes the notion that our identity is determined by what we buy, and forces us constantly to scale down our sensitivity to vulgarity, ugliness, and violence." The report expresses dismay that marketing goes directly against teachers and parents "by suggesting to students that everything in life, even their education, is ultimately about spinning and pitching and soliciting." These values are directly opposite the ones needed for children's maturation as humane adults and good citizens. The market values, say the report's authors, "are at odds with the values we try to teach our children, values essential for civilized life: that children should care about others, that they should be able to govern themselves, and that there is more to life than material things."[29]

The Political Impasse

In recent years, loud cries have rung out about a moral crisis in the nation. Alarmed by the moral relativism seen in the approaches of many parents and teachers, reformers like William Bennett have helped spur a trend toward character education in schools. His well-known *Book of Virtues* attempts to inculcate ethics in children through moralizing tales.[30] Similar books, with different emphases, have come out from the political Left.

The movement spearheaded by Tipper Gore to label music compact disks for children and teenagers did take hold. A number of groups of parents or consumers have also sprouted up to keep watch on the media and the market, making information on offensive material public and pressuring advertisers and media conglomerates. Finally, many individuals and families are changing their habits in order to provide small-scale resistance to what they see as an incoherent, amoral, selfish, and obscene culture.

There is much to be said about these approaches, but they are inadequate to the Herculean task before them. The effectiveness of these efforts will continue to be limited as long as they keep coming up against a barrier that is primarily political and ideological. Worries about the excesses and messages of advertising tend to come from the Left. Worries about moral relativism in education and the media tend to come from the Right. Worries about inappropriate media fare for children and adolescents come from many points across the spectrum, but most often from the Right when the issue is sex and from the Left when the issue is violence. In the meantime, the culture that remains strikes many as unconscionable. Dissent from both the Right and the Left is compromised by an embrace of the free market as currently arranged and a market-defined notion of freedom. Elshtain gets at this when she writes:

> On the one hand, we witness a morally exhausted Left embracing the logic of the market by endorsing the translation of *wants* into *rights*. Although the political Left continues to argue for taming the market in an economic sense, it follows the market model when social relations are concerned, seeing in any restriction of individual "freedom" or "lifestyle option," as we call it today, an unacceptable diminution of rights and free expression. On the other hand, many on the political Right love the untrammeled (or the less trammeled the better) operations of the market in economic life, but call for a state-enforced restoration of traditional mores, including strict sexual and social scripts for men and women in family and work life.[31]

In our time of political flux, such generalizations fortunately no longer completely capture the real range of positions, including centrist and independent thought (including Elshtain's) that defies traditional party lines. But it is apparent that an overly libertarian streak has splashed itself across American politics of all stripes to the detriment of our public culture. Liberals rightly worry that attempts to enforce morality could infringe, for example, on the newly won rights and freedoms of gays, and conservatives rightly worry about the potential of vast, inefficient government regulations and bureaucracies to stifle entrepreneurial initiative and ingenuity. But in resorting to the extremes of personal liberty and free market philosophy, in the absence of countervailing structures and traditions of civic and family life, as well as government pressure and regulation of the worst corporate excesses, this libertarianism paves the way for the total dominance of commercial over moral culture.

Our Alternatives

The current situation is untenable. Anyone raising young children today faces a major challenge: to raise good children in a culture that holds reprehensible behavior as the ideal. In such circumstances, the options are limited. The starkest choices are either to acquiesce and go along with the mainstream, forgetting one's qualms, or to sever one's ties completely and take up residence in some far-flung community or in another country. While the latter is tempting, real isolation is most likely elusive, given the globalization of the economy and thus of culture. Between these extremes, however, are endless possibilities for various forms of resistance and opposition, from individual revolt to collective pressure.

The idea of totally opting out of mainstream American life has a history as long as the country's, but that history is largely one of failure. The period of social reform from the 1830s to the 1850s witnessed a huge number of utopian experiments, from the transcendentalists' Brook Farm to the Oneida community in upstate New York. With the notable exception of Oneida, which had its own problems, most such experiments were very brief. This was also the case with the large number of communal living arrangements that were inspired by 1960s revolt. These efforts inevitably stumbled on the same recurrent problems: who would do the household and other chores and what the sexual guidelines would be in a noncommercial, egalitarian world of freedom. Not only do people disagree over what constitutes a utopia, they also tend to invade each others' privacy and rights when they seek to perfect individual behavior in the name of the collective. In all cases, tension with mainstream culture is omnipresent, since the founders' initial socialization took place in that culture and ties between community members and the outside world continue to exist. The dominant role of the larger culture is an insurmountable obstacle.

The problems with exile are substantial. Commitment to the nation and sheer self-defense rule it out. For an American to reject all of American culture is to reject the privileges and protections of citizenship in the longest-lasting experiment in democracy in the history of the world. It is precisely this history of democracy that gives hope for the future. As much a part of its history as its political and economic growth are this country's rich traditions, including traditions of dissent that have continually produced, along with the occasional demagogue, important democratic and humanitarian change. Genuine artistic and intellectual freedom—not the freedom to debase our public culture for the sake of individual gain—is essential for this kind of dissent, for the flourishing of culture, and for the nurture of children. A movement on behalf of the quality of life our democracy makes possible would be in the best tradition of American self-betterment and social reform.

A compelling model for beginning such an effort is the one put forth by the Motherhood Project: engaged resistance. This is a posture based on a grateful sense of belonging to and connectedness with other citizens in the nation at the same time that one opposes the negative incursions of the dominant culture and attempts to change it through peaceful debate and resistance. It includes family and individual changes, such as reducing or eliminating the time spent watching television, muting advertisements when they come on, or restricting the intrusions of the media more broadly—including "TV, cable, radio, video games, and the Internet." It includes increasing the number of activities such as sports and games that are "not media driven," making homes "commerce free zones," and refusing to have children serve as "walking billboards" with brands showing on their clothes or to let them be used for market research. It includes changing one's attitude: "We will strive to lead less media-driven, work-driven, and consumption driven lives, and more balanced, fruitful, and purposeful lives." It includes forms of collective protest such as boycotts of companies that refuse to support the goal of eliminating destructive, antisocial messages or who sponsor programs with undue sex or violence. It includes boycotts, petition and letter-writing campaigns, and exclusive patronage of companies that adopt a code of self-regulation. It includes lobbying and forming "communities of resistance" in order to "establish more spaces in which children can be safe from the entreaties of advertising and marketing." It includes meeting with advertisers in order to persuade them to support the moral culture and supporting protests, such as one that was waged against the Golden Marble award for the best advertisement aimed at children.[32]

One caveat: it will not suffice to focus on the need for a separate, protected world for children. This logic allowed the outcry against the brutal lyrics of some rap songs to be reduced to a question of age-appropriate ratings. It allows lamentations about a fundamental moral crisis to be reduced to a need for character education in schools. The obscenity of modern culture should be the concern not just of the "motherworld," but also of all those who ascribe to any kind of moral world at all. For the Motherhood Project and others like it to be effective, the quality of the wider culture beyond the child's world needs to be kept in view. It is not enough to protect children from the culture of obscenity until they come of age. The successful socialization of children is contingent upon the existence of a meaningful society and culture into which to socialize them.

Many compelling voices have pointed out that we need to find a new basis for our relations with one another. Elshtain quotes Pope John Paul II who sees "solidarity" as an alternative to the ethos of cutthroat competition and materialism that threaten to rend the basic social bonds required to sustain a society. Rather than counting on a "vague compassion" for others or "shallow distress" for their woes, solidarity would demand that we view "the 'other' . . . not just as some kind of instrument . . . but as our 'neighbor,' a 'helper' . . . to be made a sharer on a par with ourselves in the banquet of life to which all are equally invited by God."[33]

Others have suggested that we need to know more about how the media and market culture work so that we can teach our children to see through their messages and know when they are being manipulated.[34] While some of this information is undoubtedly helpful, as a major plan of action this approach risks falling into acquiescence and cynicism. A culture of resistance based mainly on negation and criticism still keeps our attention riveted on the impoverished messages and images at issue. Much more promising would be an immediate decision on the part of vast numbers of people to live completely differently. This would mean finding sources for our public philosophy other than the media and the market. It would entail refusing to let virtual experiences and relations stand in for real ones. In essence, it would mean finding a culture and a society that is made up of more than just vicious and voracious selves and marketable commodities.

Wendell Berry has eloquently articulated an ethos that constitutes a true alternative to the exploitative, self-interested one now dominant in our age: stewardship. He has elaborated at length the ways in which particular approaches of modern business (mainly agribusiness) have cut us off from our moral tradition, which was embedded in our agricultural past. This tradition, he writes, involves a profound recognition of our basic dependence on one another: it "asks us to consider that we are members of the human community and are therefore bound to help or harm it by our behavior." Berry argues that one of the primary traits of any orthodoxy is that people who have adopted it can see no other options. This means that any effective change must originate on "the margins" of that orthodoxy, and that it must present a clear alternative to the dominant thought. Using the decline of small farming as a metaphor for the larger ravages of advanced consumer capitalism, he believes that our own orthodoxy revolves around a belief in profit, affluence, immediate gains, large-scale exploitation. The alternative vision is one based on long-term sufficiency, preservation, human-scale activities, a sense of "enough." Pointing to the factors that go into making a farm a viable concern, Berry points out that one of the most essential is "the farmer's wish to remain there." We might say the same about American society at the dawn of the twenty-first century. For this country to remain viable, it will be necessary for parents to continue to wish to raise their children here.

NOTES

1. Quoted in Don Oldenburg, "Ads Aimed at Kids," *Washington Post*, 3 May 2001, p. C4.

2. Ibid.

3. Okey Ndibe, "Early Exposure to Sexual Images Ruins Children," *Hartford Courant*, 10 February 2001, p. A11.

4. Frank Rich, "Naked Capitalists," *New York Times Magazine*, 20 May 2001, pp. 51, 80.

5. Rochelle Gurstein, "Obscenity," in *A Companion to American Thought*, ed. Richard Wightman Fox and James T. Kloppenberg (Oxford: Blackwell, 1995), pp. 506–7; Rochelle Gurstein, *The Repeal of Reticence: A History of America's Cultural and Legal Struggles over Free Speech, Obscenity, Sexual Liberation, and Modern Art* (New York: Hill and Wang, 1996), pp. 39–49.

6. Gurstein, "Obscenity," p. 507; Rochelle Gurstein, "On the Obsolescence of 'Puritanism' as an Epithet," in *Reconstructing History: The Emergence of a New Historical Society*, ed. Elizabeth Fox-Genovese and Elisabeth Lasch-Quinn (New York: Routledge, 1999), pp. 56–70, originally published in *Salmagundi*; Gurstein, *Repeal of Reticence*, pp. 179–212, 288–308.

7. Gurstein, "Obscenity," p. 507.

8. Harry M. Clor, *Obscenity and Public Morality: Censorship in a Liberal Society* (Chicago: University of Chicago, 1969), p. 225.

9. Ibid., p. 225; the quote is from George Elliott, "Against Pornography," *Harper's Magazine*, March 1965, pp. 52–53.

10. Clor, *Obscenity and Public Morality*, p. 245.

11. Sylvia Ann Hewlett and Cornel West, *The War Against Parents: What We Can Do for America's Beleaguered Moms and Dads* (Boston: Houghton Mifflin, 1998), p. 149; the various sources of their compilation are cited on p. 281, n. 48.

12. Ibid., pp. 150–53.

13. Donald E. Cook et al., *Joint Statement on the Impact of Entertainment Violence on Children*, Congressional Public Health Summit Report, 26 July 2000, available through the American Academy of Pediatrics at www.aap.org/advocacy/releases/jstmtevc.htm

14. Wray Herbert and Missy Daniel, "The Moral Child," *U.S. News and World Report*, 3 June 1996, p. 52.

15. Stuart Ewen, *Captains of Consciousness: Advertising and the Social Roots of the Consumer Culture* (New York: McGraw-Hill, 1976), pp. 53, 44–45.

16. Enola Aird and David Blankenhorn, "Advertising to Minors is Major Endeavor," *Orlando Sentinel*, 6 May 2001, p. G1.

17. Ibid.

18. See Jean Kilbourne, *Still Killing Us Softly*, video produced and directed by Margaret Lazarus (Cambridge, Mass.: Cambridge Documentary Films, 1987) and her other films in her *Killing Us Softly* and her book, *Deadly Persuasion: Why Women and Girls Must Fight the Addictive Power of Advertising* (New York: Simon & Schuster, 1999).

19. Erica Goode, "Study Finds TV Alters Fiji Girls' View of Body," *New York Times*, 20 May 1999, p. A17.

20. Donna Kutt Nahas, "Eating Disorders in Men—Researchers and Clinicians Are Seeing More New Cases," *New York Newsday*, 7 November 2000, p. C5; Nanci Hellmich, "Man in the Mirror: Obsessed Body Fixation May Muscle Out Health," *USA Today*, 20 September 2000, p. 6D.

21. John Leo, "The Sex-Change Boom," *U.S. News and World Report*, 12 March 2001, p. 20; Leon R. Kass, "Preventing a Brave New World: Why We Should Ban Human Cloning Now" *The New Republic*, 21 May 2001, pp. 30–39.

22. Hewlett and West, *The War Against Parents*, pp. 131–33.

23. The Motherhood Project, Institute for American Values, "Watch Out for Children: A Mother's Appeal to Advertisers," 2 May 2001, available at www .watchoutforchildren.org/html/watch_out_for_children.html

24. Jean Bethke Elshtain, *Democracy on Trial* (New York: Basic Books, 1995), pp. 41–42.

25. Neil Postman, *Amusing Ourselves to Death: Public Discourse in the Age of Show Business* (New York: Viking Penguin, 1985), pp. 83–98.

26. Christopher Lasch, *The Culture of Narcissism* (New York: W. W. Norton, 1979), pp. xiii–xvi.

27. Pope John Paul II, "Sollicitudo Rei Socialis," *Origins* 17, no. 33 (1988), quoted in Elshtain, *Democracy on Trial*, pp. 13–14.

28. Ibid., p. 14.

29. The Motherhood Project, "Watch Out for Children," pp. 4–6, 14.

30. William J. Bennett, *Book of Virtues: A Treasury of Great Moral Stories* (New York: Simon and Schuster, 1993).

31. Elshtain, *Democracy on Trial*, p. 16.

32. Motherhood Project, "Watch Out for Children," pp. 22–23.

33. Pope John Paul II, "Sollicitudo Rei Socialis," quoted in Elshtain, *Democracy on Trial*, pp. 13–14.

34. Neil Postman, for instance, makes this suggestion at the end of his excellent critique, *Amusing Ourselves to Death*, pp. 158–63.

4

The Problem of Exposure

Violence, Sex, Drugs, and Alcohol

Stacy L. Smith and Ed Donnerstein

Recently, a rash of schoolyard shootings have taken place across the country. As a result, Americans are asking, "who is to blame for kids killing kids?" Although many point an accusatory finger at the perpetrator's parents, increased accessibility to guns, and schools' unresponsiveness to peer harassment, the mass media also have been implicated as a contributory factor. Indeed, a recent nationwide poll conducted by *Newsweek* (1999) reveals that 78 percent of those interviewed believe that the media deserve "some" or "a lot" of the blame for the recent mass shootings.[1]

What impact does exposure to media violence and other negative images of sex, drugs, and alcohol have on this country's youth? This chapter will attempt to answer this very question. One important caveat must be made before we do so, however. The mass media are only one factor that may contribute to children's and young adults' socialization. We would never argue that they are the only factor nor even the most important one. Yet research reveals consistently that exposure to the mass media can independently and interactively with other factors contribute to children's socioemotional development.

The chapter is divided into four sections. First, we will examine how

much time children spend consuming media content. Because of continued public concern, most of the research reviewed in this section will focus on the prevalence and use of the most popular mass media in the lives
of young people—television. Second, we will examine the types of negative messages children are being exposed to in the mass media. In particular, we will review content analyses of violence, sex, drugs, and alcohol. Third, we will examine the effect of exposure to these four different
types of "negative" media content. We will pay specific attention to the
impact of viewing these types of media messages on young viewers'
thoughts, attitudes, and behaviors. Finally, we will turn our attention to
the influence of the Internet in the lives of American children. We will
focus on the types of content children may be exposed to online as well
as the effects of such exposure. We will also discuss measures designed
to help reduce the risk that exposure to inappropriate Internet content
might have on children.

Patterns of Exposure

Television is a ubiquitous phenomenon in the lives of most American
kids. Nielsen data reveals that 98 percent of the households in this country have at least one television set and 76 percent have more than one.[2]
Further, the television set is on an average of seven-and-one-half hours
per day, slightly more in winter than in summer.

These figures tell us very little, however, about how much time children actually spend watching television. To address this issue, the Henry
J. Kaiser Family Foundation (1999) conducted a nationwide survey to
assess children's and adolescents' patterns of exposure to the mass
media.[3] A total of 3,155 2- to 18-year-old children or their parents were
surveyed at length about media consumption. The results reveal that
children spend an average of 2 hours and 46 minutes watching television
per day, which is far more time than they spend reading print media (44
minutes), listening to CDs/tapes (48 minutes) or the radio (39 minutes).
These figures suggest that children are watching roughly 19 hours of television programming per week or approximately 1,000 hours (one-and-
a-half months) per year.

Several factors have been found to influence youngsters' television
use. The first is age. Studies reveal a curvilinear relationship between age
and children's exposure to television.[4] The 1999 Kaiser Foundation

study found that exposure to television increases until 13 years of age and then declines throughout the remaining teenage years. The decline of television watching in later adolescence is presumably due to the increasing importance of other social activities during junior and senior high school.

The second factor is gender. Research reveals that boys report watching slightly more television than do girls.[5] Typically, these differences are explained by the larger number of male characters on television than female ones. In this situation, young males have more same-sex role models to attend to and identify with than their young female counterparts. Another explanation for boys' increased TV use is that children's programs are often filled with action and violence, two features of television that young boys are drawn to and report liking.[6]

The third factor is parents' level of education. Studies generally show that individuals with more formal education report watching less television.[7] Educated parents may be more likely to encourage their children to engage in other types of leisure-time activities, such as reading. Indeed, research reveals that children with highly educated parents are less likely to watch television than are those with less educated parents.[8]

In addition to television, children have access to at least a few other forms of mass media in their lives that are worth mentioning. According to Nielsen research, 76 percent of American households subscribe to basic cable programming in this country and 85 percent own a VCR,[9] thereby potentially bringing into the home more graphic and explicit images of violence, drugs, and sex. The use of video-game technology is also increasing. Based on the 1999 Kaiser Foundation survey, 70 percent of the children in this country have a video game player in their home, and the average child spends 20 minutes playing per day, with boys engaging in more daily interactivity (31 minutes) than girls (8 minutes).[10]

Taken together, these results reveal that children spend a lot of time with media, most frequently television. In fact, TV viewing is their number one leisure-time activity outside of sleep.

Patterns of Content

A nationwide survey of over 800 8- to 15-year-olds was undertaken recently by Nickelodeon, the Henry J. Kaiser Family Foundation, and Children Now to learn what sources adolescents rely on to get information about tough issues such as violence, sex, drugs, and alcohol.[11] Nearly 40 percent of the 12- to 15-year-olds surveyed stated that television and movies were a source of "a lot" of information about these topics. Given these findings, it becomes important to examine the media messages being sent to our children regarding these issues.

Violence

The largest and most comprehensive assessment of violence on television in the history of social science research was conducted recently for the $3.3 million National Television Violence Study, funded by the National Cable Television Association in 1994.[12] Barbara J. Wilson and her colleagues assessed violence in a composite week of television programming during the 1994/95, 1995/96, and 1996/97 viewing seasons across twenty-three popular broadcast, independent, and cable outlets. In addition to tabulating the amount of violence shown on these channels, the researchers assessed ten major contextual variables that have been found to either increase or decrease the risk of aggression, fear, and desensitization (see table 4.1).

The NTVS findings reveal four major trends in the presentation of violence. First, violence is pervasive on American television. Sixty percent of television programs feature one or more violent acts and the typical show features an average of six violent interactions per hour. Second, violence on television is often glamorized. Attractive characters are shown engaging routinely in justified violence, and the negative consequences of their aggressive behavior are rarely depicted. Almost 40 percent of violent incidents on television feature attractive characters, who are potent role models that children and adults identify with. Roughly 30 percent of violent interactions are justified or socially sanctioned. In addition, more than one-third of violent programs depict "bad" characters who are never or rarely punished for their violent actions.

Third, violence on television is sanitized and trivialized. Over half of all violent interactions on television show no physical pain to the victim. Yet more than 50 percent of the violent interactions on television would be lethal or incapacitating if they occurred in the real world. Less than 20 percent of all violent programs depict the extended pain and suffering caused by aggression, and roughly 40 percent of the violent scenes are featured in a humorous context.

Table 4.1. The Impact of Media Violence by Context Factor

	Outcome Variables		
	Learning Aggression	Emotional Desensitization	Fear
Attractive perpetrators	↑		
Attractive victims			↑
Weapons	↑		
Extensiveness/graphicness	↑	↑	↑
Justification	↑		
Rewards	↑		↑
Punishments	↓		↓
Realism	↑		↑
Humor	↑	↑	

Source: Adapted with permission from Barbara J. Wilson et al., National Television Violence Study (Thousand Oaks, Calif.: Sage, 1997), vol. 1, p. 22.
↑ = an increase of a particular outcome variable
↓ = a decrease of a particular outcome variable

A few other notable findings from NTVS should be highlighted. Across all three years, movies are the most likely genre to feature violence (90%), followed by dramatic series (74%) and children's shows (67%). Out of all genres, children's programs feature the highest rate of violent interactions per hour (13.37). However, not all children's shows concentrate equally on violence. Adventure/mystery shows have an average of 14.3 violent interactions per hour; slapstick comedies have 29.1; and superhero programs have 28.1. Social relationship and magazine style children's shows portray substantially less violence (4.2 and 1.6 violent interactions per hour respectively).[13] Although music videos have received a great deal of public criticism,[14] Smith and Boyson's 2002 secondary analysis of NTVS data shows that only 15 percent featured violence, with rap videos (29%) more likely to contain aggressive content than adult contemporary (7%), rock (12%), or rhythm and blues videos (9%).[15]

Sex

How much sex is on television? Although several studies have attempted to answer this question,[16] the most rigorous measurement of sex on TV was conducted recently by Dale Kunkel and his research team at the

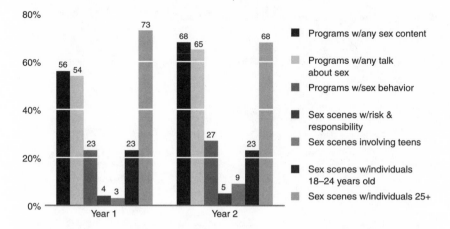

Fig. 4.1. Distribution of Sexual Messages on Television: 1998 vs. 2000. Data from Dale Kunkel et al., *Sex on TV 2: A Biennial Report to the Kaiser Family Foundation* (Menlo Park, Calif.: Kaiser Family Foundation, 2001).

University of California, Santa Barbara. Funded by the Henry J. Kaiser Family Foundation,[17] the team is conducting a biennial examination of the amount of talk about sex as well as sexual behavior on television. Every two years, the researchers sample and code a composite week of television content across ten broadcast, independent, and cable channels. In this way, they are recording the longitudinal patterns in sexual depictions on television.

The results show that the amount of sexual content on television has increased. In the course of two years, the percentage of programs featuring any type of sexual content has risen 12 percent (see fig. 4.1) and the rate of sexual scenes per hour has increased from 3.2 to 4.1. As noted in figure 4.1, the amount of talk about sex and sexual behavior in television programming has also increased over time. However, the findings reveal that when sexual intercourse is featured on television, it is most often implied and is rarely overtly depicted on screen.

In addition, the findings show that more young people on television are involved in sex. Kunkel and his team observed a significant increase in the proportion of scenes featuring sexual intercourse related behaviors involving 13- to 17-year-olds from 1998 to 2000 (3% vs. 9%, respectively). Put another way, only 3 scenes featured teen intercourse across the entire composite week in 1998 while 16 such scenes occurred in 2000. Although this pattern was observed with teens, the proportion of scenes involving sexual intercourse related behavior among young adults (18- to 24-year-olds) and adults over 25 remained unchanged.

Although sexual content seems to be more prevalent on television, messages of risk (unwanted pregnancy, sexually transmitted diseases, HIV/AIDS) and responsibility (abstinence, condom use) across the overall landscape of television programming are not. Roughly 5 percent of all scenes involving sexual content in 2000 mentioned sexual precautions, negative consequences, and/or patience, virtually unchanged since 1998. However, the findings reveal that the prevalence of risk/responsibility messages are changing significantly in programs involving teens. When teens are shown talking about intercourse that has already occurred, 33 percent of the programs include some reference to protected sex, the responsibility of sexual involvement, or the risks involved in unsafe sex. Further, a quarter of all shows in which teens engage in intercourse have some type of risk/responsibility theme in the plot.[18] These trends suggest that programmers may be becoming more sensitive in their handling of sexual portrayals involving teens in light of the serious public health concerns that face this country's youth.[19]

Some television program genres and show times are associated with greater sexual content. In 2000, movies were the most likely genre to feature programs with any type of sexual content (89%) followed by situation comedies (84%) and soap operas (80%). Situation comedies had the highest rate of conversations about sex per hour (7.3), which is higher than the rate within this genre in 1998. Movies featured the most programming with sexual behaviors (68%), with a rate of 1.5 scenes per hour. Prime time, the most popular time of day for watching television, also featured more sex. A full 67 percent of the shows in prime time featured sexual content in 1997/98 and 75 percent did in 1999/00.

In sum, this research reveals that sex—like violence—is prevalent on American television. If the average child watches 2 to 3 hours of TV daily, she or he is exposed to roughly 8 to 12 scenes involving sex or somewhere between 230 to 340 such scenes per month! Clearly, young viewers are receiving a steady stream of sexual messages on television and a high proportion of these portrayals fail to depict the risks and responsibilities involved in such mature behavior.

Drugs and Alcohol

Content analyses have also examined the amount of drugs and alcohol in entertainment media. We are only going to focus on three types of media that are popular with youth: prime-time television shows, movies, and music videos. Studies show four trends in the portrayal of substance use in prime time. First, substance use is frequent in prime time.[20] For example, one study found that 64 percent of the episodes in prime time featured some reference to alcohol in the 1986 season and 8.1 alcohol drinking acts per hour.[21] More recently, Christensen, Henriksen, and Roberts (2000) found that 71 percent of top rated prime-time situation comedies and dramas depicted alcohol use and 19 percent tobacco use.[22] Second, the typical drinker and/or smoker in prime time tends to be an adult white male professional.[23] However, at least one study of substance use suggests that women drink more wine than men do. Third, substance use is sometimes presented in rewarding contexts. Wallack et al (1990) found that roughly a quarter of the episodes featuring alcohol presented it attractively and in ways that encouraged drinking. Christensen and his colleagues' results showed that almost half of all situation comedies and dramas in prime time featuring alcohol use contextualize it with humor. Finally, the negative consequences of drinking and/or smoking are rarely shown in prime time occuring in about 17–20 percent of such shows.[24]

Other studies have looked at tobacco and alcohol use in movies. Examining two hundred of the most popular movie rentals from 1996/97, Roberts, Henriksen, and Christensen (1999) found that 93 percent of movies in the sample featured alcohol, 89 percent depicted tobacco, and 22 percent showed illicit drugs.[25] Oftentimes the substance used was glamorized, with 29 percent of all movies showing positive expressions of longing, desire, or favorable attributes of use—especially for alcohol. Less than 10 percent of all movies showed the long-term repercussions of substance use and only 13 percent of all scenes showing a young character using a substance depicted any consequences whatsoever. Perhaps most surprising, the portrayal of substance use had little influence on movie rating. Seventy-nine percent of G- or PG-rated films featured tobacco use and 76 percent showed alcohol use. Consistent with these trends, Goldstein, Sobel, and Newman (1999) found that roughly half of all animated G-rated films by five production companies released between 1937 and 1997 featured one or more depictions of tobacco or alcohol use![26]

Substance use is also featured in music videos. DuRant et al. (1997) examined alcohol and tobacco use in 518 music videos of five different genres on MTV, VH-1, CMT, and BET.[27] The researchers found that alcohol and smoking were most prevalent in videos on MTV (27% and 26%, respectively) and VH-1 (25% and 23%, respectively). Rap videos (30%) and adult contemporary videos (23%) were more likely than other genres to depict smoking and rap (27%) and rock (25%) contained the most videos with alcohol. Further, alcohol was more likely to be featured in videos that contained some form of sexuality. Finally, almost three-fourths of the videos that showed them depicted smoking (74%) or alcohol use (77%) in a positive light.

In sum, popular media are filled with positive depictions of substance use. Comparing all types of content, alcohol use seems to be more frequently portrayed on television than violence and/or sex. Although the research reviewed above only focused on popular forms of entertainment media, it is important to note that children and adolescents are also being bombarded by advertising messages for alcohol on television and for both alcohol and tobacco on billboards and in magazines.[28]

Overall, the content studies all show that glamorized messages involving violence, sex, drugs, and alcohol are prevalent in the mass media, which usually do not discuss or portray the negative consequences associated with such behaviors.

Negative Effects of Exposure

Now that we have established how much and what types of messages are featured in the media, we turn our attention to the antisocial or potentially harmful effects of exposure to violence, sex, and drugs and alcohol in the media on youth.

Violence

The number of children involved with violence in this country is staggering. As reported by the Center for Disease Control and Prevention (2000), 6,146 young people between the ages of 15 and 24 were the victims of homicide in 1997, making homicide the second leading cause of death for individuals in this age bracket.[29] Since 1988, the same report indicated that more than 80 percent of the 15- to 19-year-old homicide victims were killed with guns.[30]

Does exposure to television violence contribute to any of these alarming patterns? Research reveals that it can. Numerous experiments reveal that exposure to media violence can cause an increase in aggressive behavior.[31] For instance, Bandura, Ross, and Ross (1963) found that nursery school children exposed to a model acting violently were significantly more aggressive than were those not exposed to any violent content.[32] Similar findings have been repeatedly observed with older children and adults.[33]

Although these findings are informative, the experimental research has been strongly criticized for being highly artificial and not being externally generalizable. Several studies have documented a positive relationship between exposure to television violence and aggressive attitudes and behaviors.[34] One problem with this type of synchronous research is that the directionality between the two variables is impossible to ascertain. It is possible that exposure to television violence leads to aggression while it is also possible that aggressive children seek out and watch violent television programming.

To assess this directionality issue, several longitudinal investigations have been conducted. Many of these studies have shown that the more children watch television violence in a given year the more aggressive they behave in subsequent years.[35] For boys, one investigation—as summarized by Huesmann and Miller—revealed that viewing TV violence at age 8 was a significant and positive predictor of serious adult criminality twenty-two years later independent of social class, intellectual achievement, or parenting variables.[36] In fact, a recent meta-analysis of 217 studies revealed that media violence is positively and significantly related to aggression.[37]

Several intervening variables may affect the media violence–aggression relationship. Research reveals that children who are prone to aggression,[38] fantasize about violence,[39] identify with aggressive characters,[40] and believe television violence is realistic[41] may be more at risk for learning aggression from depictions of televised violence. In addition to learning about violent acts, another harmful effect associated with viewing media violence is desensitization. People repeatedly exposed to violence may become numb or emotionally insensitive to stimuli or events. Studies show that viewing television violence can have a significant impact on desensitization.[42] For example, one investigation found that young males who were heavy viewers of television were less aroused physiologically by exposure to media violence than were young males who were light viewers.[43] Thus, heavy viewing can affect viewers' physiological reactivity to violence.

Although these findings are important, they fail to reveal what impact exposure to media violence may have on viewers' attitudes towards real-life aggression. To address this issue, scholars have assessed the effects of exposure to media violence on viewers' tolerance of real-world aggression.[44] Drabman and Thomas (1974) exposed one group of children to an 8-minute violent excerpt while another group was not shown the video. Both groups were then given an opportunity to "monitor" two nursery school children at play.[45] The results showed that children exposed to the violent clip took significantly longer to seek help when the two children got into a physical altercation than did those who were not exposed to any violent content. Similar findings have been documented more recently.[46] Hence, even short-term exposure to media violence can numb or desensitize viewers to real-world aggression.

A third and final harmful effect of viewing television violence is fear. There are two types of fear effects. First, exposure to media violence may evoke intense fright responses in viewers, especially younger children.[47] Cantor argues that three general types of media depictions routinely evoke fear: dangers and injuries, distortion of natural forms, and experiencing the endangerment and fear of others.[48] Each of these categories is common in violent media content. Although a majority of children report being frightened by television,[49] a significant number have retroactively reported experiencing more persistent forms of emotional upset such as nightmares, sleep disturbances, bizarre thoughts, and difficulty eating.[50] Second, repeated viewing of media violence may contribute to viewers' attitudes about violent crime in the world. Studies show that heavy viewing of television is positively associated with increased estimates of individuals involved in real-world crime and violence as well as the perception that the world is a mean and dangerous place.[51]

Together, over forty years of social science research reveals that exposure to media violence can contribute to learning aggression, desensitization, and fear. This conclusion has been reached by virtually every professional organization or governmental body that has examined the topic, including the American Medical Association (1996), the American Psychological Association (1993), Centers for Disease Control (1991), and even the U.S. Surgeon General (1972).[52]

Sex

Unlike the research on television violence, the research on the effects of exposure to sexual media content is in its infancy.[53] This is surprising since the United States has the highest rate of teen pregnancy in the Western industrialized world with four out of every ten young women becoming pregnant before they reach the age of 20, according to the National Campaign to Prevent Teen Pregnancy (2000).[54] Teen pregnancy is not the only problem, however. Based on the 2000 report by the Henry J. Kaiser Family Foundation, 66 percent of all new cases of sexually transmitted diseases occur in people between the ages of 15 and 24, and as many as half of all new HIV infections are estimated to be among people under 25 years of age.[55]

Because of these alarming trends, researchers have begun to assess the impact that depictions of sex in the mass media may be having on adolescents. To date, only a few experiments have examined the impact of sexual messages on adolescents' acquisition of information. For example, Greenberg, Perry, and Covert (1983) found that 5th and 6th grade viewers of a program specifically designed by CBS to teach about sexual facts and feelings learned significantly more than did nonviewers.[56] A decade later, Greenberg, Linsangan, and Soderman (1993) exposed 9th and 10th graders to a variety of clips about prostitution and sexual activity among married characters or to a variety of clips about homosexuality and sexual activity among unmarried characters.[57] The results showed that viewers were more likely to learn the meaning of sexual words and phrases ("freebie," "solicitation," "shooting blanks") after exposure to the clips of prostitution, marital sexual sctivity, and homosexuality, which shows that adolescents are acquiring sexual information from both instructional televised messages and those produced for entertainment only.

In addition to assessing how children learn about sex, scholars have been interested in the impact of exposure to sexual content on adolescents' attitudes towards premarital sex, and they have designed experiments to test this.[58] Greeson and Williams (1986) found that adolescents exposed to music videos on MTV were more likely to agree that premarital sex was OK for teenagers than were those who did not see the videos on MTV.[59] More recently, Kalof's results (1999) revealed that undergraduate females are marginally more accepting of interpersonal violence after exposure to a video with sexual and gender stereotypical imagery than are those undergraduate females exposed to a video devoid of such content.[60]

While the research presented above has been concerned with transitory effects, at least one study has assessed the impact of massive exposure to sexual content on teens' moral evaluations. Byrant and Rockwell (1994) exposed male and female adolescents for three hours on five consecutive nights to one of three types of television content: (1) sexual relations between unmarried partners, (2) sexual relations between married partners, or (3) nonsexual relations between adults.[61] Several days after this exposure, the teens were brought back into the lab and were shown a series of video clips, some of which featured sexual improprieties. The results showed that those adolescents who had been exposed to massive doses of unmarried intercourse rated the sexual improprieties as less bad than did those teens who had seen the other types of videos. The researchers replicated these findings in a subsequent experiment utilizing a no-viewing control group.

All of this research has examined the impact of the types of images and conversations depicted routinely on broadcast television. Nielsen research, however, shows that more and more families across the country are subscribing to cable programming.[62] Those households adopting premium cable outlets (HBO, Showtime, Cinemax) may be offered a smattering of R- and X-rated content thereby potentially increasing adolescents' access to more sexually explicit and graphic portrayals. Therefore, it becomes important to assess what sort of impact more extreme depictions of sex may have on adolescent viewers.

For obvious ethical reasons, researchers cannot expose minors to graphic sexual content; however, they have conducted a series of impressive studies examining the effects of exposure to the sexualized violence of slasher films on undergraduates' emotional desensitization.[63] For example, Linz, Donnerstein, and Penrod (1984) exposed male undergraduates to five slasher films over the course of five days.[64] Each day, after they had seen the film, the team assessed the men's perceptions of and emotional reactions to the violence. The findings revealed that the men rated the last slasher film as less violent and less degrading to women and reported less anxiety and depression from viewing it than they had after the first day's viewing. This effect also "spilled over" and influenced participants' evaluations of aggression in real-world domains. Males exposed to the heavy diet of slasher films rated the victim of a violent sexual assault as significantly less injured than did those males in a nonviewing control group. These findings suggest that exposure to the admixture of sex and violence may be particularly harmful to young males who are developing beliefs and norms about dating, the opposite sex, and sexual intimacy.

In addition to this body of experimental research, at least two correlational studies have been conducted. Brown and Newcomer (1991) found that adolescents who viewed a high proportion of "sexy" television shows were more likely to have reported having had intercourse than were those who viewed a lower proportion of such programming.[65] Because the causal direction here is impossible to ascertain, other researchers have turned to examining the longitudinal relationship between these two variables. Peterson, Moore, and Furstenberg's results (1991) revealed that early exposure to television during elementary school was not a significant predictor of subsequent initiation of sexual intercourse a few years later.[66] These longitudinal findings must be viewed with caution, however. The researchers only assessed relatively general measures of overall viewing during the first period and not specific exposure to "sexy" television content.

At least three intervening variables may influence the impact of sexual content on youth. The first is age. At least one study shows that younger children have considerably more difficulty understanding sexual talk and joking on television than do older children.[67] Because of this, younger children may be less affected by exposure to such depictions than their older counterparts. The second is perceived reality. Theory suggests and research supports the hypothesis that realistic depictions have more influence on viewers than do fantastic ones.[68] It should follow that adolescents' level of perceived realism of sexual content should also moderate its impact. Teens who perceive sexual depictions on television to be highly realistic may experience more dissatisfaction or disappointment when their own initial sexual experiences are not like those on television. Indeed, Baron (1976) found a negative relationship between high school students' perceptions of media characters' sexual prowess and pleasure and satisfaction with their initial coital experience.[69] The third is family environment. Bryant and Rockwell's results (1994) revealed that active family communication during home viewing decreased the negative effects of teens' exposure to fifteen hours of nonmarital sexual content on their moral evaluations.[70] Thus, families who discuss sexual content in the media may help inoculate their children from potentially harmful effects of repeated exposure.

Drugs and Alcohol

The two most frequently used drugs by children and adolescents are alcohol and tobacco.[71] In fact, reports reveal that first use of alcohol and tobacco begins early in life—around age 13 for drinking and 16 for smoking.[72] Children report experiencing a lot of peer pressure to try these drugs in elementary school. For instance, 30 percent of students in grades 4–6 indicate that they have received "a lot" of pressure from classmates to drink beer, and 34 percent have received "a lot" of pressure to try cigarettes.[73] Using such drugs can have lethal consequences later in life. Roughly 100,000 deaths occur each year in the United States due to excessive alcohol consumption, and cigarette smoking took the lives of 2.2 million individuals between 1990 and 1994.[74]

Given the lifelong consequences of using alcohol and tobacco, it becomes important to assess whether or not entertainment media contributes to their use among children and teens.[75] To date, at least three experiments have shown that exposure to substance use in entertainment programming can have an immediate effect on children.[76] For example, Kotch, Coulter, and Lipsitz (1986) examined the impact of exposure to drinking or nondrinking scenes on 5th and 6th grade children's attitudes towards alcohol. The results showed that boys exposed to scenes with alcohol being consumed were more likely to state that the good aspects of drinking outweighed the bad than were those boys exposed to scenes without such depictions.[77] Pechmann and Shih (1999) exposed some 9th grade nonsmoking students to clips from movies that featured smoking and others to the same clips that had the smoking segments carefully edited out.[78] Immediately after exposure, the students' beliefs about smokers were assessed. The results showed that students exposed to the scenes with tobacco use believe that others perceive smokers as significantly higher in terms of status (intelligent, smart, rich, successful) and vitality (healthy, clean, good-smelling) than did those students exposed to the scenes without tobacco use. In a follow-up experiment using feature length films with or without smoking, the authors not only replicated the status findings but also documented that exposure to films with smoking increases students' intention to smoke. These studies show that viewing scenes depicting alcohol and tobacco use may have a pronounced short-term impact on children's attitudes and beliefs about drinking and smoking. Survey research also has been conducted to investigate the relationship between exposure to entertainment media and children's consumption rates. Some research has documented that exposure to entertainment television is related to substance use. Assessing only males, Tucker (1985) found a positive relationship between viewing television and drinking. Heavy viewers of TV reported more alcohol use per month than did light viewers even after the researcher controlled for demographic variables.[79]

While not all studies of adolescents have documented a positive association between seeing characters drink on screen and drinking,[80] at least two longitudinal studies reveal that exposure to alcohol at early ages can influence later use. In New Zealand, Connelly, Casswell, Zhang, and Silva (1994) examined the longitudinal relation between viewing in general and recall of alcohol messages in particular (advertisements, entertainment messages) at ages 13 and 15 and consumption of alcohol at age 18.[81] For females only, early exposure to television in general was a significant and positive predictor of later wine and spirit consumption. In the United States, Robinson, Chen, and Killen (1998) assessed media use (television, music videos, VCR) of nondrinking 9th graders and their alcohol use 18 months later.[82] According to the Robinson et al. (1998, p. 3), the results showed that "controlling for the effects of age, sex, ethnicity, and other media use, each increase of 1 hour per day of television viewing [at initial assessment] was associated with a 9 percent average increased risk of starting to drink alcohol during the next 18 months, each increase of 1 hour per day of music video viewing [at initial assessment] was associated with a 31 percent average increased risk of starting to drink alcohol during the next 18 months."[83]

In summary, this body of evidence suggests that entertainment messages filled with depictions of alcohol and tobacco can have a significant negative effect on children's attitudes, beliefs, and even substance use behaviors.

The Internet

Throughout this chapter, we have discussed the impact that various media have on children's and adolescents' attitudes, beliefs, and behaviors. We have seen the enormous ability of the media to transcend the influence of parents and peers in providing information (sometimes correct, but often not) about the world in which they live. The research and findings we have discussed so far, however, deal only with fairly traditional forms of media such as television or film. As we are all aware, newer technologies, in particular the Internet, have created a new dimension for researchers to consider when they examine the effects of problematic media content. Because the Internet is highly interactive, these effects could be stronger than those of the traditional media.[84]

Unlike traditional media, the Internet gives children and adolescents access to just about any form of content they want. They need only learn how to find it. For the first time, these individuals will be able (with some work) to view almost any form of sexual behavior, violent content, or advertising. Furthermore, this viewing can be done in the privacy of their own rooms with little knowledge of their parents. For decades, parents and others have been concerned about the potentially harmful influence on children and adolescents of exposure to sexual and violent media content. Today, these children and adolescents have access to such content using a technology about which they are often more sophisticated and knowledgeable than their parents. Too often we hear of computer-phobic adults who posses little knowledge of this expanding technology. Such resistance to the technology combined with a limited knowledge base will make finding solutions to potential problems such as easy access to sexual images even more difficult.

Before discussing this new addition to our media world, it is important to point out that the research on the effects of the Internet—both positive and negative—is limited. Because the technology is so new we have few studies on the effects of Internet content to draw on. Second, it is extremely difficult to conduct such studies because of the problems of determining a proper sample. Finally, finding ways to deal with possible harmful effects are complicated by the global nature of this medium.

It is important to note that we take the position that the Internet and all its various components are extremely informative and useful. This is one technology that we want our children to have access to and be knowledgeable about. It is exceedingly educational and almost indispensable in today's society. Like any new technological advance, it will have some downsides, but they should in no way prevent continued advancement of the technology or the teaching of children and adults about its vast usefulness and value. We strongly emphasize that in all respects the Internet is a very powerful information and instruction technology and one which we must continue to develop. We want the reader to continue to keep in mind that only a small part of the content available on the Internet may be considered potentially harmful to children. This small fraction must be discussed, however, since computers make searching for and finding this material much easier than ever before.

Surfing the Net

In their report on media use in the home, the Kaiser Foundation study (1999) found that 69 percent of children live in homes with computers and 45 percent of these homes have some form of Internet access.[85] Overall use of the Internet has increased 50 percent a year since 1990. Between 1999 and 2002, there is an expectation of a 155 percent increase in Internet use for 5- to 12-year-olds and a 100 percent increase in use for teens.[86] There is every indication that 50 percent of children, even as young as 5, will be online within the next few years.

The Internet is a technology that seems to differentiate (at least for now) the young from the old. In its most recent survey of online use, the Pew Foundation (2001) found that only 15 percent of individuals 65 years and older were online, compared with 75 percent of individuals 18 to 29 years of age.[87] According to surveys, children and adolescents 9 to 17 years old are also regular Internet users [88]and indicate that they actually prefer their computers to television or telephones. Of course this should not come as a surprise to many of us, since the computer now functions as both a television and a telephone.

More recent analyses are beginning to indicate that children and adolescents are spending more of their time with computers and less time with television.[89] In addition, computer time is more likely to be spent engaging in activities like games, chat rooms, e-mail, and Web surfing than it is for school-related activities.[90] Communication with others (e-mail) is perhaps the major reason for Internet use.[91] This encourages strangers to communicate with youngsters through newsgroups, list-serves, and chat groups.

Will the Internet, with all its varying components, replace television as the medium of choice? A recent study by the National Association of Broadcasters (2000) indicates that a faster Internet connection will draw people more deeply into the Web—and away from their TVs and radios.[92] In the average American home (without a broadband Internet connection), individuals spend about a third of their media time with television and 28 percent with radio. Only 11 percent of media time is spent on the Internet. But in a home with broadband access, such as a cable modem or DSL, people typically spend 21 percent of their media use time online, almost 24 percent watching television, and 21 percent listening to the radio.

Is television dead? No, not really. But as technology changes and high-speed connections become more popular (and less expensive) the computer and the Internet may replace other media as the main source of entertainment and information. Live video transmissions are now routine, and our ability to access on demand full-length violent movies, video games, and anything else we desire in "entertainment" is right around the corner.

Internet Dangers

While over half of parents believe being online is more positive then watching TV,[93] they may be unaware that

- Of the 1,000 most visited sites, 10 percent are adult-sex oriented.
- 44 percent of teens have seen an adult site.
- 25 percent of teens have visited a site promoting hate groups.
- 12 percent have found a site where they receive information on how to buy a gun.
- Many child-oriented sites have advertisements.
- Violent pornography has increased over the years in both newsgroups and Web sites, and access to violent pornography has become easier.[94]

Even if parents were aware of these data, children and adolescents conduct many of their online activities alone, in an anonymous context, and without (as we have already noted) parental supervision. Areas for concern on the Internet do not differ from those of traditional media: concerns about sex, violence, sexual violence, and tobacco and alcohol advertisements. We would expect the effects of exposure to these stimuli on the Internet to be at least the same as on traditional media, if not enhanced, since the interactive nature of the Internet can lead to more arousal and more cognitive activity.[95] More important, search engines on the Internet provide easy access to materials that were once considered difficult for children and adolescents to get ahold of.

One of the most controversial types of Internet content is sexual material, which has raised concerns about child exploitation. Such material ranges from photographs to the Internet equivalent of telephone sex, sometimes with a live video connection. Sending sexual information by e-mail or posting it on bulletin boards by those targeting children has been a long-term issue. Adult Web sites that feature hard-core sexual depictions are of equal concern. According to one estimate, such sites are a half-billion-dollar industry and half of the spending on the Internet is in this area. Some suggest that adult-sex sites are the "king" of advertising and are among the sites most searched for by users.[96] In their discussion of the potentially harmful effects on children of exposure to sexual media, Malamuth and Impett (2001) note how easy it is for 9- to 15-year-olds to access sexually explicit materials via the Internet.[97] This is not to imply that children did not seek out and find sexual content before the Internet. Today, however, the process is easier, faster, more anonymous, and likely to bring to your computer screen anything you want.

There have been discussions recently[98] of the possibility of some form of sexual addiction occurring with the proliferation and use of sexually related Internet sites. One argument is that the anonymity of the Internet could foster such addictive behavior. The research however, does not demonstrate that such addiction occurs, and if it does, only a relatively small minority of users are affected. Still, there is no question that this is one area that needs further study.[99]

Concern about children's and adolescents' use of the Internet is not limited to sexual content.[100] Other perceived dangers come from information on Satanism and religious proselytizing as well as drugs and gambling. Religious cults, which only a few years ago would have had a limited audience, can now reach out to a worldwide following. Offshore gambling is now a major e-commerce business. A credit card or a money order (something teenagers can purchase) allows access to any one of hundreds of offshore casinos.

Terrorism is another issue of concern. Some online archives provide instructions for making bombs or other weapons. Kip Kinkel, the teenager who killed his parents and two high school classmates in Oregon, described himself in his e-mail profile as someone who liked "watching violent cartoons on TV, sugared cereal, throwing rocks at cars" and his favorite occupation was "surfing the Web for information on how to build bombs." A proliferation of hate speech and hate groups have become easily accessible on the Web. Not only is the reach of white supremacist groups changing, but so are their targets for membership. According to a report from the Southern Poverty Law Center (1999), Internet hate groups have risen over 60 percent in recent years.[101]

Alcohol and tobacco advertisements and Web sites dedicated to smoking and drinking are another problem. Many of these sites use promotional techniques that are considered quite appealing to adolescents. In a recent report in this area, the Center for Media Education (1999) not only identified numerous sites dedicated to smoking and alcohol use that would be influential to teens, but also found that these sites were not readily shielded by blocking software.[102] The enforcement of government regulations on tobacco and alcohol advertising has been of significant help in more traditional media such as television. This has not been the case with respect to the Internet, and as we discuss later, is not likely be an effective tool to combat advertising, which exists within a global context.

Children's privacy is another major issue. A series of reports from the Center for Media Education (2001), cites growing concern that many Web sites, even those aimed directly at children (under age 13), are requesting personal information without asking for parental permission.[103] In fact, less than 25 percent of these sites asked children for their parents' permission to disclose such information as e-mail address, phone numbers, and home address, as well as information about their parents. According to the Annenberg Public Policy Center (2000), more than 50 percent of children are willing to give out information about their parents in exchange for a free gift offered on a Web site.[104]

What We Can Do

There are three major approaches to dealing with the problem of children's and adolescents' access to inappropriate Internet content. The first is government regulation restricting the content. The second is technology including blocking software and some form of rating system. Third—and what we believe to be the most important—is media literacy for parents and their children.

Government Regulation. Within the United States, the First Amendment protects offensive speech, including sexually explicit materials, from censorship. In general, the U.S. Courts have struck down most content restrictions on books, magazines, and films. There are of course exceptions such as "obscenity," child pornography, and certain types of indecent material depending on the time, place, and manner of the presentation. In 1996, Congress passed a bill regulating Internet content, primarily in the area of pornography. The Supreme Court of the United States ruled on the Communications Decency Act in 1998, and as expected, held it to be unconstitutional and an infringement on freedom of speech. Likewise, other courts have ruled that service providers, such as America On Line, could not be held liable for the sending of pornographic materials over the Internet. It is obvious that the courts are well aware that government regulation in this area would be difficult or nearly impossible to enforce given not only the vastness of materials available but also the global scope of the Internet.

Blocking Technology. Another solution to this problem has been the development of software that is designed to block unwanted sites. This blocking software can block access to known adult sites, for instance, or to any site containing predetermined words such as sex, gambling, or other words that are associated with unwanted content. There are a number of these types of software available which perform these and other functions, but none of these blocking systems is completely effective. The Web changes quite rapidly and software designed for today may not be entirely appropriate tomorrow. In one test of the effectiveness of blocking adult sites,[105] it was found that one program was able to block out eighteen of twenty-two selected sites. Other programs were able to block about half the adult sites, and one of the tested programs did not block any of the sites. Furthermore, either transposing letters or renaming the Web browser on the hard disk often defeated those blocking e-mail or chat group communications. In a more recent test of these products by *Consumer Reports*,[106] there was some improvement in the ability of this type of software to block objectionable materials that contain sexually explicit content, violently graphic images, or that promote drugs, tobacco, crime, or bigotry. Far more troubling, however, was the finding that filters appeared to block legitimate sites based on moral or political value judgments. Furthermore, since this software blocks certain word strings or known sites, it may also block extremely educational Web pages. As the report rightfully concludes, filtering software is no substitute for parental supervision.

Media Literacy. The role of parents in working with their children and becoming familiar with this technology is critical. Children can be taught critical viewing skills in their schools so that they learn to better interpret what they encounter on the Web. The same techniques used to mitigate media violence or the appeals of advertisements can also be effective in this area. In addition, a large number of professional organizations concerned with the well being of children and families have begun to take a more active role in reducing the impact of harmful Internet content (e.g., American Academy of Pediatrics, American Medical Association Alliances). Within this new arena of technology, we should take a lesson from our findings on media violence interventions. Research on intervention programs has indicated that we can reduce some of the impact of media violence by empowering parents in their roles as monitors of children's television viewing. These studies indicate that parents who view programs with their children and discuss the realities of violence, as well as alternatives to aggressive behaviors in conflict situations, can actually reduce the negative impact (increased aggressiveness) of media violence.[107] The same type of positive results can be obtained when parents begin to monitor, supervise, and participate in their children's Internet activities.

Conclusion

The purpose of this chapter has been to review what we know about the problem of the exposure of children and adolescents to the mass media. We reviewed research suggesting that viewing or interacting with media content involving violence, sex, drugs, and alcohol can have a negative impact on young viewers. However, the nature or way in which these depictions are presented also matters. By showing the consequences or repercussions of violence, sex, and drug or alcohol use, the mass media can be effective in educating children and teens about the risks and responsibilities involved in such mature behavior. In addition to traditional media like television and film, we also discussed children's and adolescents' involvement with the Internet. Because research on the effects of interacting with this new mass media is still in its infancy, we call on social scientists to keep investigating the positive *and* negative effects of the Internet in the lives of America's youth.

NOTES

1. John Leland et al., "A Lower Body Count," *Newsweek* (23 August 1999), p.46.

2. Nielsen Media Research, *2000 Report on Television: The First 50 Years* (New York: Nielsen, 2000).

3. Donald F. Roberts, Ulla G. Foehr, Victoria J. Rideout, and Mollyann Brodie, *Kids & Media @ the New Millennium: A Comprehensive National Analysis of Children's Media Use* (Menlo Park, Calif.: The Henry J. Kaiser Family Foundation, 1999).

4. Aletha C. Huston et al., *Big World, Small Screen: The Role of Television in American Society* (Lincoln: University of Nebraska Press, 1992).

5. John Condry, *The Psychology of Television* (Hillsdale, N.J.: Lawrence Erlbaum, 1989); Roberts et al., *Kids & Media*, p. 20.

6. Jack Lyle and H.R. Hoffman, "Children's Use of Television and Other Media," in *Television and Social Behavior: Reports and Papers*, vol. 4, ed. Eli A. Rubinstein, George A. Comstock, and John P. Murray (Washington, D.C.: U.S. Government Printing Office, 1972), pp. 129–256; Jack Lyle and H.R. Hoffman, "Explorations in Patterns of Television Viewing by Preschool-age Children," in ibid., pp. 257–74; Richard Potts, Aletha C. Huston, and John C. Wright, "The Effects of Television Form and Violent Content on Boys' Attention and Social Behavior," *Journal of Experimental Child Psychology* 41, no. 1 (1986): pp. 1–17.

7. Condry, *Psychology of Television*; Robert Kubey and Michael Csikszentmihalyi, *Television and the Quality of Life: How Viewing Shapes Everyday Experience* (Hillsdale, N.J.: Lawrence Erlbaum, 1990).

8. Roberts et al., *Kids & Media*, p. 24.

9. Nielsen Media Research, *2000 Report*.

10. Roberts et al., *Kids & Media*, p. 20.

11. Kaiser Family Foundation, "Talking with Kids about Tough Issues: A National Survey of Parents and Kids," 2001, available at www.kff.org/content/2001/3105/summary.pdf.

12. Barbara J. Wilson et al., "Violence in Television Programming Overall: Uni-

versity of California, Santa Barbara Study," *National Television Violence Study*, 3 vols. (Newbury Park, Calif.: Sage Publications, 1997–1998) 1: pp. 1–268; 2: pp. 3–204; 3: pp. 5–220.

13. Barbara J. Wilson et al., "Violence in Children's Television Programming: Assessing the Risks," *Journal of Communication* 52, no. 1 (2002): pp. 5–35.

14. American Academy of Child and Adolescent Psychiatry, "The Influence of Music and Music Videos" (2000), available at www.aacap.org/publications/factsfam/musicvid.htm; Tipper Gore, *Raising PG Kids in an X-rated Society* (Nashville, Tenn.: Abingdon, 1987).

15. Stacy L. Smith and Aaron Boyson, "Violence in Music Videos: Examining the Prevalence and Context of Physical Aggression," *Journal of Communication* 52, no. 1 (2002): pp. 61–83.

16. For a review of these studies, see Bradley S. Greenberg and Linda Hofschire, "Sex on Entertainment Television," in *Media Entertainment*, eds. Dolf Zillmann and Peter Vorderer (Mahwah, N.J.: Lawrence Erlbaum, 2000), pp. 93–111.

17. Dale Kunkel et al., *Sex on TV: A Biennial Report to the Kaiser Family Foundation* (Menlo Park, Calif.: Kaiser Family Foundation, 1999); Dale Kunkel et al., *Sex on TV 2: A Biennial Report to the Kaiser Family Foundation* (Menlo Park, Calif.: Kaiser Family Foundation, 2001).

18. Kunkel et al., *Sex on TV 2*, p. 50.

19. Ibid., p. 51.

20. Anna R. Hazan and Stanton A. Glantz, "Current Trends in Tobacco Use in Prime-time Fictional Television," *American Journal of Public Health* 85 (1995): pp. 116–17; Alan Mathios, Rosemary Avery, Carol Bisogni, and James Shanahan, "Alcohol Portrayal on Prime-time Television: Manifest and Latent Messages," *Journal of Studies on Alcohol* 59 (1998): pp. 305–10; Nancy Signorielli, "Drinking, Sex, and Violence on Television: The Cultural Indicators Perspective," *Journal of Drug Education* 17 (1987): pp. 245–60.

21. Lawrence Wallack, Joel Grube, and Patricia A. Madden, "Portrayals of Alcohol on Prime-time Television," *Journal of Studies on Alcohol* 51 (1990): pp. 428–37.

22. Peter G. Christenson, Lisa Henriksen, and Don F. Roberts, *Substance Use in Popular Prime-time Television* (Washington, D.C.: Office of National Drug Control Policy, 2000).

23. Hazan and Glantz, "Current Trends"; Mathios et al., "Alcohol Portrayal"; Wallack et al., "Portrayals of Alcohol."

24. Christenson et al., *Substance Use*; Wallack et al., "Portrayals of Alcohol."

25. Don. F. Roberts, Lisa Henriksen, and Peter G. Christenson, *Substance Use in Popular Movies and Music* (Washington, D.C.: Office of National Drug Control Policy, 1999).

26. Adam O. Goldstein, Rachel A. Sobel, and Glen R. Newman, "Tobacco and

Alcohol Use in G-rated Children's Animated Films," *The Journal of the American Medical Association* 281, no. 12 (1999): pp. 1131–36.

27. Robert H. DuRant et al., "Tobacco and Alcohol Use Behaviors Portrayed in Music Videos: A Content Analysis," *American Journal of Public Health* 87, no. 7 (1997): pp. 1131–35.

28. Diane. P. Hackbarth, Barbara Silvestri, and William Cosper, "Tobacco and Alcohol Billboards in Fifty Chicago Neighborhoods: Market Segmentation To Sell Dangerous Products To the Poor," *Journal of Public Health Policy* 16, no. 2 (1995): pp. 213–30; Patricia A. Madden and Joel W. Grube, "The Frequency and Nature of Alcohol and Tobacco Advertising in Televised Sports, 1990 through 1992," *American Journal of Public Health* 84, no. 2 (1994): pp. 297–99; Donald E. Strickland, T.A. Finn, and M.D. Lambert, "A Content Analysis of Beverage Alcohol Advertising: I. Magazine Advertising," *Journal of Studies on Alcohol* 43, no. 7 (1982): pp. 655–82.

29. Centers for Disease Control, *Youth Violence Facts*, 2000, available at www.cdc.gov/ncipc/factsheets/yvfacts.htm, p. 1.

30. Ibid.

31. For a review of these studies, see Robert M. Liebert and Janice Sprafkin, *The Early Window*, 3rd ed. (New York: Pergamon Press, 1988).

32. Albert Bandura, Dorothea Ross, and Shelia A. Ross, "Imitation of Film-mediated Aggressive Models," *Journal of Abnormal and Social Psychology* 66, no. 1 (1963): pp. 3–11.

33. Richard H. Walters and Edward L. Thomas, "Enhancement of Punitiveness by Visual and Audiovisual Displays," *Canadian Journal of Psychology* 17, no. 2 (1963): pp. 244–55.

34. Leonard D. Eron, "Relationship of TV Viewing Habits and Aggressive Behavior in Children," *Journal of Abnormal and Social Psychology* 67, no. 2 (1963): pp. 193–96; Jeannie J. McIntyre and James J. Teevan, "Television Violence and Deviant Behavior," in *Television and Social Behavior*, vol. 3, eds., George A. Comstock and Eli A. Rubinstein (Washington, D.C.: U.S. Government Printing Office, 1972) pp. 383–435; Jack McLeod et al., "Adolescents, Parents, and Television Use: Adolescent Self-report Measures from Maryland and Wisconsin Samples," in ibid., pp. 173–238.

35. Monroe M. Lefkowitz et al., "Television Violence and Child Aggression: A Follow-up Study," in ibid., pp. 35–135; Rowell Huesmann, Jessica Moise, Cheryl L. Podolski, and Leonard Eron, *Longitudinal Relations between Children's Exposure To Television Violence and Their Later Aggressive and Violent Behavior in Young Adulthood: 1977–1992.* Paper presented at the annual meeting for the International Communication Aggression, Jerusalem, Israel, July 1998.

36. L. Rowell Huesmann and Lori S. Miller, "Long-term Effects of Repeated Exposure To Media Violence in Childhood," in *Aggressive Behavior*, ed. L.R. Huesmann (New York: Plenum Press, 1994), pp. 153–85, especially p. 168.

37. Haejung Paik and George Comstock, "The Effects of Television Violence on Antisocial Behavior: A Meta Analysis," *Communication Research* 21, no. 4 (1994): pp. 516–64.

38. L. Rowell Huesmann and Leonard D. Eron, "Cognitive Processes and the Persistence of Aggressive Behavior," *Aggressive Behavior* 10, no. 3 (1984): pp. 243–51; L. Rowell Huesmann et al., "Stability of Aggression over Time and Generations," *Developmental Psychology* 20, no. 6 (1984): pp. 1120–34.

39. Huesmann and Eron, "Cognitive Processes," pp. 243–51.

40. Ibid.

41. Huesmann et al. *Children's Exposure to Television Violence.*

42. Margaret H. Thomas et al., "Desensitization to Portrayals of Real-life Aggression as a Function of Exposure to Television Violence," *Journal of Personality and Social Psychology* 35, no. 6 (1977): pp. 450–53.

43. Victor B. Cline, Roger G. Croft, and Steven Courrier, "Desensitization of Children to Television Violence," *Journal of Personality and Social Psychology* 27, no. 3 (1973): pp. 360–65.

44. Margaret H. Thomas and Ronald S. Drabman, "Toleration of Real Life Aggression as a Function of Exposure to Televised Violence and Age of the Subject," *Merrill-Palmer Quarterly* 21, no. 3 (1975): pp. 227–32.

45. Ronald S. Drabman and Margaret H. Thomas, "Does Media Violence Increase Children's Toleration of Real Life Aggression?" *Developmental Psychology* 10, no. 3 (1974), pp. 418–24.

46. Kenneth W. Hirsch and Fred Molitor, "Children's toleration of real-life aggression after exposure to media violence: A replication of the Drabman and Thomas studies," *Child Study Journal* 24, no. 3 (1994): pp. 191–207.

47. Joanne Cantor, "Fright reactions to mass media," in *Media Effects*, eds. Bryant Jennings and Dolf Zillman (Hillsdale, N.J.: Lawrence Erlbaum, 1994), pp. 213–45.

48. Ibid., p. 222.

49. Barbara J. Wilson, Cynthia Hoffner, and Joanne Cantor, "Children's Perceptions of the Effectiveness of Techniques to Reduce Fear from Mass Media," *Journal of Applied Developmental Psychology* 8, no. 1 (1987): pp. 39–52.

50. Joanne Cantor, *Mommy, I'm Scared* (San Diego: Harcourt Brace, 1998), see pp. 12–19; K. Harrison and J. Cantor, "Tales from the Screen: Enduring Fright Reactions to Scary Media," *Media Psychology* 1, no. 2 (1999): pp. 117–40.

51. For review, see George Gerbner et al., "Growing up with Television: The Cultivation Perspective," in Jennings and Zillmann, eds., *Media Effects*, pp. 17–42.

52. American Medical Association, *Physician Guide to Media Violence* (Chicago: AMA, 1996); American Psychological Association, *Violence and Youth: Psychology's Response* (Washington, D.C.: APA, 1993); Centers for Disease Control, *Position Papers for the Third National Injury Conference: Setting the National Agenda for Injury*

Control in the 1990s (Washington, D.C.: Department of Health and Human Services, 1991); Surgeon General's Scientific Advisory Committee on Television and Social Behavior, *Television and Growing up: The Impact of Televised Violence* (Washington, D.C.: U.S. Government Printing Office, 1972).

53. Aletha C. Huston et al., *Measuring the Effects of Sexual Content in the Media: A Report to the Kaiser Family Foundation* (Menlo Park, Calif.: Kaiser Family Foundation, 1998); Bradley S. Greenberg, Jane D. Brown, and Nancy L. Buerkel-Rothfuss, eds., *Media, Sex and the Adolescent* (Cresskill, N.J.: Hampton Press, 1993).

54. National Campaign to Prevent Teen Pregnancy (2000), *Facts and Stats*, available at www.teenpregnancy.org/genlfact.htm, p. 1.

55. Kaiser Family Foundation (2000). *Sexually Transmitted Diseases in the United States: Facts*, available at www.kff.org, p. 2.

56. Bradley S. Greenberg, Kathy L. Perry, and Anita M. Covert, "The Body Human: Sex Education, Politics, and Television," *Family Relations* 32, no. 3 (1983): pp. 419–25.

57. Bradley S. Greenberg, R. Linsangan, and Anne Soderman, "Adolescents' Reactions to Television Sex," in Brown and Buerkel-Rothfuss, eds., *Media, Sex, and the Adolescent*, pp. 196–224.

58. Larry E. Greeson and Rose A. Williams, "Social Implications of Music Videos for Youth: An Analysis of the Content and Effects of MTV," *Youth and Society* 18, no. 2 (1986): pp. 177–89; Linda Kalof, "The Effects of Gender and Music Video Imagery on Sexual Attitudes," *The Journal of Social Psychology* 139, no. 3 (1999): pp. 378–85.

59. Greeson and Williams, "Social Implications."

60. Kalof, "Effects of Gender."

61. Jennings Bryant and Steven C. Rockwell, "Effects of Massive Exposure to Sexually Oriented Prime Time Television Programming on Adolescents' Moral Judgment," in *Media, Children, and the Family: Social Scientific, Psychodynamic, and Clinical Perspectives*, eds. Dolf Zillmann, Jennings Bryant, and Aletha C. Huston (Hillsdale, N.J.: Lawrence Erlbaum, 1994), pp. 183–95, especially p. 187.

62. Nielson Media Research, *2000 Report*.

63. Dan Linz, Ed Donnerstein, and S. Michael Adams, "Physiological Desensitization and Judgments about Female Victims of Violence," *Human Communication Research* 15, no. 4 (1989): pp. 509–22; Dan Linz, Ed Donnerstein, and Steven Penrod, "Effects of Long-term Exposure to Violent and Sexually Degrading Depictions of Women," *Journal of Personality and Social Psychology* 55, no. 5 (1988): pp. 758–68; Charles R. Mullin and Dan Linz, "Desensitization and Resensitization to Violence against Women: Effects of Exposure to Sexually Violent Films on Judgments of Domestic Violence Victims," *Journal of Personality and Social Psychology* 69, no. 3 (1995): pp. 449–59.

64. Dan Linz, Ed Donnerstein, and Steven Penrod, "The Effects of Multiple

Exposures to Filmed Violence against Women," *Journal of Communication* 34, no. 3 (1984): pp. 130–47.

65. Jane D. Brown and Susan F. Newcomer, "Television Viewing and Adolescents' Sexual Behavior," *Journal of Homosexuality* 21, no. 1–2 (1991): pp. 77–91.

66. James L. Peterson, Kritin A. Moore, and Frank F. Furstenberg, "Television Viewing and Early Initiation of Sexual Intercourse: Is There a Link?" ibid., pp. 93–119.

67. L. Teresa Silverman-Watkins and Joyce N. Sprafkin, "Adolescents' Comprehension of Televised Sexual Innuendos," *Journal of Applied Developmental Psychology* 4, no. 4 (1983): pp. 359–69.

68. Charles Atkin, "Effects of Realistic TV Violence vs. Fictional Violence on Aggression," *Journalism Quarterly* 60, no. 4 (1983): pp. 615–21; L. Rowell Huesmann, "An Information-Processing Model for the Development of Aggression," *Aggressive Behavior* 14, no. 1 (1988): pp. 13–24.

69. Steven J. Baron, "Sex on TV and Adolescent Sexual Self-Image," *Journal of Broadcasting* 20, no. 1 (1976): pp. 61–68.

70. Bryant and Rockwell, "Effects of Massive Exposure."

71. Vic C. Strasburger, *Adolescents and the Media* (Thousand Oaks, Calif.: Sage, 1995).

72. American Lung Association. (2001). *Fact Sheet: Teenage Tobacco Use*, available at www.lungusa.org/tobacco/teenager_factsheet99.html; National Council on Alcoholism and Drug Dependence. (1999). *Youth, Alcohol, and Other Drugs*, available at www.ncadd.org/youthalc.html.

73. Ibid., p. 3.

74. Schneider Institute for Health Policy, *Substance Abuse* (Princeton, N.J.: Schneider Institute, 2001).

75. Most of the research on media messages involving drugs or alcohol has focused on the impact of either advertising or entertainment portrayals. Because the focus of this chapter is on the effects of entertainment media on children, we will only cover the latter. For an excellent review of advertising effects, see Vic C. Strasburger, "Children, Adolescents, Drugs and the Media," in, *Handbook of Children and the Media*, eds. Dortothy G. Singer and Jerome L. Singer (Thousand Oaks, Calif.: Sage, 2000), pp. 415–45.

76. Robert G. Rychtarik et al., "Alcohol Use in Television Programming: Effects on Children's Behavior," *Addictive Behaviors* 8, no. 1 (1983): pp. 19–22.

77. Jonathan B. Kotch, Martha L. Coulter, and Angela Lipsitz, "Does Televised Drinking Influence Children's Attitudes toward Alcohol?" *Addictive Behaviors* 11, no. 1 (1986): pp. 67–70.

78. Cornelia Pechmann and Chuan F. Shih, "Smoking Scenes in Movies and Antismoking Advertisements before Movies: Effects on Youth," *Journal of Marketing* 63, no. 3 (1999): pp. 1–13.

79. Larry A. Tucker, "Television's Role Regarding Alcohol Use among Teenagers," *Adolescence* 20, no. 79 (1985): pp. 593–98, especially p. 596.

80. Charles Atkin, John Hocking, and Martin Block, "Teenage Drinking: Does Advertising Make a Difference?" *Journal of Communication* 34, no. 2 (1984): pp. 157–67.

81. George M. Connolly et al., "Alcohol in the Mass Media and Drinking by Adolescents: A Longitudinal Study," *Addiction* 89, no. 10 (1994): pp. 1255–63.

82. Thomas N. Robinson, Helen L. Chen, and Joel D. Killen (1998). Television and Music Video Exposure and Risk of Adolescent Alcohol Use, available at www.pediatrics.org/cgi/content/full/102/5/e54.

83. Ibid., p. 3.

84. Haejung Paik, "The History of Children's Use of Electronic Media," in Singer and Singer, eds, *Handbook of Children and the Media*, pp.7–27.

85. Roberts et al., *Kids & Media*.

86. Paik (2001).

87. Pew Foundation, *The Pew Internet and American Life Project: The growth of the Internet population in America in the last half of 2000* (Philadelphia, Pa.: The Pew Charitable Trusts, 2001).

88. Roberts et al., *Kids & Media*.

89. Kaveri Subrahmanyam et al., "New Forms of Electronic Media," in Singer and Singer, eds., *Handbook of Children and the Media*, pp.73–99.

90. Roberts et al., *Kids & Media*.

91. Subrahmanyam et al., "New Forms."

92. National Association of Broadcasters, *The Broadband Revolution: How Superfast Internet Access Changes Media Habits in American Households* (Washington, D.C.: National Association of Broadcasters, 2000).

93. Todd Tarpley, "Children, the Internet, and Other New Technologies," in Singer and Singer, eds., *Handbook of Children and the Media*, pp.547–56.

94. Ragnbild T. Bjornebekk and Tor A. Evjen, "Violent Pornography on the Internet," in Cecilia Feilitzen and Ulla Carlsson, eds., *Children in the New Media Landscape* (Goteborg, Sweden: UNESCO, 2000) pp. 185–210.

95. L. Rowell Huesmann, "An Information-processing Model for the Development of Aggression," *Aggressive Behavior* 14, no. 1 (1988): pp. 13–24.

96. Mark Griffiths, "Sex on the Internet," in Feilitzen and Carlsson, eds., *Children in the New Media Landscape* pp.169–84.

97. Neil Malamuth and Emily A. Impett, "Research on Sex in the Media," in Singer and Singer, eds., *Handbook of Children and the Media*, pp. 269–87.

98. Griffiths, "Sex on the Internet."

99. Ibid.

100. Ed Donnerstein, "What's Out There in the Media: The Internet," in *Caring*

for Children in the Media Age, Jay Squires and Todd Newlands, eds. (Sydney: University of New South Wales, 1998).

101. Southern Poverty Law Center, *Hate Group Web Sites on the Rise* (Montgomery, Ala.: Southern Poverty Law Center, 1999).

102. Center for Media Education, *Alcohol and Tobacco on the Web: New Threats to Youth* (Washington, D.C.: Center for Media Education, 1999).

103. Center for Media Education, *Children's Online Privacy Protection Act: The First Year* (Washington, D.C.: Center for Media Education, 2001).

104. Annenberg Public Policy Center, *The Internet and the Family 2000* (Philadelphia: Annenberg Pubic Policy Center, 2000).

105. Consumer Reports, *Internet Blocking Software* (Yonkers, N.Y.: Consumer Union of the United States, May 1999).

106. Consumer Reports, *Digital Chaperones for Kids* (Yonkers, N.Y.: Consumer Union of the United States, March 2001).

107. Ed Donnerstein, Ron G. Slaby, and Leonard D. Eron, "The Mass Media and Youth Aggression," in *Reason to Hope: A Psychosocial Perspective on Violence and Youth* Leonard D. Eron, Jacquelyn H. Gentry, and Paul Schlegel, eds. (Washington D.C.: American Psychological Association, 1994), pp. 219–50.

5

Equipment for Living

How Popular Music Fits in the Lives of Youth

Peter G. Christenson

A few years ago my son, who was then eight, developed a fascination with rap music in general and with the controversial artist Snoop Doggy Dogg in particular. I knew enough about Snoop's unsavory lyrics and numerous scrapes with the law to become concerned about this infatuation. At one point I blurted: "Jesse, Snoop's nothing more than a common hoodlum!" Jesse replied: "I know, Dad, but I can separate the man from his music." I believe Jesse was saying something like this: Music is "just music," not what people say about the messages in the lyrics, the reputation of the artist, or any presumed evil influences on kids. He, the listener, was in control, and I, the parent, was overreacting.

At the most fundamental level, this chapter surrounds the issue between me and my son, that is, whether today's popular music is to be seen simply as a voluntary pastime pursued by a sophisticated young audience who can take the embedded messages with a grain of salt, or whether music plays a central role in the socialization of young people and thus carries the power to exert a significant influence on their values and behavior. Either way, two things are certain: one, that many, if not most, adolescents are deeply involved in music—that it matters to them—and two, that our society is just as deeply embroiled in a bitter and divisive debate over popular music's messages and cultural influence. American adolescents spend a great deal of time with music and music videos, probably as much as they spend with television, the only close media competitor. But their involvement with music extends well beyond sheer time expenditure. Music alters and intensifies their moods, provides much of their informal language, dominates their conversations, and provides the ambiance at their social gatherings. Music styles define the crowds and cliques they run in. Moreover, for better or worse, music personalities provide models for how they should think and act.

A good indication of how much popular music really matters to young people was provided in a 1990 report by Donald Roberts and Lisa Henriksen of Stanford University. They asked a sample of junior and senior high school students from Northern California what media they would choose to take with them if they were stranded on the proverbial desert isle. The students selected a first, second, and third choice from the following list: TV set, books, video games, computer, newspapers, VCR and videotapes, magazines, radio, and music recordings and the means to play them. Since radio is almost exclusively a music medium among adolescents, radio and music recordings were combined into a single "music" category. Music came out well ahead of television (which placed second overall) at all grade levels. Over 80 percent of the total sample made music one of their first three choices, and music was the first choice for nearly half. Among 11th graders, music was selected first twice as frequently as television.[1] One researcher has written: "In terms of both the sheer amount of time devoted to it and the meanings it assumes, it is music, not television, that is the most important medium for adolescents."[2] Given that time spent listening to popular music reaches parity with that spent viewing television as early as 5th or 6th grade, one could add "and many children" to the end of the sentence.[3]

To be sure, most adults—critics, parents, researchers, and others—view television as the center-stage medium in childhood and adolescence. Perhaps this is because television has pictures: in other words, Tennyson may have been right when he observed, "Things seen are mightier than things heard." Perhaps it is due in part to television's "visibility" in another sense. Much of young people's TV viewing takes place in the company of parents or other adults. Moreover, even if parents are not actually present they often encounter their children's favorite programs inadvertently as they scan through the channels with the remote control. In contrast, young people's music listening seldom occurs in the presence of adults, and parents are unlikely to expose themselves incidentally to their children's favorite music — indeed, many take pains to avoid it.[4]

Both the research community and the public at large seem to be paying increased attention to popular music's importance in the socialization process. In large part, this increased attention stems from the highly controversial nature of the lyrics, video imagery, and personalities associated with today's popular music. Rap and heavy metal music, especially, have drawn repeated condemnations for demeaning women, glorifying violence and drug use, and legitimizing racism and homophobia. Rock music has always drawn fire for its various excesses, but the "modern era" of outrage can be traced to 1985, when a group of parents under the leadership of Tipper Gore voiced their concerns about the influence of "porn rock" before the Senate Commerce Committee, in the process moving the record industry to institute a system of parental warnings on explicit lyrics. A decade later the Senate Juvenile Justice Committee listened to a similar set of worries from a contingent of citizens outraged by "gangsta rap." In 1995 Senator Robert Dole opened his presidential campaign by declaring war on Hollywood's "nightmares of depravity," with rap music just as high on his enemies list as movies or TV.[5] Rock music has been implicated in the string of tragic school shootings (apparently several of the shooters shared an obsession with the music of hard-edged rock performers such as Marilyn Manson), and the rap/hip-hop culture has been blamed for poor math and reading scores among inner-city youth.[6] Whatever the merits of the various accusations, it is clear that serious attention must be given to the role of popular music in contemporary adolescence.

Amount of Music Use

As was already noted, most children and adolescents report that popular music is at least as important to them as television, and generally more so. Precisely how much time is spent with music, however, is a complicated issue. Some of the research on time expenditure has found more TV viewing than music listening, and some has given the edge to music.[7] A recent national survey of over 2000 8- to 18-year-olds conducted for the Henry J. Kaiser Family Foundation indicates that the comparison depends on age. For those between 8 and 13, average daily TV time was just over 3½ hours, compared to about 1½ hours of music listening. For 14- to 18-year-olds, however, TV and music consumption were about the same: 2½ hours daily. In other words, for this group, time with television was about an hour less than for the younger group, and time with music about an hour more.[8]

The Kaiser study is particularly strong because of its large-scale national random sample: most previous estimates have been based on smaller, and often rather unrepresentative, groups of respondents. However, even the best-designed studies may underestimate young people's popular music listening if they fail, as the Kaiser study did, to take into account the unique capacity of music to operate as secondary, background activity. Often, music simply "appears" in the adolescent's environment. A teenager may drive to school while chatting with a friend, all the while "listening" to music from a car radio. Kids may congregate for a stated purpose—a car wash, a day on the beach—but the boombox is still there, and music is often an integral part of the occasion. There is a question, of course, whether background listening ought to count as true *exposure*, but those who would argue against its inclusion might take up this simple challenge: turn off the "background" music when adolescents are studying, chatting, or doing chores. The response will generally be strong and immediate.

When a conscious attempt is made to measure *all* listening, whether in the background or foreground, levels of exposure to music turn out to be at least as high as TV among children in late grade school and considerably higher among adolescents. In the same study mentioned above, Roberts and Henriksen had high school students provide the standard estimate of how much time they spent on a typical day consuming various mass media, including television and music. After these initial estimates were made, participants were asked this question focusing on music: "Now that you have thought some about your music listening, give us another estimate . . . Include the time you do nothing but listen, and the time that music is on in the background when you work, do homework, visit, are in a car, and so on." Based on this estimate including background time, music occupied from 3 to almost 4 hours per day, depending on age and gender. Music time exceeded television time by amounts ranging from ½ hour (for 9th grade boys) to almost 2 hours (for 11th grade girls).[9]

Depending on the question asked, then, preadolescents and adolescents spend somewhere between 2 and 4 hours a day with popular music, compared to 2 or 3 hours watching television. Age makes a big difference. Even though many young people develop a serious interest in popular music as early as 1st or 2nd grade, music consumes much more time in preadolescence and adolescence.[10] Girls listen more than boys (and substantially more by high school), and in most studies African American and Hispanic youth report listening more than white youth.[11] Finally, it should be noted that despite the considerable attention given by critics and researchers to music videos, music video viewing occupies only about 15 to 30 minutes a day.[12]

Popular Music Uses and Gratifications

In his 1962 essay, "Popular Songs and the Facts of Life," S.I. Hayakawa wrote these words about the role of blues music in the African American community of the time: "I am often reminded by the words of blues songs of Kenneth Burke's famous description of poetry as 'equipment for living.' In the form in which they developed in Negro communities, the blues are equipment for living humble, laborious, and precarious lives of low social status or no social status at all—nevertheless, they are valid equipment."[13] Contemporary popular music provides no less valid equipment for living the life of an American adolescent.

How, then, do young people use music in their lives? At the simplest, most global level, children, adolescents, and adults—all of us, in other words—listen to music because it gives us pleasure. This pleasure can take many forms. Music can make a good mood better and allow us to escape or "work through" a bad one. It can relieve tension, provide escape or distraction from life's problems and complications, keep us company when we're alone, fill the time when there's nothing much to do, and ease the drudgery of repetitive, menial tasks and chores, including, to the chagrin of many parents, studying and homework. Music also fills a variety of functions in social situations: it fills uncomfortable gaps in conversations, provides topics of conversation, and makes parties or social gatherings more lively and comfortable. Music also stimulates dancing, singing, clapping, and other forms of direct participation. Listeners frequently identify in a personal way with the stories told in song lyrics. They also learn new language, expose themselves to different cultures, and respond to the political and social messages embedded in popular songs. Music preferences and tastes are used to form and solidify friendships, express resistance against adult authority, identify subcultures, and mark psychological and physical boundaries both within youth culture and between the youth and adult worlds. Popular music is, in other words, a very versatile piece of equipment. For the purposes of the following discussion, however, it is useful to focus on these four general categories: affective uses, social uses, cultural uses, and music video uses.

Affective Uses

When adolescents talk about what music does for them, they invariably invoke some reference to the way it makes them *feel*. The importance of this emotional or affective impact has been observed in a number of studies, but perhaps the best information on the issue comes from Professor Keith Roe's work with Swedish adolescents. He presented twelve possible reasons for listening to music and asked students how much each reason applied to them. Using factor analysis, Roe found that most of the variability in the original array could be organized into three underlying dimensions: (a) atmosphere creation and mood control (to relax and stop thinking about things, get in the right mood, set a social atmosphere, and dancing); (b) silence-filling and passing the time when there's nothing else to do; and (c) attention to lyrics. Of the three, atmosphere creation and mood control emerged as the most important, with time-filling second and attention to lyrics a distant third.[14] A similar pattern seems to hold even as early as middle grade school. A few years ago, I conducted a study in which 1st-grade through 6th-grade school children explained to interviewers why they liked listening to music. The children's responses were recorded and later placed into categories. Although many of the children answered with a generic, "I just like it," those who provided a more specific answer most often mentioned atmosphere and mood control. Next in frequency were background and passing time, followed by lyrics. By 6th grade the relative frequency of the three types of response was quite close to that reported by Roe: about 40 percent mentioned atmosphere and mood control, 20 percent mentioned passing time, and just under 10 percent cited the meaning in the lyrics.[15]

The research suggests, then, a principle that might be labeled "the primacy of affect." That is, for most young people, popular music use is motivated primarily by the desire to control mood and enhance emotional states. When teens want to be in a certain mood, when they feel lonely, when they seek distraction from their troubles, music tends to be the chosen medium.[16] As in many aspects of popular music use, gender specifies the nature of emotional management. Consistently, males are more likely than females to use music to increase their energy level and seek stimulation—that is, to get "pumped up" or "psyched up." Females are more likely to listen in order to lift their spirits when they're down or lonely, or to use music to work through a somber mood.[17] Larson and his colleagues wrote: "For girls, whose listening tastes are more often directed toward ballads and love songs, music is not elevating, but rather is associated with sadness, depression and sometimes anger. While boys appear to use music to energize themselves, young adolescent girls' use of music may be driven more by a need to both explore and cope with new concerns and worries that accompany this age period, perhaps especially those surrounding the intimate relations that are so often the themes of these songs."[18]

The practice of matching negative music with negative moods applies to many boys as well. Male heavy metal fans, for example, often choose music that deepens rather than reverses their negative emotional states. Jeffrey Arnett asked a sample of male heavy metal fans whether they were more likely to listen to heavy metal when they were in a "particular mood." Fewer than 10 percent said they tended to listen when in a positive mood, versus almost half who said they were most likely to listen when they were angry. One respondent said he sought out "full-blown thrashing metal" when he was "mad at the world."[19]

At first glance this process seems rather dysfunctional. In his theory of mood management, Dolph Zillman argues, logically enough, that people generally choose media experiences that produce more positive moods, while avoiding those that promote aversive ones. Yet it is clear that people routinely consume troubling, unpleasant, even depressing media fare, including popular music.[20] Zillman's essentially hedonic principle would have little trouble with cases where the immersion in sad or angry music serves a purgative function, allowing teens to work through and out of negative mood states. In fact, many of the angry listeners in Arnett's study claimed to experience such an effect. But how does one explain the use of music to make bad moods even worse?

Mary Beth Oliver has described two mechanisms that may help to explain the phenomenon. The first process, "downward social comparison," posits that although we are normally disturbed by media content in which bad things happen to good people, on occasion such material may have the positive effect of making our own plight seem less awful by comparison. Obviously, popular music provides a wealth of texts well suited for downward comparison. An adolescent who has been snubbed by a boyfriend or girlfriend or who is experiencing conflict with parents can easily find a song that depicts an even more desperate situation than his or her own. The second process described by Oliver requires making a distinction between the negative mood itself (grief, anger, loneliness) and what she calls a "meta-mood," that is, one's *feelings about the feelings*. Oliver argues that meta-moods may be positive even though the feelings that generate them are negative. In other words, one may be sad yet feel good about it or at least justified in the sadness. Under some circumstances, then, the affective rewards of music listening may be located in these meta-moods: listening to sad, angry, or depressing songs may contribute to a sense that not only is it all right to feel this way, but this is the right way to feel.[21]

It is crucial, however, to distinguish between the *motivations* for and the actual *effects* of listening. Teens may find it somehow rewarding and validating to wallow in their misery or heighten their anger through music, and they may well have the subjective feeling that the music has helped them deal with, make sense of, even defuse their negative emotions. Nevertheless, the net emotional effects of the experience may remain negative. Few people, we suspect, would say it is a good thing to deepen an adolescent's anger or depression. This process may also entail some serious behavioral consequences. As Zillman has shown, a person in a heightened state of physiological arousal or excitation will tend to experience ensuing stimuli more intensely than a person who is less aroused: the initial arousal level "transfers" to the new situation. Thus, in an experimental study, college students who were aroused before listening to exciting music experienced a more intense reaction to the music than those who had not been previously aroused.[22]

In other words, kids who are already "pumped up" will get more energized by high energy music than kids who are aren't already in an agitated state. But the process doesn't end there: it seems quite possible that the experience of music may heighten arousal levels even further, thus setting the stage for the transfer of an even higher state of excitement to situations and stimuli that follow. More generally, one could envision a cycle of emotion in which pre-existing intense mood states increase the intensity of responses to music, which in turn (given the right music) intensifies the initial mood state. Indeed, such a cycle may have been at work in the numerous documented cases of adolescents committing suicide or violent crimes after listening to suicidal or violent music. Almost without exception, these cases involve youth who are initially depressed or angry, then listen to high intensity music with suicidal or violent themes, then, with tragic consequences, transfer their mood states into action.[23]

Social Uses

Popular music is inseparable from adolescent social life: many argue, in fact, that the social uses and meanings of popular music are the real key to its special niche in the lives of youth.[24] Donald Roberts and I distinguish between the "quasi-social" uses and "socializing" uses of popular music listening. The term *quasi-social* applies to situations in which a person is listening alone but in which listening nonetheless serves goals and needs revolving around social relationships. The best example of this is when music is used to replace or invoke the presence of absent peers, thus relieving feelings of loneliness. In one study, two-thirds of a sample of college respondents said they listened either "somewhat" or "very frequently" in order to feel less alone when they were by themselves. The same study showed this use of music to be significantly more frequent among girls than for boys.[25] Solitary music listening may also prepare adolescents for *future* peer interactions and relationships. To a large extent, those who know little about teen pop culture and current music trends are consigned to the periphery of teen culture, whereas pop music "experts" tend to have more friends and enjoy enhanced status in the adolescent social structure.[26] Solitary listening, obviously, can feed the expertise that contributes to these social rewards. It is important to note in this context that most popular music listening occurs *alone*, not in the presence of peers or family.[27]

Popular music is an essential ingredient in adolescent socializing. Music is used to accompany courtship and sexual behavior; it provides the basis for friendships; and in larger gatherings, such as parties, dances, or clubs, it supplies atmosphere, reduces inhibitions, stimulates conversation, and, of course, moves participants to dance. It is virtually impossible to imagine a teen party without popular music. Adolescents differ in the extent to which they incorporate popular music into social interactions. Females are somewhat more likely than males to use music in a socializing context; and, on average, females report more interest in dancing.[28] African American youth are not only more involved with music generally than whites, but are also more involved in dancing and more likely to consider the ability to dance as an important personal attribute.[29] The use of music in social contexts also varies according to music taste and subculture membership. For example, an ethnographic study of dance club behavior revealed very different patterns of interaction between heavy metal fans, who engaged in relatively little cross-sex communication of any kind, and a crowd referred to as "yuppies" or "preppies," who were much more likely to engage in boy-girl chatting and dancing.[30]

Cultural Uses and Music Preferences

Popular music also expresses, creates, and perpetuates the various "us-them" distinctions that develop between groups and subcultures. The most basic such distinction is between youth and adults, and there is ample evidence that an adolescent's degree of involvement with popular music—and particularly with "adult-disapproved" music forms such as heavy metal and rap—correlates positively with peer orientation and negatively with orientation toward parents and other adults, including school authorities.[31] James Lull, who has published a number of studies on youth and music, maintains that popular music's *essential* significance lies in its power to express opposition to adult authority and mainstream cultural values: "Generally, young people use music to resist authority at all levels, assert their personalities and learn about things that their parents and the schools aren't telling them."[32] Similarly, Lawrence Grossberg argues that the basic "work" of rock music is to unite adolescents in opposition to the straight, boring, adult world. True rock music (as opposed to pop), he says, represents freedom from the restraints of authority and the right to seek pleasure in one's own way and in the moment.[33]

There may, however, be some reason to question how broadly this "oppositional" use applies. Most kids are not in a state of open warfare against their parents, not alienated from the adult and school culture, and not on the fringe of adolescent culture—in other words, they are not rebelling.[34] Without question, some 15-year-old boys crank up their favorite death metal album at least in part to enrage their parents. Yet when adolescents are asked directly why they listen to music or why they like a certain musician, song, or genre, relatively few say that it is because music expresses their conflict with authority. Many teens, one suspects, pursue adult-disapproved personal styles and music preferences not so much to offend or distance themselves from adults as to cultivate a public *image* of rebelliousness and independence. Even if things at home are running smoothly enough, status is gained by making a show of conflict with parents and the adult world. Thus, for instance, we find that adolescents report much "tougher," more rebellious music tastes in the presence of their peers than they report individually in private.[35] This tension between basic respect for parental authority and the need to project an independent public image is illustrated by Kotarba and Wells's description of young adolescents' arrival at a Houston all-ages dance club. Too young to drive, many of these young patrons depended on their parents to deliver them. Obviously, then, parents were aware of what their children were doing and had permitted it. The kids insisted, however, on being dropped off a full city block away and then walking to the club alone or with their friends. As one said: "It isn't cool to have everyone see your mother driving you to Roma's."[36]

There is no question, however, about the connection between popular music and group differences *within* teen culture. Every American high school is divided into subgroups, and often these are identified with a specific type of music. For those who are unsuccessful in school or alienated from the mainstream (racial and ethnic minorities, for instance), music allegiance is much more than one cultural marker among many—it is a primary means for expressing solidarity, pride, and defiance. Thus, it makes sense to speak of alternative, punk, rave, hip-hop, heavy metal, or rasta subcultures because, for such groups, music often forms the primary focus of group identity. The use of music to express subgroup resistance to the mainstream is not limited to the high school setting. One study found that rap music gave black students in predominantly white universities an important focus of resistance against the dominant authorities and cultural values of the university. To these students and others who either can't or choose not to fit into the mainstream, music provides a sense of power and insurgence.[37]

The Uses of Music Videos

As already noted, watching music videos is for most adolescents an occasional diversion rather than a constant obsession, thus suggesting that the fears often expressed about the impact of music videos may be exaggerated. Three factors, however, elevate the importance of music videos: First, the visual information in music videos may have more potential to shape viewers' attitudes and perceptions of social reality than does the music alone. Second, because videos occupy the eyes, music video viewing is more likely a foreground than a background activity. Third, although the overall average viewing time for music videos is less than 30 minutes a day, a segment of perhaps 5–15 percent of adolescents watch *several hours a day.* These highly absorbed viewers stand a much greater chance of being influenced.

Most writers and commentators reason from the energy and intensity of the visual element that the pictures are more central to the pleasure of music videos than the music itself. Marsha Kinder, for example, maintains that because music videos' uniqueness is based on their pulsing, discontinuous dreamlike visual images, these images must be the "primary source of pleasure."[38] The research on music video uses and gratifications, however, generally shows the music itself to be at least as important as the visual component. Moreover, when visuals have been cited as a source of pleasure, they are often relegated to the ancillary role of shedding light on a song's meaning.

This is not to suggest that pure visual stimulation is unimportant—the pictures are provocative and they are noticed. However, the research suggests that the visual themes and images in music videos are not taken seriously as a source of knowledge about the world. Adolescents do not use music videos as a "school of life" on important moral issues or on how to conduct social relationships. Rather, the information they seek deals with the stylistic details of teen culture—fashion trends, dance moves, and popular music itself. The research finds strong racial and gender differences in teen orientation to music videos. Blacks and females are more likely than whites and males to say they find music videos instrumental in their lives, and they are particularly likely to cite music videos as a way to stay on top of current teen culture trends. Black adolescents are almost twice as likely as whites to watch music videos for information about dancing. These differences, along with the others reported earlier, confirm a general pattern: blacks and females are more involved in all aspects of popular music, both in terms of time and emotional investment, than whites and males. Black females are the most involved subgroup of all.[39]

The Messages in the Music

Most of the criticism now being aimed at popular music and music videos stems from something in their "content." With the popular song, this means lyrics—sometimes specific words, sometimes more general images or portrayals. With music videos, of course, visual information gets most of the attention, but the issues involved span the same range from the specific (for example, how women are dressed) to the general (how women are treated in relationships). It would not take any of us very long to find something in the messages and imagery of the music media that we would just as soon not have young people hear or see. Content matters because the words and images in the music media carry obvious implications for adolescent socialization.

Some qualifications and warnings are in order at the outset of any discussion of the messages contained in popular music: First, to a great extent the "message" of popular music resides not in certain words or pictures but in the "sound"—the melodic and rhythmic qualities that differentiate popular music from other music and pop music genres from one another. Indeed, what most of us probably think of as the story or the "message" is often ignored during the music listening or video viewing process. Second, music and messages about music come through various channels other than stereos, radio stations, and the MTV network. Movies, talk shows, album cover art, pop magazines, rock concerts, even posters and T-shirts are all part of the extended music culture and are involved in its discourse. An especially important (and little researched) aspect of this expanded concept of the popular music culture surrounds the reputations and actions of musicians themselves, many of whom exhibit in their personal lives the very sort of problematic values and attitudes for which their music is criticized. Finally, we should all be aware that our adult interpretations of lyrics or music videos often do not correspond to the message that children and adolescents may see. A number of studies have shown wide discrepancies not only between adult and adolescent readings of music texts, but also between different groups of young listeners.[40]

Even so, for a significant minority of listeners, the meaning of lyrics (or the "message" of a music video) is every bit as crucial in their pleasure as the melody or beat. Lyrics are mentioned as a primary gratification by many youth and a secondary gratification by most.[41] For better or worse, then, lyrics and music videos are often attended to, processed, discussed, memorized, even taken to heart. Given the controversy surrounding heavy metal and rap music, it is interesting to note that heavy metal and rap fans report much higher levels of interest and attention to lyrics than teens in general. In fact, two interesting patterns emerge from the research on attention to lyrics: First, the more important music is to an adolescent, the more weight he or she gives to lyrics as a music gratification. Second, attention to lyrics is highest among fans of oppositional or controversial music, whether it be 1960's protest rock or the heavy metal and rap of today. In other words, the more defiant, alienated, and threatening to the mainstream a music type is, the more closely its words are followed.[42]

Themes of Love and Sex

Today as always, the most common theme in popular music is the "boy-girl issue"—courtship, romance, falling in and out of love, and increasingly in recent years, sex. Of course, the concern about popular music content has not arisen from its natural predilection for love and courtship themes but the directions those themes have taken. Different critics complain about different things here: some lament the displacement of Platonic love by overt sexual depiction; others bemoan the sad and pessimistic portrayal of relationships; still others worry about the stereotypical way in which lyrics describe the women (and sometimes the men) involved in the relationships. Whatever the specific complaint, it is clear that the way popular music deals with the boy-girl issue has changed significantly. Popular music—and this will surely surprise no one—is much less romantic and much more overtly sexual than it once was. It is indeed a long way from the Everly Brothers' plaintive "Whenever I want you, all I have to do is dream" (1958) to lines like these rap hits:

Well, if it's on, it's on, baby bring some friends / We can all get butt naked in the Holiday Inn / How you like it, from the front, from the back, how you like to ride? ("How U Like It," Mr. Marcelo featuring Masta P, 2000)

You know how we do, bitches in them see-through dresses on / Double shots of Henny rock, all night lemon drops / Til they touchin', have 'em touchin' other women's spots . . ./ All night ménage à trois, who came to get ride, who came to get high, what the fuck ("In the Club," Beanie Sigel featuring DJ Clue, 2000)

Evil dick likes warm, wet places / Evil dick don't care about faces / Evil dick likes young, tiny places / Evil dick leaves gooey, telltale traces ("Evil Dick," Body Count, 1992)

Although this level of explicitness certainly doesn't characterize all current popular music, it is nonetheless indicative of a general trend toward more open and often graphic depiction of the physical component of relationships. Perhaps even more important, the majority of songs depicting sex are sung in a *male* voice. Thus, the message may not be so much one of mutual sexual gratification, but of the sexual exploitation of females.[43]

Studies of music videos also offer up a great deal of sexual imagery, and these portrayals, too, are increasingly provocative and unambiguous. To be sure, there is little sexual content of the sort that would receive an R rating if it were to appear on a movie screen. Rather, as Christenson and Roberts wrote: "Sex in music videos is more a matter of titillation than consummation, a sex of bikinis and lingerie, pouty looks, flirtation, suggestive dancing, necking, undulation, crotch-grabbing and snaking up against street lamps."[44] A 1994 study by John Tapper and his colleagues found "sexual appeal" imagery, that is, the presence of implicit or explicit sexual images or symbolism, in about 30 percent of the videos in several hours sampled off various music video channels. There were large differences between genres: about half of pop, soul, and rap videos contained sexual appeal imagery versus 23 percent of alternative music videos, 14 percent of classic rock videos, and only 8 percent of heavy metal videos.[45] A similar analysis of videos from the year 1990 led the researchers to conclude that the most salient message of music videos is: "Whether you are male or female, act sexual."[46] Like song lyrics, music videos are usually constructed from the perspective of male fantasy: thus, women are much more likely than men to wear provocative clothing and be the objects of sexual pursuit.[47]

Violence

Parents and citizens' groups also criticize popular music for glorifying violence. Gang and street violence are often a central theme in rap music, as in these lines: "What you ain't heard, boy, I ride with these niggas, I die with these niggas/ Do a drive-by with my 45 'cause I'm down with these niggas" ("Down 4 My Niggas," C-Murder, 2000). Violent references also occur in other genres, too, particularly heavy metal.[48] It is not known specifically what proportion of songs incorporate violence, although it is probably not a great proportion of the very most popular. Only 8 percent of the songs in an analysis of top hits from 1980 to 1990 contained references to violence, and violence or death formed the primary focus in fewer than 1 percent.[49] On the other hand, this study ended about the time that rap—the genre most known for incorporating violent themes—broke into the mainstream. Given rap's huge popularity, the percentage of songs with significant levels of violent imagery is probably higher today than it was a decade ago.

Music videos also present violent themes and imagery with reasonable frequency. A 1984 report by the National Coalition on Television Violence claimed that violent or hostile behavior occurred about 18 times an hour in MTV programming. Another study conducted at about the same time found that just over half of music videos contained representations of violence, with about 10 percent displaying guns, chains, knives, or other dangerous weapons. The research suggests that similar levels of violence exist today. When violence does occur, moreover, it typically incurs no consequences.[50]

Related to violence are the repeated portrayals, especially in hard rock, heavy metal, and rap videos, of frustration, anger, and defiance against symbols of authority. One doesn't need to watch MTV for very long to see examples of a sort of "in your face" adolescent rebellion against parental figures, teachers, businessmen, police, politicians, or other representatives of entrenched power. Susan Bleich and her colleagues argue that among rock music's many themes "none is more obtrusive . . . than that of adolescent defiance of freedom-curtailing impositions by persons or institutions in power."[51] As noted previously, one can argue that this stand against adult authority is natural and predictable—in a sense, it's what rock 'n' roll is all about. Even so, the prevalence of this message carries obvious implications for the relationship between the generations.

Substance Use

Even though popular music has often been linked to substance use—particularly illicit drugs—little systematic research has been conducted on substance use themes in music lyrics or music videos. This seems an especially important omission given the importance of popular music to children and adolescents.

Alcohol. Alcohol use has always played a central role in American popular music. In his book on predominant themes in the history of American popular music, Lee Cooper (1991) lists scores of songs with a primary focus on drinking, titles such as: "Chug-a-lug" (recorded by Roger Miller in 1964), "Margaritaville" (Jimmy Buffett, 1977), "Scotch and Soda" (Ray Price, 1983), and "Red Red Wine" (Neil Diamond, 1968). Many more examples could easily be compiled, ranging from early blues through contemporary rock, rap, and country music. And this only considers songs that incorporate drinking as a major theme: many more incorporate references to alcohol in the context of other subject matter.

A recent study published in 1999 by the Office of National Drug Control Policy (ONDCP) provides the latest and most extensive data on the frequency of alcohol and illicit drug references in popular music. The research examined the lyrics of the top thousand songs of 1996 and 1997, two hundred each from these categories of music: Hot-100 (pop), rap, heavy metal, country, and alternative rock. Overall, 17 percent of the songs contained some reference to alcohol. There were, however, sizeable differences according to music type: 47 percent of rap songs contained alcohol references, compared to 4 percent of heavy metal, 10 percent of alternative rock, 12 percent of Hot-100, and 13 percent of country-western.[52] Obviously, alcohol appears much more often in rap than in other genres. One scholar has suggested rap music promotes drinking as an "accoutrement of identity, pleasure, sensuality and personal power." The author quotes these lines from "8-Ball" by NWA:

"Old English 800, cuz that's my brand / Take it in a bottle, 40, quart or can / Drink it like a madman, yes I do."[53]

Rap music videos are also more likely to show alcohol use than are videos from other genres. A study of over 500 music videos recorded from three different networks reported that 27 percent of rap videos showed one or more characters drinking, followed by rock (25%), country (21%), adult contemporary (19%), and rhythm and blues (17%). About one in five (19%) of the entire sample of 500 videos portrayed drinking by a lead singer. Moreover, several videos showed repeated shots of both drinking and tobacco use by a lead singer.[54]

Illicit Drugs. Popular music has long been associated with illicit drug use. Indeed, it is impossible to separate the progressive rock of the late 1960s and early 1970s from the controversies surrounding drug lyrics (both real and purported) such as the Beatles' "Lucy In the Sky With Diamonds" or the Byrds' "Eight Miles High."[55] More recent examples of drug references are just as easy to come by. For example:

I don't get angry when my mom smokes pot,
Hits that bottle and goes back to the rock
(Sublime, "What I Got," 1996)

Pass the hay [marijuana] you silly slut,
Blaze it up so I can hit that bud,
Get me zoned and I'll be on,
Cuz I love to smoke upon hay
(Crucial Conflict, "Hay," 1997)

I'm a thug, I'm a die high,
I be out in Jersey, puffin' Hershey
(Puff Daddy, "Can't Nobody Hold Me Down," 1997)

Interestingly, given the salience of drugs in the popular music culture, the ONDCP study provides the first quantitative evidence regarding the frequency of drug references in music. That study found illicit drug references in 18 percent of the one thousand songs examined in the study, with dramatic differences between genres, ranging from 63 percent of top rap songs to less than 1 percent of country songs. In terms of the *nature* of the portrayals, the study concluded that drug use tended to be treated in a neutral context, more or less as a normal aspect of life. Direct condemnation of drugs occurred in only a handful of songs, and clear references to the negative consequences of use were equally rare.[56]

As noted above, the influence of popular music must be considered to include not just the music itself, but also the reputation of the musicians, whose substance use habits are often quite familiar to young fans. Thus, actual drug use by musicians is a matter of considerable concern, especially given the tendency for many youth to adopt musicians as role models. A 1996 *Newsweek* cover story on celebrities' drug involvement associates a number of artists with heroin use, even suggesting that the effect is to glamorize heroin use, even when its use leads to death, as it has for a number of rock musicians.[57] One thing is certain: whether or not the popular music culture glamorizes substance use, it certainly does not condemn it.

Some Effects of Popular Music and Music Videos

This section focuses on research directly related to the impact of popular music and music videos on youth. It should be pointed out, however, that the music *uses* mentioned earlier in this chapter are, at some level, also *effects* and that most of these effects of music listening are benign or at worst neutral. That is, if kids say music helps them relax, or makes their parties more fun, or just gets them through a boring day, we should probably take them at their word. Particularly important in this context is the clear and well-documented impact of music on adolescent mood states (which, as noted previously, may not always be so benign). The following discussion centers on "content-related" effects—effects that connect logically to the messages embedded either in music lyrics or music video imagery. As we will see, most of the research on content-related music effects surrounds the attitudinal and behavioral impact of the more extreme and negative messages in today's popular music, in particular the messages embedded in hard rock, heavy metal, and rap. This bias is worth at least a note in passing: without question, more attention must be given to the impact of other sorts of music and messages.

A number of studies report positive associations between adolescents' music preferences and various individual characteristics. For example, college students whose tastes run to mainstream pop and dance music appear to be more extroverted than those with other music tastes, while those oriented to hard rock seem to have a greater need than other students to seek excitement and stimulation.[58] Heavy metal fans have been studied more extensively than any other music subculture, and it turns out that a preference for heavy metal music is associated with a variety of troublesome attitudes and behaviors, including drunk driving, casual sex, experimentation with marijuana and cocaine, conflict with parents and school authorities, anti-establishment attitudes, permissive sexual attitudes, Satanic beliefs, and low levels of trust in others (see chap. 6).[59] A survey of white college students showed those favoring rap music to be more aggressive and less trusting in others than students who preferred genres such as country, classic rock, or alternative rock music.[60] These correlational findings, though, do not necessarily warrant the conclusion that music exposure has produced the various differences reported. It seems just as likely that these associations result either from the action of a third variable (for instance, social class or family environment) or that the arrow of causation runs the opposite direction—in other words, that personal characteristics come first and exposure to a certain type of music follows. For that reason, the balance of this section concentrates on the experimental research now emerging on the impact of the music media.

Although most experimental studies have dealt with music videos, some attention has been given to the effects of music alone. In one study, three identical groups of college students wrote "stories" about a series of ambiguous pictures while listening to one of three types of music: aggressive music with aggressive lyrics, aggressive music with non-aggressive lyrics (for example, Christian heavy metal music), or non-aggressive music with non-aggressive lyrics. The music played continuously for 20 minutes while the students wrote their stories, after which they took a paper-and-pencil test designed to measure their level of general hostility. Counter to expectation, no group differences emerged either in level of hostility expressed in the stories or in scores on the hostility scale. The researchers explained this result by suggesting that the students simply had not paid attention to the lyrics.[61]

Another music-only study found an effect of listening to heavy metal music, but not the effect expected. The investigators set out to test whether listening to sexually violent heavy metal would increase acceptance of sex-role stereotypes and sexually violent behavior. Groups of undergraduate males listened either to sexually violent heavy metal, Christian heavy metal rock, or classical music, then filled out a questionnaire measuring sex-role stereotyping, adversarial sexual beliefs, and rape myth acceptance. Surprisingly, it did not matter whether participants heard sexually violent heavy metal lyrics or Christian heavy metal lyrics—exposure to either type of heavy metal produced more negative attitudes toward women on the various measures than did listening to classical music. The fact that the two types of heavy metal produced the same effect suggests that students were reacting to the sound only and that the sound elicited a response something like: "That's heavy metal, and if it's heavy metal, then it must be sexual and violent." The "message" of a song, then, may lie not so much in the actual lyric content, but in the content listeners infer based on musical qualities.[62]

Experiments on responses to music videos have demonstrated effects on a variety of cognitive and attitudinal measures. As previously mentioned, a primary concern of researchers has been the potential impact of violent and sexual imagery, and various studies have shown effects in these areas. Larry Greeson and Rose Ann Williams compared the responses of a group of high school students who viewed 30 minutes of music videos with high concentrations of sex, violence, and anti-establishment themes to another group who saw the same amount of videos randomly taped off the air. They found that 7th and 10th graders who had watched the "high impact" hard rock videos reported a higher level of approval of premarital sex than the comparison group. Among 10th graders, the high impact videos also reduced disapproval of violence. Exposure to rock videos with violent themes has also been shown to increase college males' level of antagonism and disrespect toward women.[63]

A series of studies conducted by Christine and Ranald Hansen have shown that exposure to rock videos can exert a variety of short-term effects on how college students judge people in purportedly unrelated contexts. Among their findings: (a) exposure to rock videos with defiant and antisocial imagery increased students' acceptance of actual rude and defiant behavior; (b) exposure to music videos displaying highly gender-stereotyped behavior increased the tendency to apply gender-stereotyped rules in judging the subsequent behavior of "real" men and women; and (c) watching various types of "sexy" music videos caused students to rate characters in sexually neutral television commercials as being more physically attractive and sexier.[64]

Research on the impact of viewing rap music videos tends to report the same kind of results. In one experiment, three identical groups of 11- to 16-year-old lower income African American youth watched either eight violent rap videos, eight nonviolent rap videos, or served as a control group who saw no videos. The violent videos contained images of both weapons and violent acts. The nonviolent videos focused on dancing and partying, featuring scantily clad female hangers-on fawning over the male performers. After participants viewed the videos and completed a brief "memory test," the important dependent measures were applied under the guise of a separate study on decision-making skills. The boys were presented with two brief stories, then asked to comment on what the parties involved should have done in the situations described. One story recounted an incident in which a young man physically assaults both his girlfriend and an old male friend of hers after seeing the two exchange a friendly hug and kiss. The second scenario involved an exchange between two old high school friends, one living simply and working hard in college, the other driving a BMW and wearing extravagant clothes and jewelry—a "player," in other words. Exposure to the rap videos influenced attitudes toward both violence and academic aspirations, at least as indicated in the students' responses to the scenarios. The boys who had viewed the violent videos were more likely than those in either the nonviolent video group or the no-video control group to condone the attack against the girl's old friend and to say they would have done the same thing. Boys who watched either type of rap video were less likely than those in the control group both to want to be like the young man attending college and to believe he would ever finish school.[65]

Rap is also very popular among white youth, and a pair of studies by Dolph Zillman and his colleagues indicate that exposure to rap videos can influence whites' attitudes toward African Americans and their culture. The first study employed an elaborate experimental procedure to examine the effect of politically radical rap music on race-related political attitudes. First, under the impression that their task was to evaluate music videos, white and African American high school students saw one of three sets of music videos: popular rock videos, nonpolitical rap videos, or radical political rap videos. The students later participated in a purportedly unrelated study of student politics in which they responded to one of six ostensible candidates for student office. Three of the candidates were white, and three were African American. Within each race, the candidates took one of three political stances: a racially liberal stance, a racially radical stance, or a neutral stance. The videos had no effect on the political attitudes of African American adolescents. White participants, however, were influenced. Exposure to the radical political rap videos dramatically increased white listeners' support for the message of racial harmony advocated by an African American candidate and decreased their acceptance of a conservative white candidate arguing against affirmative action. As the authors note, this finding runs contrary to the frequently voiced claim that radical rap makes white kids more racially defensive.[66]

The second study raised the issue of female artist rap videos' possible influence on how white listeners perceive African American women. The specific concern of the research was the influence of the sexually provocative videos being produced by female rap artists such as Salt-n-Pepa and Yo-Yo. The authors note the debate between those who see such videos as a celebration of female sexual openness and empowerment and others who say these sexualized portrayals are merely more of the same female sexual exploitation and degradation so common in videos by male artists. Students viewed the music videos in one context, then later participated in a second and supposedly unrelated "person perception" study. The participants, who were all white college students, were assigned randomly to one of three groups: a control group who did the person perception study without watching any videos, and two experimental groups, one of which watched four "sexually enticing" videos by female rap artists, and the other of which viewed four "devoted love" videos by female rap artists.

In the person perception phase, students were shown a series of slides of women, some white and some African American, and were asked to form trait judgments of the women based on their physical appearance. The results showed that the African American women in the slides were given significantly more negative ratings by those who had seen the sexually titillating rap videos than by those in either the control group or the devoted love group. In other words, they were judged to be less attractive, less assertive, less faithful, less positive in general. No such differences appeared in the judgments of white women. In the words of the authors: "Female Black rappers who dwell on sexual sensuality appear to do this at the expense of white audiences' less favorable perception of uncounted Black women. This outcome is consistent with the claim of Black leaders who feel that rappers give Blacks a bad rap."[67]

In summary, then, we find both correlational and experimental evidence that exposure to popular music and music videos can produce measurable content-related effects. It is important to acknowledge that the volume of research on the influence of popular music is very small compared to the research on the effects of television. In addition, and as most of the authors acknowledge, the generality of the experimental findings is compromised by their contrived procedures and settings and by their short time-frame. These studies must be supplemented with research conducted in the real world of adolescents and over a long enough period of time to address the persistence of any effects. These caveats aside, the general sense of the research reported here runs very much in parallel with the literature on the effects of TV. Indeed, it is increasingly apparent that, like watching television, exposure to popular music and music videos may, under certain circumstances and with certain groups of youth, exert an important cognitive, affective, and behavioral influence. Given the prevalence of negative messages in both lyrics and video images, there is a legitimate cause for concern about the specific nature of this influence.

Does this mean that the searing guitar music parents hear behind their kids' bedroom doors and the pink-haired, tongue-pierced dervish exploding across the music video screen are turning young people into monsters? Obviously not. Most kids are fine most of the time, and although music matters to them, it is primarily a source of pleasure rather than a problem. They listen not to analyze lyrics and learn about the world, not to seek guidance on how to live their lives, not to facilitate social interaction, but simply because they like it. To be sure, popular music does teach them things, does help them to sort out emotions and feelings, and so on. It is the medium that matters most to adolescents, not least because it talks about the things that matter most to them—love, sex, loyalty, independence, friendship, authority—with an honesty and directness they don't often get from adults. One thing is certain: for most of today's adolescents, popular music functions not just as "equipment for living," but as the essential equipment for living.

NOTES

1. Donald Roberts and Lisa Henriksen, "Music Listening Versus Television Viewing among Older Adolescents," paper presented to the International Communication Association, Dublin, Ireland, June 1990.

2. Keith Roe, "The School and Music in Adolescent Socialization," in *Popular Music and Communication*, ed., J. Lull (Beverly Hills, Calif.: Sage Publications, 1987), pp. 212–30.

3. Peter Christenson, "Childhood Patterns of Music Use and Preferences," *Communication Reports* 7, no. 1 (1994): pp. 136–44.

4. Ibid.

5. Richard Lacayo, "Violent Reaction," *Time* (12 June 1995): pp. 25–30.

6. Leo Hubbard, "Professor Gives Hip-Hop a Bad Rap," *The Skanner* (Portland, Ore.), 26 May 1999, p. 9.

7. Peter Christenson and Donald Roberts, *It's Not Only Rock & Roll: Popular Music in the Lives of Adolescents* (Cresskill, N.J.: Hampton Press, 1998).

8. Donald Roberts, "Media and Youth: Access, Exposure, and Privatization," *Journal of Adolescent Health* 27, no. 2 (2000): pp. 8–14.

9. Roberts and Henriksen, "Music Listening Versus Television Viewing."

10. Peter Christenson, Peter DeBenedittis, and Thomas Lindlof, "Children's Use of Audio Media," *Communication Research* 12, no. 3 (1985): pp. 327–43; Christenson and Roberts, *It's Not Only Rock & Roll*; Roberts, "Media and Youth: Access, Exposure, and Privatization."

11. Jane Brown, Kim Childers, Karl Bauman, and Gary Koch, "The Influence of New Media and Family Structure on Young Adolescents' Television and Radio Use," *Communication Research* 17 (1990): pp. 65–82; Christenson and Roberts, *It's Not Only Rock & Roll*; Roberts and Henriksen, "Music Listening."

12. Peter Christenson, "Preadolescent Perceptions and Interpretations of Music Videos," *Popular Music and Society* 16, no. 3 (1992): pp. 63–73; Reed Larson and Robert Kubey, "Television and Music: Contrasting Media in Adolescent Life," *Youth and Society* 15, no. 1 (1989): pp. 13–31; Ellen Wartella, Katherine Heinz, Amy Aidman, and Sharon Mazzarella, "Television and Beyond: Children's Video Media in One Community," *Communication Research* 17, no. 1 (1990): pp. 45–64.

13. S.I. Hayakawa, *The Use and Misuse of Language* (Greenwich, Conn.: Fawcett, 1962), p. 161.

14. Keith Roe, "Swedish Youth and Music: Listening Patterns and Motivations," *Communication Research* 12, no. 3 (1985): pp. 353–62.

15. Christenson, "Childhood Patterns."

16. Christenson and Roberts, *It's Not Only Rock & Roll*; Reed Larson, Robert Kubey, and Joseph Colletti, "Changing Channels: Early Adolescent Media Choices and Shifting Investments in Family and Friends," *Journal of Youth and Adolescence* 18, no. 6 (1989): pp. 583–599; Jack Lyle and Heidi Hoffman, "Children's Use of Television and Other Media," in *Television in Day-to-day Life: Patterns of Use*, ed., Eli Rubinstein, George Comstock, and John Murray (Washington, D.C.: Government Printing Office, 1972), pp. 129–256.

17. Jeffrey Arnett, "Adolescents and Heavy Metal Music: From the Mouths of

Metalheads," *Youth and Society* 23, no. 1 (1991): pp. 76–98; Larson, Kubey, and Colletti, "Changing Channels"; Keith Roe, "Swedish Youth and Music"; Alan Wells, "Popular music: Emotional Use and Management," *Journal of Popular Culture* 24, no. 1 (1990): pp. 105–17.

18. Larson, Kubey, and Colletti, "Changing Channels."

19. Arnett, "Adolescents and Heavy Metal Music."

20. Dolph Zillman, "Mood Management: Using Entertainment to Full Advantage," in *Communication, Social Cognition and Affect*, ed. Lewis Donohew, Howard Sypher, and E. Tory Higgins (Hillsdale, N.J.: Erlbaum, 1988), pp. 147–71.

21. Mary Beth Oliver, "An Examination of the Enjoyment of Negative-Affect Producing Entertainment," paper presented to the International Communication Association, Dublin, June 1990.

22. Joanne Cantor and Dolph Zillman, "The Effect of Affective State and Emotional Arousal on Music Appreciation," *Journal of General Psychology* 89, no. 1 (1973): pp. 97–108.

23. See Christenson and Roberts, *It's Not Only Rock & Roll*, for a discussion of these incidents.

24. Simon Frith, *Sound Effects: Youth, Leisure and the Politics of Rock 'n' roll* (New York: Pantheon, 1981); James Lull, "Listeners' Communicative Uses of Popular Music," in *Popular Music and Communication*, James Lull, ed. (Newbury Park, Calif.: Sage, 1987), pp. 140–74; Roe, "Swedish Youth and Music."

25. Walter Gantz et al., "Gratifications and Expectations Associated with Popular Music among Adolescents," *Popular Music and Society* 6, no. 1 (1978): pp. 81–89.

26. Hanna Adoni, "The Functions of Mass Media in the Political Socialization of Adolescents," *Communication Research* 6 (1978): pp. 84–106; Roger Brown and Michael O'Leary, "Pop Music in an English Secondary School System," *American Behavioral Scientist* 14, no. 3 (1971): pp. 401–13; Joseph Dominick, "The Portable Friend: Peer Group Membership and Radio Usage," *Journal of Broadcasting* 18, no. 2 (1974): pp. 164–69.

27. Christenson and Roberts, *It's Not Only Rock & Roll*; Larson and Kubey, "Television and Music."

28. Raymond Carroll et al., "Meanings of Radio to Teenagers in a Niche-programming Era," *Journal of Broadcasting and Electronic Media* 37, no. 2 (1993): pp. 159–76; Gantz et al., "Gratifications and Expectations"; Roe, "Swedish Youth and Music"; Wells, "Popular Music."

29. Yasui Kuwahara, "Power to the People, Y'all: Rap Music, Resistance, and Black College Students," *Humanity and Society* 16, no. 1 (1992): pp. 54–73; James Lull, "Popular Music and Communication: An Introduction," in *Popular Music and Communication*, 2nd ed., ed. James Lull (Newbury Park, Calif.: Sage, 1992), pp. 1–32.

30. Joseph Kotarba and Laura Wells, "Styles of Adolescent Participation in an

All-ages Rock 'n' roll Nightclub: An Ethnographic Analysis," *Youth and Society* 18, no. 4 (1987): pp. 398–417.

31. Christenson and Roberts, *It's Not Only Rock & Roll.*

32. Lull, "Listeners' Communicative Uses of Popular Music," p. 153.

33. Lawrence Grossberg, "Rock and Roll in Search of an Audience," in Lull, ed., *Popular Music and Communication,* pp. 175–97.

34. Shirley Feldman and Glen Elliott, eds., *At the Threshold: The Developing Adolescent* (Cambridge: Harvard University Press, 1990).

35. Leif Finnas, "Do Young People Misjudge Each Others' Musical Taste?" *Psychology of Music* 15 (1989): pp. 152–66.

36. Kotarba and Wells, "Styles of Adolescent Participation," pp. 402–3.

37. Kuwahara, "Power to the People, Y'all."

38. Marsha Kinder, "Music Video and the Spectator: Television, Ideology, and Dream," *Film Quarterly* 38, no. 4 (1984): pp. 2–15.

39. Peter Christenson, "Preadolescent Perceptions and Interpretations of Music Videos," *Popular Music and Society* 16, no. 3 (1992): pp. 63–73; Jane Brown, Kenneth Campbell, and Lynn Fischer, "American Adolescents and Music Videos: Why Do They Watch?" *Gazette* 37, no. 1 (1986): pp. 19–32; Se-wen Sun and James Lull, "The Adolescent Audience for Music Videos and Why They Watch," *Journal of Communication* 36, no. 1 (1986): pp. 115–25.

40. Jane Brown and Laurie Schultze, "The Effects of Race, Gender and Fandom on Audience Interpretations of Madonna's Music Videos," *Journal of Communication* 40, no. 2 (1990): pp. 88–102; see Christenson and Roberts, *It's Not Only Rock & Roll,* for a general discussion of the "problem" of interpretation.

41. Christenson and Roberts, *It's Not Only Rock & Roll;* Gantz et al., "Gratifications and Expectations"; Roe, "Swedish Youth and Music."

42. Arnett, "Adolescents and Heavy Metal Music"; Christenson and Roberts, *It's Not Only Rock & Roll;* Kuwahara, "Power to the People, Y'all."

43. Donald Roberts and I discuss the importance of the male voice at some length in our book, *It's Not Only Rock & Roll.*

44. Christenson and Roberts, *It's Not Only Rock & Roll,* p. 142.

45. John Tapper, Esther Thorson, and David Black, "Variations in Music Videos as a Function of Their Musical Genre," *Journal of Broadcasting and Electronic Media* 38, no. 1 (1994): pp. 103–14.

46. Rita Sommers-Flanagan, John Sommers-Flanagan, and Britta Davis, "What's Happening on Music Television?: A Gender Role Content Content Analysis," *Sex Roles* 28, no. 2 (1993): pp. 745–53 (quoted on p. 752).

47. S. Seidman, "An Investigation of Sex-Role Stereotyping in Music Videos," *Journal of Broadcasting and Electronic Media* 36, no. 2 (1992): pp. 209–16.

48. Yumi Wilson, "Death Metal, Gangsta Rap, Grunge Rock Have a Common Theme: Violence," *San Francisco Chronicle,* 31 May 1994, pp. E1, E3.

49. Donald Roberts, David Kinsey, and Sheila Gosh, "Themes in Top 40 Songs of the 1980's," unpublished manuscript, Stanford University, Department of Communication, 1993.

50. Richard Baxter et al., "A content analysis of music videos," *Journal of Broadcasting and Electronic Media* 29, no. 3 (1985): pp. 333–40; National Coalition on Television Violence, *NCTV Music-video Monitoring Project* (Marlboro, Mass.: National Coalition on Television Violence, 1984); Barry Sherman and Joseph Dominick, "Violence and Sex in Music Videos: TV and Rock 'n' Roll," *Journal of Communication* 36, no. 1 (1986): pp. 79–93; Tapper, Thorson, and Black, "Variations in Music Videos."

51. Susan Bleich, Dolph Zillman, and James Weaver, "Enjoyment and Consumption of Rock Music as a Function of Rebelliousness," *Journal of Broadcasting and Electronic Media* 35, no. 3 (1991): pp. 351–366 (quoted on p. 351).

52. Donald Roberts, Lisa Henriksen, and Peter Christenson, *Substance Use in Popular Movies and Music* (Washington, D.C.: Office of National Drug Control Policy, 1999).

53. Denise Herd, "Contesting Culture: Alcohol-related Identity Movements in Contemporary African American Communities," *Contemporary Drug Problems* 20, no. 4 (1993): pp. 739–758.

54. Robert DuRant et al., "Tobacco and Alcohol Use Behaviors Portrayed in Music Videos: A Content Analysis," *American Journal of Public Health* 87, no. 7 (1997): pp. 1131–35.

55. For a good description of the history of the controversies surrounding drugs and rock music, see Ed Ward, Geoffrey Stokes, and Ken Tucker, *Rock of Ages: The Rolling Stone History of Rock and Roll* (New York: Rolling Stone Books, 1986).

56. Roberts, Henriksen, and Christenson, *Substance Use in Popular Movies and Music.*

57. Karen Schoemer, "Overdosing on Fame: Heroine is Now a Style as Well as a Substance," *Newsweek*, 15 July 1996, p. 53.

58. David Rawlings and Vera Ciancarelli, "Music Preference and the Five-Factor Model of the NEO Personality Inventory," *Psychology of Music* 25, no. 2 (1997): pp. 120–32.

59. Arnett, "Adolescence and Heavy Metal Music"; Peter Christenson and Boreas van Nouhuys, "From the Fringe to the Center: A Comparison of Heavy Metal and Rap Fandom," paper presented to the International Communication Association, Albuquerque, May 1995; Thomas Gordon, Ernest Hakanen, and Alan Wells, "Music Preferences and the Use of Music to Manage Emotional States: Correlates with Self-Concept Among Adolescents," paper presented to the International Communication Association, Miami, May 1992; Christine Hansen and Ranald Hansen, "Constructing Personality and Social Reality through Music: Individual Differences among Fans of Punk and Heavy Metal Music," *Journal of Broad-*

casting and Electronic Media 35, no. 3 (1991): pp. 335–50; Graham Martin, Michael Clarke, and Colby Pearce, "Adolescent Suicide: Music Preference as an Indicator of Vulnerability," *Journal of the Academy of Child and Adolescent Psychiatry* 32, no.3 (1993): pp. 530–35.

60. Alan Rubin, Daniel West, and Wendy Mitchell, "Differences in Aggression, Attitudes Toward Women, and Distrust as Reflected in Popular Music Preferences," *Media Psychology* 3, no. 1 (2001): pp. 25–42.

61. Catherine E. Wanamaker and Marvin Reznikoff, "Effects of Aggressive and Nonaggressive Rock Songs on Projective and Structured Tests," *Journal of Psychology* 123, no. 6 (1989): pp. 561–70.

62. Janet St. Lawrence and Doris Joyner, "The Effects of Sexually Violent Rock Music on Males' Acceptance of Violence Against Women," *Psychology of Women Quarterly* 15, no. 1 (1991): pp. 49–63.

63. Larry Greeson and Rose Ann Williams, "Social implications of music videos for youth: An analysis of the content and effects of MTV," *Youth and Society* 18, no. 1 (1986): pp. 177–89; Dena Peterson and Karen Pfost, "Influence of Rock Videos on Attitudes of Violence Against Women," *Psychological Reports* 64, no. 1 (1989): pp. 319–22.

64. Christine Hansen and Ranald Hansen, "The Influence of Sex and Violence on the Appeal of Rock Music Videos," *Communication Research* 17, no. 2 (1990): pp. 212–34; Christine Hansen and Ranald Hansen, "How Rock Music Videos Can Change What Is Seen When Boy Meets Girl: Priming Stereotypic Appraisal of Social Interactions," *Sex Roles* 19, no. 5–6 (1988): pp. 287–316; Christine Hansen and Walter Krygowski, "Arousal-augmented Priming Effects: Rock Music Videos and Sex Object Schemas," *Communication Research* 21, no. 1 (1994): pp. 24–47.

65. James D. Johnson, Lee Jackson, and Leslie Gatto, "Violent Attitudes and Deferred Academic Aspirations: Deleterious Effects of Exposure to Rap Music," *Basic and Applied Social Psychology* 16, no. 1–2 (1995): pp. 27–41.

66. Dolph Zillman et al., "Radical Rap: Does it Further Ethnic Division?" ibid., pp. 1–25.

67. Su-lin Gan, Dolph Zillman, and Michael Mitrook, "Stereotyping Effect of Black Women's Sexual Rap on White Audiences," *Basic and Applied Social Psychology* 19, no. 3 (1997): pp. 381–99.

6

Music at the Edge

The Attraction and Effects

of Controversial Music on Young People

Jeffrey Jensen Arnett

G oing back at least to the rise of jazz in the early twentieth century, popular music has been a source of public concern for its possible effects on young people. Adults in every decade since have expressed the fear that the music embraced by the young may be morally corrupting and provoke them into deviant behavior. Although popular music has changed dramatically over the past century, it has been consistently portrayed as a force leading the young into temptation and separating them from the influence of their parents, teachers, and other adult authorities. First jazz, then the rock 'n' roll of the 1950s, then the rock music of the 1960s, through punk in the 1970s, heavy metal in the 1980s, and rap in the 1990s—each of these popular music genres has, in its turn, been regarded by adults as outrageous, offensive, and dangerous, while these very qualities have led many young people to greet the music with enthusiasm.

Why are so many young people attracted to music at the edge—music that many of their elders consider outrageous, offensive, and dangerous? Are the concerns expressed by adults over such music legitimate, or a consequence of sensationalism and of adults' amnesia over how their own music was regarded when they were young? These are the questions this chapter will address.

Rieff's "Transgressive"

As a theoretical tool to analyze the appeal of diverse types of popular music over the past century, I will use Philip Rieff's idea of the *transgressive*.[1] According to Rieff, something that is transgressive violates cultural norms and expectations. All cultures have *interdicts*, which are prohibitions, social rules, commands for what one must not do. Transgressive acts violate the interdicts. Some degree of transgressive behavior is inevitable in any culture; but in Rieff's view, interdicts are healthy and necessary for a culture to flourish or even to survive. Rieff expressed the concern that American society in the late twentieth century began to elevate transgressive behavior to the level of virtue while systematically undermining the force of the interdicts. In Rieff's view, this placed American society on the road "from civilization to barbarism—from a not-doing of what is not to be done to a routine doing of precisely that" (p. 47).

This is Rieff's idea, in a nutshell. I think it is potentially valuable for analyzing the appeal of edge music to adolescents, but I wish to do more than simply apply Rieff's idea. Although Rieff introduced the idea of the transgressive he did little to develop it theoretically, and I wish to develop it here so that it can be applied to edge music. Also, rather than accepting Rieff's conclusions about the moral decline of American society and the role of popular music in that putative decline, I wish to analyze this claim critically and consider the extent to which social science research can cast light on this question.

What is it that makes the transgressive appealing, especially to the young? One source of its appeal is that the interdicts it violates often include restrictions on sexual behavior, and being transgressive often involves experiencing sexual pleasure, or at least sexual fantasies and sexually suggestive behavior. For adolescents, at an age when sexual maturity has been reached and sexual desire is new and strong but interdicts limit their sexual behavior, anything that invites them to defy the interdicts and enjoy their sexuality is likely to have a powerful transgressive appeal.

Another aspect of the appeal of the transgressive is the excitement inherent in violating the interdicts. There may be something about violating cultural norms that is inherently thrilling, especially to the young. Scholars of the phenomenology of crime, especially Jack L. Katz,[2] have shown that for many criminals the primary appeal of the crime is not in the material rewards it may yield but in its psychological rewards—the excitement of it, the thrill of it, the challenge of mastering a potentially chaotic situation. For many noncriminals, too, taking voluntary risks is often experienced as pleasurable. Words such as exciting and thrilling can be used to describe this state, but the best description of it is a word from the French, *frisson*, which has connotations of physical/sensual excitement experienced as a consequence of taking an illicit risk. So, the appeal of the transgressive exists partly in the frisson that young people experience when they violate an interdict.

Why does experiencing the transgressive induce a frisson in the young and not the old? Or, to put it another way, why is the promise of frisson enough to inspire transgressive behavior in the young but not the old? One reason is that the young are newly autonomous from their parents, newly conscious of their own growing power for self-directed behavior. Consequently, behaving transgressively inspires a frisson in them because it is connected to their new powers, it acts as a declaration of their independence, in a way it would not for adults.

Perhaps more importantly, behaving transgressively carries fewer social penalties for the young than for adults. In American society, as in most societies, transgressive behavior is condoned for the young but not for adults. A young person who is transgressive is often tolerated, sometimes even admired, by others. She or he is simply exhibiting the natural exuberance of youth, living life to the fullest.

In contrast, an adult engaging in the same behavior as this hypothetical young person would be regarded as reprehensible, shameful, possibly psychologically disordered. Adults are supposed to have settled into the conventional, responsible, predictable patterns of behavior expected of adults. For example, in my research on how people conceptualize the transition to adulthood, a majority of people from adolescence through middle age believe that becoming an adult means giving up transgressive behavior such as getting drunk or trying illegal drugs.[3] Thus, few adults could enjoy a transgressive frisson without having it overshadowed by shame and censure. In contrast, young people can enjoy the frisson of the transgressive more fully because they know that there is an implicit cultural belief that they are at a time of life when behaving transgressively is condoned, perhaps even approved.

Although behaving transgressively means violating the interdicts, and therefore acting in a way that society regards as morally wrong, in another sense transgressive acts are imbued with virtue by those engaged in them. What makes the transgressive virtuous, a statement of moral courage, is that interdicts are often seen as suppressing our natural, healthy human urges, and consequently the transgressive is seen as true, genuine, authentic. As Robert Pattison describes,[4] this is an idea that originated with the Romanticism of the eighteenth century, but it was adopted with enthusiasm in the twentieth century by devotees of popular music, especially rock. In both rock and Romanticism there is, in Pattison's words, a "heroism of excess" (p. 122). The heroes are those who are willing to break the limits of nature and society—those who are willing to take the risk of the transgressive.

Jazz

Jazz was the music of the youth culture from the early years of the twentieth century through the 1940s, although its dominant form changed, from New Orleans jazz to Swing to Bop. In the Lynds' *Middletown* study of the 1920s,[5] music and radio topped the lists of interests of high school boys and girls of all social classes, and jazz was the music they listened to. Young people from the 1920s through the 1940s bought jazz records in large numbers, packed the dance halls and concert halls to hear their favorite jazz bands, and made pop icons out of musicians such as Louis Armstrong, Benny Goodman, Ella Fitzgerald, and Duke Ellington.[6]

What made jazz so popular, and to what extent was its appeal transgressive? Certainly the brilliance and creativity of the musicians played a large part in its appeal. But in addition to this, jazz was seen from the beginning by both its fans and its critics as highly sensual music, music that would stimulate sexual desire. This characteristic of jazz was due to the music qualities of the songs, not the lyrics. Many of the most popular jazz songs had no lyrics at all, and when there were lyrics they were usually innocuous. The sexual quality of jazz derived from the music, the beat of it, the energy, the intensity.

The other quality that made jazz sexually charged was that it was music to dance to.[7] In dancing to jazz, the young demonstrated its sexually transgressive power. Jazz dancing was spontaneous, energetic, and intense, like the music, and partners grasped each other tightly and moved rapidly. The combination of jazz music and dancing was intoxicating to the young, and deeply disturbing to their elders. Both adults and young people recognized the transgressive quality of jazz, especially with regard to sexuality, but adults feared it while the young embraced it with enthusiasm. A newspaper of the 1920s represented the adult view of jazz dancing this way: "The music is sensuous, the embracing of the partners—the female only half-dressed—is absolutely indecent; and the motions—they are such as may not be described with any respect for propriety, in a family newspaper."[8]

Jazz may also have been transgressive to young whites because of its association with African Americans. It grew out of spirituals and blues, two other types of music created by African Americans, and nearly all the early jazz musicians were black. Even after white musicians discovered and embraced jazz, most of the prominent performers and innovators continued to be African Americans.[9] Given the strict racial segregation of American society during this period, most young whites would have had little contact with blacks, and jazz being black music may have added to its allure for them as something mysterious, exciting, daring—in short, transgressive.

Rock 'n' Roll

By the end of the 1940s jazz had developed into a music form that was far different from what it had been in its early years. Improvisation had become much more daring and creative, to a point where it often retained little connection to a primary melody and rhythm, as had been the style in early jazz. This change may have made jazz more interesting and complex musically, but it also made it esoteric; and young people looking for a lively melody, a driving beat, and a song they could dance to had to look elsewhere.

By the mid-1950s they had found what they were looking for. It was called rock 'n' roll, and it was personified in a young white, former delivery-truck driver named Elvis Presley. Like jazz, rock 'n' roll was created by African Americans, and like jazz it grew out of the blues. Elvis had grown up in the South listening to early rock 'n' roll being performed by black musicians, and he incorporated the sensuality and power of their singing styles into his own. Although Elvis was the dominant rock 'n' roll star of the 1950s, African American performers such as Chuck Berry and Little Richard were also popular.

Like jazz, the transgressive quality of rock 'n' roll was in the music, not the lyrics. The lyrics of rock 'n' roll classics like "Hound Dog," "Johnny B. Goode," and "Tutti Frutti" contain nothing offensive. But like jazz, the music of rock 'n' roll was perceived by both its fans and its critics to be sexually arousing. The pounding beat of rock 'n' roll, the loud, raw sound of the electric guitars (amplified to unprecedented levels with new technology), and the passionate vocal styles of the singers seemed like an invitation to be transgressive, to violate the interdicts that restricted the sexuality of the young.

Also, like jazz, rock 'n' roll was dance music, and the dancing styles that accompanied rock 'n' roll added to its transgressive appeal. Rock 'n' roll dance styles were largely borrowed from jazz and shared with jazz dancing high energy, frequent close contact between partners, and a reliance on spontaneous, unscripted dance movements. This style of dancing reinforced and extended the transgressive sexual power of the music.

Something in rock 'n' roll that departed from jazz and made it considerably more transgressive than jazz was the style of the performers. Jazz music may have been transgressive, but the performers usually did not dress provocatively or move provocatively on stage. On the contrary, jazz musicians usually dressed up for their performances and sat in chairs on stage except when soloing. In contrast, the performance style of rock 'n' roll augmented its transgressive quality. Elvis, influenced by black blues musicians he had seen, developed a performance style of bracing himself against the microphone stand and thrusting his pelvis back and forth in an unmistakably sexual way (hence the nickname "Elvis the Pelvis"), his legs pumping rhythmically, his body shaking with sensuality.

It was this transgressive performance style, even more than the music, that inspired alarm and antipathy among adults toward rock 'n' roll. When Elvis appeared on the *Ed Sullivan Show* in 1956, adolescents responded with enormous enthusiasm, but adult critics attacked his performance as lewd and obscene. Jackie Gleason, a popular TV performer of the day, sneered, "The kid has no right behaving like a sex maniac on a national show." [10] Newspaper editorials expressed concern about the potential effects on the young: "When Presley executes his bumps and grinds, it must be remembered that even the twelve year old's curiosity may be overstimulated" (p. 34). But it was precisely this "overstimulation" that made Elvis wildly popular among young people. His performance style, more than the words or the music of his songs, seemed to represent a powerful sexuality ready to burst, and the transgressive appeal of it was fascinating and irresistible to young people, not only in the United States but all over the world.

Rock

Scholars who write about popular music usually make a distinction between the "rock 'n' roll music" of the 1950s and the "rock music" that began in the 1960s and continues today.[11] Rock is less blues-based than rock 'n' roll and more diverse musically, incorporating elements of country, folk, and even classical music, along with new instruments such as synthesizers. The beginning of rock is usually marked with the rise to prominence of the Beatles in 1964.

Rock in the 1960s and early 1970s possessed a strong transgressive appeal. As Simon Frith observed, rock offered "a collective excitement, an illicit, immediate sense of solidarity and danger, an un-bourgeois lack of caution, an uncalculated honesty . . . Rock offers the fantasy of a community of risk."[12] Rock performers exhibited their "heroism of excess" by flaunting their willingness to violate the limits of society.

Sex was a transgressive area for rock, as it had been for jazz and rock 'n' roll. Once again, the transgressiveness was not so much in the lyrics as in the music and the style of the performers. The beat became more intense and more visceral as technological advances made the electric guitars more grinding, the drums and bass guitar more pounding, and the whole thing louder. The styles of the performers became more extreme; the sexual exhibitionism of performers such as Jim Morrison of the Doors soon made Elvis's hip-shaking seem relatively tame.

In addition to sex, rock extended the transgressive into three other areas: drugs, politics, and Satan. By the late 1960s, there was a strong association between rock music and illegal drugs. Many performers were rumored to use drugs; and two well-known performers, Jimi Hendrix and Janis Joplin, died of drug overdoses. A genre of rock known as acid rock developed (*acid* being slang for the drug LSD), in which the music suggested the psychological state experienced under a hallucinogenic drug.

Although rock was transgressive with regard to sex, the link to drugs was perhaps even more transgressive because of the illegality of drug use and the potential for a deadly overdose.

Rock was also transgressive in the political views it expressed. With rare exceptions, jazz songs were not political, nor were rock 'n' roll songs. But rock came to prominence during a time of extraordinary political tension in the United States, a decade of civil rights protests, race riots, political assassinations, and the Vietnam War; and these tensions were reflected in rock songs. Some rock songs openly advocated political revolution, some protested American involvement in the Vietnam War, some expressed cynicism about the integrity of political leaders, such as the Who's "Won't Get Fooled Again." Rock songs such as these were transgressive in rejecting the authority of political leaders and political institutions.

The other form in which rock was transgressive in the 1960s and early 1970s was in its use of Satan. Satan is, of course, the ultimate transgressor, described in the Bible as a rebel against God and ever since a symbol of rebellion and resistance against what is held up by society as good, holy, and moral. The power of Satan as a symbol of the transgressive perhaps made it inevitable that he would eventually be used by rock performers. The first rock performers to exploit this potential were the Rolling Stones. Through songs such as "Sympathy for the Devil" and album titles such as *Their Satanic Majesty's Request*, the Stones promoted an image of themselves as transgressors by associating themselves with the ultimate transgressor. Bands such as Led Zeppelin and Black Sabbath also used Satanic symbolism to give themselves an aura of transgressive appeal.

Punk

By the mid-1970s, rock had lost a considerable part of its transgressive power. Performance styles that seemed sexually transgressive in 1965 were tame, even comical, by 1975; thus the band Kiss became popular by carrying rock performance styles to a satirical extreme. Drug use also no longer possessed the novelty in 1975 that it had in 1965, and its transgressive appeal may have diminished with the widely publicized overdoses of several rock performers. Most political content disappeared from rock after the draft for the Vietnam War ended in 1972. Thus by the mid-1970s, the transgressive appeal of rock had waned, and there was an opening again for something newly transgressive.

Along came punk. It became hugely popular in Britain beginning in 1976, and also had followings in Europe and the United States, although not to the same extent as in Britain.[13] Punk was selfconsciously transgressive. Its aim was to be outrageous, to shock anyone who could be shocked, to offend everyone capable of offense, to break deliberately every taboo.[14]

Unlike jazz, rock 'n' roll, and rock, for which the music was more important to fans than the lyrics, in punk the music counted for little. It was loud, crude, and simple. Punk performers freely admitted their lack of musical talent or skill: not just admitted it, but wore it as bona fides of their authenticity. Rock music was perceived as having become overproduced, too smooth, too technical, too safe, a big business, and punk's crudeness was its response.[15]

It was in the lyrics of the songs that punk was most transgressive. Topics of the songs varied widely and included unemployment, racism, the British monarchy, and sex, but the undercurrent of all the songs was anger, aggressiveness, hatred, nihilism. Songs about sex went beyond the transgressiveness of rock by blending sex with hatred: "If you don't want to fuck me, fuck off," went one lyric. In other songs the anger and hatred was presented with a lighter touch, by blending it with humor. "God save the Queen/She ain't no human bein'," went the lyrics to one highly popular song by the Sex Pistols. This kind of transgressive humor, aggressively ridiculing cultural icons, was key to punk's popularity. As Michael Brake observed, "Punk offered a parody, a taunting portrayal of popular culture . . . It was healthily cynical."[16]

The style of punk was also blatantly and deliberately transgressive. Performers adopted names such as Johnny Rotten and Sid Vicious, and spit and even vomited on stage. Performers and fans alike sought to be shockingly transgressive in their appearance. Parts of the head were shaved and the remaining hair dyed in loud colors and spiked into plumes of various designs. "Jewelry" included safety pins through the nose or ears. Stage props included articles of sexual fetishism and bondage and Nazi swastikas. Punk performers were not sympathetic to neo-Nazis—on the contrary, punk performers were active in the Rock Against Racism movement—but the swastika was useful as a transgressive device, another way to provoke outrage.

Punk may have shown the limits of the appeal of the transgressive. Its appeal in Britain was brief, and may have been due in part to the anger generated among the young by the economic recession of the late 1970s; as the recession waned, so did punk. It never achieved much popularity in the United States, perhaps because it was too transgressive. Its failure in the United States and its brief popularity in Britain suggests that the transgressive can only be enjoyed within certain limits—if it violates the standards of society but not too far. On the other hand, maybe the appeal of punk was brief and limited because the music itself had little appeal, and transgressiveness alone was not enough to carry it for very long.

Heavy Metal

Heavy metal music originated in the 1960s with groups such as Led Zeppelin, Iron Maiden, and Black Sabbath, but it reached the peak of its popularity in the 1980s when heavy metal bands such as Metallica topped the charts. During the 1980s heavy metal gained considerable notoriety when heavy metal songs were criticized by the Parents Music Resource Center (PMRC), a group headed by the wives of influential politicians, and the songs were discussed in Congressional hearings on whether the content of popular songs should be regulated by the government. It was also during the 1980s that heavy metal inspired the development of a distinct youth subculture, whose members were identifiable from their black concert T-shirts and their fervent devotion to heavy metal music. They called themselves "metalheads" or "headbangers." The description of them here is based on my research, in which I interviewed them about heavy metal and other topics.[17]

Heavy metal was transgressive musically in its loudness and its abrasiveness. Technological advances made possible a new level of rawness in the electric guitar, a bass guitar of staggering power, a thunderous drum beat, and an unprecedented volume for all of it, including the vocals. To most people the loudness and abrasiveness of heavy metal made it offensive, but these same qualities were embraced enthusiastically by metalheads, who often used words such as *intense, fast, energy,* and *loud* to explain why they liked the music. The fact that most non-fans abhorred the music only made it more appealing to the metalheads because it placed them in an exclusive, daringly transgressive minority.

Lyrically, heavy metal was transgressive in multiple ways. Many songs contained political content, and as in punk this content was transgressive in attacking the legitimacy of a variety of social institutions. Songs attacked corruption in politics, religion, and the legal system and deplored the destruction of the environment by multinational corporations. Metalheads admired heavy metal performers for having the transgressive courage to present the unvarnished truth about what the world is like—in all its rottenness. "I think one of the reasons people are so hard on [heavy metal] is that it really tells the truth," one metalhead told me. "It tells the truth about everything, and people don't want to hear it." By being devoted fans of the songs, metalheads viewed themselves as sharing in the declaration of the messages and therefore possessing transgressive courage themselves.

Some heavy metal songs used Satan as a way of being transgressive. Slayer was the best-known band to use Satan frequently, in songs such as "At Dawn They Sleep," which described how "Satanic soldiers strike their prey / Leaving corpses waiting for the change." However, the use of Satanism in heavy metal songs was viewed by metalheads not as daringly transgressive but as a kind of promotional device. When I asked them about the reputation of heavy metal for promoting Satanism, the question was routinely greeted with derision. "I laugh at it," said one metalhead. "It's funny because it's all a fake, a gimmick to get them ahead." Another said "no heavy metal band really believes in Satan. It's all a ploy to sell albums." So, although Satan was used by some heavy metal bands in an effort to be transgressive, for most heavy metal fans he had little appeal as a transgressive figure.

Heavy metal lyrics were most transgressive in their violence. In my analysis of heavy metal songs, violence was the most common theme. The music of heavy metal was well suited to expressions of violence: the rough, distorted guitar sound, the pounding bass and drums, and the towering volume of it all was exceptionally effective in portraying death, war, destruction, and other violent themes. In the Metallica song "One," a war casualty recalls the landmine that has "Taken my arms / Taken my legs / Taken my soul / Left me with life in hell." In "Bloodbath in Paradise," Ozzy Ozbourne depicts the murders committed by Charles Manson and his followers, and the victims who "wake from the dead as you lie bleeding / Murdered in your bed." Slayer, the most violent of the popular heavy metal bands, often depicted brutal violence, as in "Kill Again," which describes the singer "Lift the gleaming blade / Slice her flesh to shreds / Watch the blood flow free."

Such songs marked a new level of transgressiveness in popular music. No popular songs had depicted scenes of such violence and brutality. Heavy metal was popular for a variety of reasons, including the creativity and musical talent of the performers and the political content of the songs, but the violent quality of the music and lyrics was certainly part of its transgressive appeal.

Rap

Rap music (also called "hip-hop") began in the late 1970s as street music in New York City.[18] It started out as disc jockeys "rapping" (speaking rhythmically) spontaneous lyrics to a background of a lively beat and perhaps a repeated line of music and only gradually developed into songs that were recorded. It was not until the late 1980s that rap attained widespread popularity. By the mid-1990s a wide variety of rap groups appeared on the lists of top-selling albums, and by the end of the 1990s rap equaled rock in popularity among the young.[19] It is far and away the most popular current genre among young blacks and Latinos, but whites also comprise a substantial proportion of rap fans.

Music does not have a great deal of importance in most rap songs. Often, the musical background to a song consists of little more than "samples" borrowed from other, non-rap songs and set to a pounding beat. Few rap performers play a musical instrument. What matters most in rap, and what gives it transgressive power, is the lyrics. Although not all rap songs have transgressive themes, the themes that have given rap its greatest popularity and notoriety as "gangsta rap" are transgressive themes of sexual exploitation and violence.

Sexual exploitation of women was an occasional theme in rock, punk, and heavy metal songs, but gangsta rap songs carried this theme to a new transgressive extreme by adding a deeper edge of contempt and routinely blending sex with violence. Women in rap songs are often referred to as "hos" (whores) and "bitches." Rap lyrics rage and rant against women for deception, dishonesty, sexual temptation, and sexual resistance. Sexuality is frequently portrayed as the man's successful assertion of power over a woman. Women are depicted being raped, beaten, knifed, and shot. The women are dehumanized and portrayed as deserving whatever contempt and violence they get.

In addition to sexual violence against women, other kinds of violence are the theme of gangsta rap songs. Most of the prominent rap performers are African Americans, and rap often depicts scenes of violent confrontations among young men in poor, urban, largely black areas. Performers describe murders they have committed, brag about evading others' murder attempts, and warn adversaries not to cross them or face potential violence. Certain groups such as homosexuals and Asian Americans are singled out for contempt and threats. In "Black Korea," Ice Cube warns Korean inner-city merchants, "You better pay respect to the Black fist / Or I'll burn your store right down to a crisp."

Although some rock, punk, and heavy metal songs also contained lyrics with violent themes, gangsta rap was more transgressive by putting violence at the heart of the genre. However, rap performers have generally portrayed this violence as having a political undertone, claiming the lyrics reflect the grim realities of life in American inner cities. That is, they have sought to portray the violence in the songs as transgressive politically, and therefore virtuous, rather than as simply transgressive for the sake of gaining attention and selling recordings. According to Chuck D, the leader of Public Enemy, "Rap is Black America's TV station. It gives a whole perspective of what exists and what Black life is about."[20] However, critics of rap have argued that rap performers contribute to the stereotype of young black men as potentially violent.[21]

In the context of the framework of the present chapter, it could be argued that a large part of the appeal of rap is the frisson that rap fans obtain from their association, through rap, with the culture of young black urban males and its perceived values of toughness, excitement, danger, and violence. For young, black, urban males, rap may be an expression of the conditions of life they experience, but for the great majority of rap fans who are not part of that culture the appeal of rap may lie in its transgressiveness, in its association with a cultural environment they perceive as more dangerous and exciting than the one they experience themselves.

Is Transgressive Music a Problem?

A distinct pattern is evident in the history of the transgressive appeal of youth music presented here. A transgressive music appears; young people embrace it enthusiastically, while adults express alarm and concern; the music loses its transgressive appeal as it ceases to be novel, and/or as society's boundaries for what is considered transgressive expand enough to contain the music so that it is no longer threatening; then a newly transgressive music appears; and so on.

This progression is unmistakable, but how should we interpret it? Rieff made his own view clear. He saw the interdicts gradually failing and the transgressive gradually triumphing in American society. We now put all interdicts and transgressive terms in quotation marks, he argued, which suggests that we no longer take them seriously. The result will be that we have "made ambiguous and entirely problematic all orders in which we might conceivably live."[22] He viewed the arts, including music, as contributing to the problem. "When imagination grows transgressive, then it expresses itself in brutalities, however technically refined. Even more terrible: among consumers of the products of such imaginative efforts, even the most technically-refined brutalities are transformed into direct actings-out of what the artist has only imagined" (pp. 100–101).

In contrast, most social scientists since Rieff have made light of the pattern in which what is transgressive gradually becomes acceptable, seeing this pattern as evidence that adults' concerns over the potentially damaging effects of transgressive music should not be taken seriously.[23] According to this view, the criticisms of heavy metal and rap made in recent years will, in time, look as silly and overblown as criticisms of jazz and rock 'n' roll look from our perspective today. Young people are always doing things adults do not want them to do, and adults always worry needlessly that this means the young are in moral danger. Plus ça change . . .

The research evidence on the effects of youth music, including transgressive music, are covered by Peter Christenson in chapter 5. The perspective I will offer here is based on my own research.[24] However, my main goal here is to emphasize the limitations of the available research, or in fact any research that might be done in the future, for casting light on some of the most crucial issues regarding transgressive music.

The focus of my research on youth and music has been on fans of heavy metal music, and the relation of heavy metal to the lives of the metalheads demonstrates the complexity of the roles that music can play in the lives of young people. One of the findings of my research is that metalheads are more likely than fans of other types of music to take part in a variety of types of risk behavior. They report higher rates of risky driving, risky sexual behavior, substance use, and criminal behavior (such as theft), compared to young people who prefer other types of music. Thus the transgressiveness reflected in their enthusiasm for heavy metal music is also reflected in their participation in risk behavior.

Is heavy metal music one of the influences responsible for the higher rates of risk behavior among metalheads? Does listening to transgressive music lead them to be transgressive in other aspects of their lives? It might be tempting to see the correlation here as causation and draw this conclusion. Other evidence from my research, however, suggests quite a different interpretation. I asked the metalheads directly about the effects of the music. Specifically, I asked them, "Do you listen to heavy metal when you are in any particular mood?" and "Does listening to heavy metal put you in any particular mood?"

Most commonly, metalheads reported that they listen to heavy metal especially when they are angry. This is hardly surprising, given the angry quality of both the music and lyrics of most heavy metal songs. But the surprise comes in their responses to the second question. Typically, adolescents who said they listen to heavy metal especially when they are angry, sad, or anxious also said the music has the effect not of inflaming their anger but of *calming them down*. They consciously use the music for this cathartic effect, to purge themselves of negative emotions. "It's sort of like taking a tranquilizer," said one.

Often they described the cathartic process with considerable insight: "It kind of releases the aggression I feel," said one boy. "It's a way to release some of your pressures, instead of going out and starting a fight with somebody, you know? Or taking it out on your parents or your cat or something like that." Many spoke of a particular song or group that was especially useful for its cathartic effect. Despite the nihilistic quality of the lyrics of most heavy metal songs, not one of the metalheads I interviewed said the songs made him feel sad or hopeless.

Does this mean we should all relax, then, and not be concerned about the effects of transgressive music on young people? Heavy metal was more transgressive than jazz, rock 'n' roll, or rock, and at least as transgressive as punk. If heavy metal has a calming, cathartic effect, then arguably these other types of once-transgressive music posed even less danger. And if heavy metal is cathartic, perhaps the violent content in rap is also not worthy of concern and may even be cathartic as well.

There are two reasons to hesitate before reaching this conclusion. One is that a given type of music, even a particular song, can be used in numerous ways depending on who is listening to it, what they seek from it, and how they interpret it. As media researchers have increasingly emphasized in recent years, it is important to consider the uses and gratifications that media provide to those who consume them, rather than looking simply for effects. In the case of transgressive music, even if it appears to be used for harmless purposes by some or most of its listeners, there may be those for whom it interacts with their own pre-existing tendencies or psychopathology in dangerous ways.

With regard to heavy metal and rap, the violent content of the songs may have a harmless or cathartic effect on most listeners, but this does not rule out the possibility that some would respond to this content as an inspiration to violence. Currently in the California court system there is a case in which three teenage boys are accused of murdering a girl. The boys were ardent fans of the heavy metal band Slayer, and the method of the murder allegedly bore a strong resemblance to a Slayer song that exhorts the listener to murder a blonde virgin. Rieff's warning of "direct actings-out of what the artist has only imagined" seems suddenly and terribly apt.

What if heavy metal has had a harmless or positive effect on nearly all the millions of adolescents who have listened to it, but for a handful of metalheads with unusual psychological tendencies, the songs have served as a trigger to violence? Then the issue becomes a more complex one, not easily answered by the social sciences: How far does the right to freedom of expression extend, and at what point—if any—should it be abridged in order to shield those who are potentially vulnerable to content that would not incite the vast majority?

The other reason to exercise caution before dismissing concerns about transgressive music is that its effects may be subtle and gradual, difficult to measure with the methods of the social sciences. Young people may defend their enjoyment of transgressive music by saying it is "just music" or "just lyrics" without even realizing how their characters and worldviews may be shaped by it. What if heavy metal and rap have a cathartic effect on young listeners, who report the music relieves their anger; but, at the same time, listening to many songs describing violent scenes contributes to shaping their characters and worldviews, making them harsher, coarser, more brutish, more vulgar? Here again the issues become difficult for the social sciences to answer. A longitudinal study might assess changes over time in character and worldviews, but any effects of transgressive music may be too interwoven with other influences to be discernible, even though it may be genuine and enduring.

Those of us who have at least partial sympathy for Rieff's grim analysis may draw some comfort from the historical analysis presented here. The history of popular music in the twentieth century shows the allure of the transgressive to young people and how society has sometimes responded to transgressive music by widening the scope of what is considered acceptable, moving the interdicts farther out so that transgressive music becomes mainstream and loses its edge. This is what happened with jazz, rock 'n' roll, and rock. However, this history also suggests that the flexibility of the interdicts is not unlimited. As the transgressive emphasis of edge music moved from sex to violence after the early 1970s, the interdicts became more resistant. Punk flamed briefly and then died without becoming mainstream. Heavy metal had its heyday and then faded, not because it became mainstream, but because its transgressive allure withered under a barrage of scorn and satire (e.g., *Wayne's World*, *This Is Spinal Tap*, *Beavis & Butthead*). The future of rap remains to be seen, but thus far "gangsta rap" remains out of the cultural mainstream and the target of considerable criticism, perhaps only awaiting a gifted satirist to bring it down. In any case, it appears that Rieff's fear of an inexorable course from civilization to barbarism, led by transgressive music, is by no means inevitable.

NOTES

1. Philip Rieff, *Fellow Teachers* (New York: Harper & Row, 1972).

2. Jack L. Katz, *Seductions of Crime: Moral and Sensual Attractions of Doing Evil* (New York: Perseus, 1990).

3. Jeffrey Arnett, "Conceptions of the transition to adulthood: Perspectives from adolescence to midlife," *Journal of Adult Development* 10, no. 2 (2001).

4. Robert Pattison, *The Triumph of Vulgarity: Rock Music in the Mirror of Romanticism* (New York: Oxford University Press, 1987).

5. Robert S. Lynd and Helen Merrell Lynd, *Middletown: A Study of Modern American Culture* (1927; reprint New York: Harvest, 1957).

6. Geoffrey C. Ward, *Jazz: A History of America's Music* (New York: Knopf, 2000).

7. Ibid.

8. Frank L. Allen, *Only Yesterday: An Informal History of the 1920s* (New York: Harper and Row, 1964), p.5.

9. Ward, *Jazz*.

10. Paul Lichter, *The Boy Who Dared to Rock: The Definitive Elvis* (New York: Dolphin, 1978), p. 22.

11. Simon Frith, *Sound Effects: Youth, Leisure, and the Politics of Rock 'n' Roll* (New York: Pantheon, 1981).

12. Ibid., p. 217.

13. Roger Sabin (ed.), *Punk Rock: So What?* (New York: Routledge, 1999).

14. Michael Brake, *Comparative Youth Culture: The Sociology of Youth Cultures and Youth Subcultures in America, Britain, and Canada* (London: Routledge and Kegan Paul, 1985).

15. Frith, *Sound Effects*.

16. Brake, *Comparative Youth Culture*, p. 79.

17. Jeffrey Arnett, *Metalheads: Heavy Metal Music and Adolescent Alienation* (Boulder, Col.: Westview Press, 1996).

18. Venice Berry, "Redeeming the Rap Music Experience," in *Adolescents and Their Music: If Its Too Loud, You're Too Old*, J.S. Epstein, ed. (New York: Garland, 1995); Jeffrey L. Decker, "The State of Rap: Time and Place in Hip Hop Nationalism," in *Microphone Fiends: Youth Music & Youth Culture*, A. Ross and T. Rose, eds. (New York: Routledge, 1994).

19. Donald F. Roberts, Ulla G. Foehr, Victoria J. Rideout, and Mollyann Brodie, *Kids & Media @ the New Millennium: A Comprehensive National Analysis of Children's Media Use* (Menlo Park, Calif.: The Henry J. Kaiser Family Foundation, 1999).

20. Decker, "The State of Rap," p. 103.

21. Berry, "Redeeming the Rap Music Experience"; David Samuels, "The Rap on Rap," *The New Republic*, 11 November 1991.

22. Rieff, *Fellow Teachers*, p. 39.

23. Examples are Lorraine E. Prinsky, "Leer-ics or Lyrics: Teenage Impressions of Rock 'n' Roll," *Youth and Society* 18, no. 1 (1987) and James R. McDonald, "Censoring Rock Lyrics: A Historical Analysis of the Debate," *Youth and Society* 19, no. 2 (1988).

24. Arnett, *Metalheads*.

7

Video Games and Aggressive Behavior

Craig A. Anderson

Rule the streets of Prohibition-era America with your own brand of violence and greed as you build the perfect organized crime machine. It's terribly wrong. Of course, that's what makes it fun.
—Advertisement for *Gangsters 2: Vendetta*

In 2002 the video game industry turned 30. The first commercial video game—*Pong*—appeared in 1972. As older readers of this chapter may recall (along with the author), *Pong* was an electronic ping pong game in which one or two players tried to hit an electronic ball back and forth with electronic paddles.

Media violence was, of course, quite a large industry prior to the arrival of video games, and the early video games were, for the most part, nonviolent. In recent years, violent video games have added considerably to the total media violence that was mostly found on television, in movies, and in music. Today, youth between the ages of 8 and 18 spend over 40 hours per week using some type of media, not counting what they use for school or homework assignments.[1] Television is the most frequently used electronic medium, but video games are rapidly gaining in popularity and in total time spent per week. In the United States, the average 2- to 17-year-old child plays console and computer video games 7 hours a week.[2] In 1999, 2.5 percent of entering college men reported playing video games over 20 hours per week.[3] More than 191 million video games worth $6.5 billion were sold in 2000 .[4]

Violent Video Games: History and Content

The history of video games can be divided into three eras.[5] The first era (1977–85) was dominated by Atari console video games. The first video games contained little violence. What violence existed was largely abstract, such as shooting alien spaceships. Indeed, Nolan Bushnell, the founder of Atari, recently noted that "We had an internal rule that we wouldn't allow violence against people. You could blow up a tank or you could blow up a flying saucer, but you couldn't blow up people."[6] Another factor involved in the relatively low amount of violence in the early video games was that the computing power of the console games was so low that only simple graphics could be displayed.

But as graphics became better and the potential for profits became larger, more frequent violence began to appear, even in children's games. The second era (1985–95) was dominated largely by the Nintendo console games. Even Nintendo's seemingly innocuous *Super Mario Brothers* games included the capacity to destroy harmful creatures that got in the way of the main characters by jumping on top of them or by throwing fireballs at them. One pair of studies showed that college students typically think of competitive events as more aggressive than cooperative ones and that competitive instructions dramatically increased their propensity to kill these on-screen creatures.[7]

In this second era, violent content began to appear in more and more games. The computing power of console game systems increased, enabling more complicated graphics, including more realistic portrayals of violence. It was also during this era that video games became common on desktop computers and in hand-held mini-games systems such as Game Boy. As it became apparent to manufacturers that violent games sold well, the level of violence in the games also increased. Truly violent video games came of age in this era with the killing games *Mortal Kombat, Street Fighter*, and *Wolfenstein 3D*.[8] The goal in such games is to maim, wound, or kill opponents. For example, 1993's *Mortal Kombat* (and its successors) entails a series of fights to the death between the game player and various opponents. Particularly popular are the various "fatal" moves that a player can use to finish off an opponent, such as ripping out a beating heart or popping off the head and spine. Both Sega and Nintendo released home console versions of the popular arcade game *Mortal Kombat* at about the same time. However, Nintendo released a sanitized version of the game, removing the most graphically violent features and the worst of the fatal moves; Sega released the full version. The Sega version outsold the Nintendo version by about three to one. When Nintendo released *Mortal Kombat 2*, it included all of the blood and gore and fatal moves of the Sega version. This time, the Nintendo version outsold the Sega version, possibly because more people had the Nintendo hardware.

Some of the basic characteristics and labels of video games also emerged in this era. *Mortal Kombat* represents a type of game now known as "third-person fighting" games. It is a "third-person" game because the player can see the character that he or she is controlling. It is a "fighting" game because virtually all of the game action consists of fighting other game characters. A variety of third-person fighting games were very popular in this era. *Street Fighter* is one such game. As in *Mortal Kombat*, the main theme is that the player engages in a series of fights with various opponents. Another interesting feature of many third-person fighting games is that the player can choose who he or she wants to "be" from an array of male and female characters. In part, this was an attempt to attract more female consumers. It was believed that part of the reason that so few girls and young women played video games was that the vast majority of the early games had only male heroes.

Wolfenstein 3D was one of the first very popular three-dimensional "first-person shooters." In *Wolfenstein 3D* the human hero can choose from an array of weaponry including a revolver, a knife, automatic weapons, and a flamethrower. There are a number of different levels and versions of this game, but the basic story line is similar. In *Wolfenstein 3D*, you are B.J. Blascowitz, an American soldier caught and taken prisoner while trying to infiltrate a top-secret Nazi experimentation lab. In one version, you have to shoot your way out of the prison and kill everything that moves. Your goal is to get out alive so you can tell the Allies what the Nazis are doing. In another version, your goal is to use these weapons to kill Nazi guards in Castle Wolfenstein in order to advance through a number of levels; the ultimate goal is to kill Adolph Hitler. The graphics of this game are very violent; a successful player will see multiple bloody murders and hear victims scream and groan. This game is "3D" because the character can move through a three-dimensional setting, opening doors, turning around and retracing steps, and so on. It is "first-person" because the player "sees" the world through the eyes of the character she or he is controlling. The player can see his or her own hands and arms, as well as the weapons being used, but does not see his or her whole character. It is called a "shooter" because most of the action involves shooting enemies with one kind of weapon or another, though the player can also fight with hands or nonshooting weapons such as knives.

We currently are in the third video game era (1995–present). The console game market is largely dominated by the Sony Playstation and Playstation 2. Their graphic capabilities have been greatly enhanced not only by improvements in computer technology but also by Sony's decision (emulated by others) to switch from cartridge-based systems to CD-ROM–based systems. The growth of video gaming on computers has been phenomenal in recent years. The best selling video games are usually available on computers as well as on console systems. Many games can now be downloaded from the Internet. This includes "demo" versions of extremely violent games that include most or all of the most graphic features of the full game. Such demos can be downloaded at no charge by virtually anyone with a computer and a modem, at no charge.

As one might have expected given prior trends, even more graphically violent games are now available to players of all ages and, indeed, are marketed to young children as well as teens and adults. For example, a recent "mystery shopper" study conducted by the U.S. Federal Trade Commission had underage children (13–16), unaccompanied by an adult, attempt to purchase games rated as Mature (17 or older) from various retail outlets. They were successful in 85 percent of the 380 stores sampled. Similar results have been obtained by others.[9]

Many of the early games have been updated with more realistic graphics, more weapons, and more gore. Newer versions of *Mortal Kombat, Wolfenstein 3D,* and *Street Fighter* have been released several times. One of the newest of the violent games is *Soldier of Fortune*. This computer-based 3D first-person shooter game is most noteworthy for its attempt to accurately portray real life responses of people to the physical traumas performed in the game. For instance, a shotgun blast to the arm from close range results in a graphically realistic portrayal of the arm being ripped from its socket, leaving exposed bone and sinew dangling, and lots of blood gushing from the wound.

Another fairly recent 3D first-person shooter is *Duke Nukem*. This is an extremely violent game, with provocative pictures of almost-nude women and disgusting alien piglike things that carry shotguns and disintegrate into little piles of blood and gore. The aliens have taken over Hollywood and you (the player) must take it back. The player assumes the role of Duke Nukem. To win the game, you blast away at the aliens, their flying warships, and anything else that strikes your fancy, including semi-nude women chained to pillars who, in some cases, beg to be killed. One notable feature of this game is that it is one of the first to pair extreme violence with sex.

Other types of violent games currently available to most children and adolescents include games that train players in how to conduct terrorist attacks, how to lead an antiterrorist assault team, how to fly modern fighter aircraft, and how to plot assassinations. For instance, in *Rainbow Six*, the player trains and leads a unit of secret U.S. government antiterrorists through a series of scenarios. This game, based on author Tom Clancy's Rainbow Six novels, teaches many of the skills needed by such real-life military units.

There are many wonderful educational, nonviolent strategy, and sports games available, but the most heavily marketed, sold, and played video games are extremely violent in nature, involving brutal mass killings as the primary goal in winning the game. This has been true at least since the early 1990s. For example, one mid-1990s study found that 4th grade girls (59%) and boys (73%) report that the majority of their favorite games are violent ones.[10] Many of the nonviolent games are very exciting and challenging, and when marketed with the same intensity as the violent games, have sold very well. For instance, there are a number of nonviolent racing games, such as the various versions of Indy Car and NASCAR racing games. Of course, there are also some driving/racing games that are extremely violent. For example, in *Carmageddon*, one of the main goals is to run over as many pedestrians as possible. One gets extra points for particularly spectacular kills.

Some of the better games may actually teach some useful skills; and as these games have become more sophisticated, they begin to resemble training simulators. Some of the driving games, for instance, may well improve the driving skills of the game player. Similarly, there are a number of nonviolent flight simulation games that have been very popular. Indeed, a few years ago my son (then in middle school) attended one of the NASA week-long space camps along with a large number of other kids. The activities included learning about a number of aspects of space flight and exploration, including a simulated mission on board a simulated space shuttle. In the year prior to attending the space camp, my son had spent a number of hours with the nonviolent flight simulator game *Flight Unlimited*. At space camp, he was the only "shuttle pilot" to successfully "land" the space shuttle at the completion of his team's simulated mission. The skills and knowledge gained while playing *Flight Unlimited* almost certainly aided him in landing the space shuttle in one piece.

Of course, the same technology that helps people learn how to fly a plane or drive a car can also be used to train people how to behave in a variety of antisocial ways. Most flying games are basically first-person shooters in the sky (for example, those involving fighter planes and bombers) or in space (Star Wars–based video games and other types of fantasy space war games). Though such games may teach some motor skills, the inclusion of a violent theme may well also teach some fairly antisocial perspectives on how one should deal with disagreement and interpersonal conflict.

Exposure to Violent Video Games

Though video games are now, like movies, subject to industry ratings, numerous problems remain. The rating systems differ by outlet (video arcade vs. console and home computer); they are not well understood by parents or children; they are not reliably enforced; and they apparently have little impact on the marketing efforts of the companies that produce the games. As mentioned above, a Federal Trade Commission study found that M-rated games were easily available to children under 17. This same study found that over 90 percent of surveyed companies producing M-rated games target children under 17 in the marketing of such games.[11]

Two additional problems concern the assignment of ratings and underlying assumptions of the rating systems. First, a recent study showed that the video game ratings provided by an "independent" board funded by the video game industry do not match those provided by other adults and game-playing youngsters.[12] Many games involving violence by cartoon-like characters are classified by the industry as appropriate for general audiences, a classification with which adults and youngsters disagree. Furthermore, games rated E (Everyone) can contain any of the following descriptor categories: Mild Animated Violence, Mild Realistic Violence, Animated Violence, Realistic Violence, Animated Blood, and Realistic Blood. The only two categories of violence that are prohibited in E games are Animated Blood and Gore, and Realistic Blood and Gore. Teen games (13 and older) may contain either of these types of violence as well.

Second, it is assumed that cartoon violence is not harmful to younger children. A long history of research on other forms of media violence (TV, movies), however, has demonstrated that such cartoon violence is indeed harmful to children.[13]

Finally, there is a problem with lack of parental oversight. Ninety percent of teens in grades 8–12 report that their parents never check the ratings of video games before allowing their purchase, and only 1 percent of the teens' parents had ever prevented a purchase based on its rating. Furthermore, 89 percent reported that their parents never limited time spent playing video games.[14]

Negative Effects of Media Violence

Though many educational nonviolent TV shows and video games clearly have positive effects on young people,[15] the potential negative effects of violent video games drives most current public discussions of media violence. The recent school shootings in Paducah, Kentucky; Jonesboro, Arkansas; and Littleton, Colorado, played a major role in stimulating such discussions, largely because the shooters were students who habitually played violent video games. Eric Harris and Dylan Klebold, the Columbine High School shooters, enjoyed the bloody video game *Doom*. In fact, Harris created a customized version of *Doom* with two shooters, extra weapons, unlimited ammunition, and victims who couldn't fight back—features that are eerily similar to the actual shootings at Columbine High.

The video game industry denies any link between playing violent video games and aggression, of course, just as the TV and movie industries continue to deny links between their violent products and aggression. For example, in a May 12, 2000, CNN interview, Doug Lowenstein, president of the Interactive Digital Software Association, said, "I think the issue has been vastly overblown and overstated, often by politicians and others who don't fully understand, frankly, this industry. There is absolutely no evidence, none, that playing a violent video game leads to aggressive behavior."

In fact, the research literature on the effects of media violence in general (including TV and movie violence) is quite large and conclusive. By 1975, eighty studies had been published on the effects of media violence on aggressive behavior. A meta-analysis of those early studies clearly showed that there was no room for doubt: exposure to media violence causes increases in aggression, and this relation between media violence and aggression exists in both laboratory and in real-world settings. One particularly disturbing aspect of the more general question about media violence concerns the misinformation typically presented in the news media. By 1975, the scientific community had ample evidence of a significant (and causal) link between media violence (mostly on TV) and aggressive behavior. In subsequent years, the scientific evidence has grown even stronger. But news media reports on the link between exposure to media violence and aggression have moved in the opposite direction over time. On average, more recent news reports imply that media violence effects are weaker than did earlier news reports.[16]

The state of scientific knowledge about a research question changes over time as more research is conducted. One reason is that, over time, there are improvements in research instruments and research design. Another is that, in general, a larger sample of studies provides a more accurate picture of the true hypothesized effect than a smaller sample of studies. For example, a single study of the link between smoking and lung cancer using 500 people provides one picture. But 100 studies, each using 500 people, would provide a much more accurate over-all picture. After many studies have been conducted, one can examine the results of the studies to get an idea of what was known by a particular date. For example, we can get an idea of the best scientific estimate of the relation between smoking and lung cancer in 1960 by averaging the results of all smoking–lung cancer studies that had been published by 1960. We can similarly look at the best estimates in 1965, 1970, and so on, each time averaging the results of all studies published by that date. By plotting such repeated estimates across time, we can then see how the state of scientific knowledge about that research question changed over time.

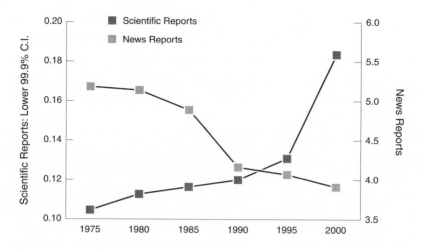

Fig. 7.1. Scientific vs. News Reports of the Effect of Media Violence on Aggression. Based on data reported in Brad J. Bushman and Craig A. Anderson, "Media Violence and the American Public: Scientific Facts Versus Media Misinformation," *American Psychologist* 56, no. 6/7 (2001): pp. 477–89.

We can then ask whether news reports about the research question match the scientific evidence and whether changes in news reports over time reflect changes in the state of scientific knowledge. The most direct way to do this is to gather all of the news reports (for example, all newspaper articles) on the research question, rate each on its conclusions concerning this question, and then average those ratings for various time periods. This is precisely what Brad Bushman and I have done with the research question of whether exposure to media violence is linked to aggression.

Figure 7.1 displays the shifts in the accumulated scientific knowledge base about media violence effects on aggression since 1975; it also displays the shifts in the news reports about the scientific evidence linking media violence and aggression. The Scientific Reports line in the figure displays a very conservative estimate of the true relation between media violence and aggression. In a sense, it can be thought of as what a skeptic might conclude from the research. A score greater than zero indicates that a statistical summary of all studies published by that date yielded a highly significant result that increased exposure to media violence was linked to increases in aggression. A score of zero would indicate that there appears to be no link between media violence and aggression. A negative score would indicate that increased exposure to media violence is linked to decreases in aggression. The Scientific Reports line shows that since 1975, even a skeptical assessment of the research literature would conclude that media violence is linked to increases in aggression. It also shows that as additional research studies were conducted, evidence of this link has grown stronger.[17]

The News Reports line in figure 7.1 is the average rating of all relevant written news reports (newspapers, magazines) over the preceding five-year period. These averages were based on a 21-point rating scale with verbal anchors at −10 (the article said that viewing violence causes a decrease in aggression), −5 (urged parents to encourage their children to consume violent media), 0 (the article said that there was no relation between media violence and aggression), +5 (urged parents to discourage their children from consuming violent media), and +10 (the article said that viewing violence causes an increase in aggression). If news reports accurately reflected the actual state of scientific knowledge, the two lines in figure 7.1 should be parallel. At worst, the news media reports should show the same pattern as the scientific evidence but with a lag of a few years. In fact, as the state of scientific knowledge supporting a significant and causal link between media violence and aggression grew stronger, news media reports actually grew weaker.

The central question of this chapter concerns whether or not playing violent video games has an impact on aggressive behavior and on other aggression-related variables, such as aggressive feelings. Research specifically focusing on the effects of exposure to violent video games has been slowly accumulating in recent years. The first comprehensive meta-analysis of these studies was published by my colleague Brad Bushman and me.[18] Results of this meta-analysis of studies of violent video games, and a more recent analysis conducted for this chapter, are the focus of the next sections.

Negative Effects of Violent Video Games

Meta-analysis is a set of statistical procedures used by researchers to combine results across studies in order to test specific hypotheses. It is less subject to the specific biases or expectations of the reviewer than is the older style narrative review. For instance, one can summarize statistically the results of all empirical studies that have examined the effects of violent video games on aggressive behavior. In addition to getting a more accurate statistical estimate of the effect under consideration, meta-analysis also allows the researcher to test whether certain characteristics of the studies are systematically related to the effect under consideration. For example, one can ask whether the effect of violent video games on aggressive behavior is greater for males than it is for females.

Effects for Adults and Children Combined

Our meta-analysis uncovered thirty-two research reports on the effects of violent video games on aggression and aggression-related variables. These thirty-two reports included forty-six independent samples of participants. Over 3,800 individuals participated in these studies; slightly more than half (57%) were children under 18. These studies focused on five types of dependent variables. Of most interest, of course, is aggressive behavior. Across the various studies, the types of aggressive behavior assessed varied widely. For example, in some studies children's fighting behaviors were observed in a free play period that took place after the children had played either a violent or nonviolent video game. In other studies, aggressive behavior was assessed by standard laboratory aggression tasks, by teacher ratings, by self-reports of violent criminal behaviors, by self-reports of aggressive (but not criminal) behavior, and by parent reports. Three additional aggression-related variables assessed in some studies were: aggressive affect (e.g., anger), physiological arousal (e.g., heart rate), and aggressive cognition (e.g., thoughts about aggression). Finally, several studies assessed the effects of violent video games on subsequent prosocial (helping) behavior.

Overall, the results showed that exposure to violent video games significantly increases aggressive behavior, aggressive affect, physiological arousal, and aggressive cognition. The results also showed that exposure to violent video games significantly decreases prosocial behavior. Finally, the results showed that the effects of playing violent video games did not systematically differ for adults versus children, males versus females, or for true experiments versus correlational studies. In other words, exposure to violent video games seemed to have roughly the same effect on everyone, and to show up in all types of studies.

Though these results are quite clear, there are several more specific questions that need to be addressed. For instance, even though the results found no difference in the magnitude of violent video game effects on children versus adults, a motivated skeptic (e.g., representatives of the Interactive Digital Software Association) could argue that only studies that have used children under age 18 should be included. Furthermore, in traditional meta-analyses an attempt is made to include all possible studies, despite their potential methodological shortcomings. For example, consider an experiment in which children play either a violent or a nonviolent video game and are then observed while playing with other children to see who is most likely to fight. In such a study, it is important that the nonviolent video game be as much fun and as easy as the violent game. In some studies, however, the nonviolent game appears to be less fun and more difficult. If the research domain being examined is sufficiently large, one can do statistical tests to see whether such a shortcoming reliably produces unusual results. The new analyses in the next section attend to these issues.

Results of a New Meta-analysis

I conducted a new meta-analysis for this chapter for three primary reasons. First, several new studies of violent video games are now available for inclusion in the meta-analysis. Second, despite the earlier finding of similar effects for children and adults, many people would like to see more specific analyses of video game effects on children. Third, the earlier meta-analysis included as many studies as possible, including some with potential methodological shortcomings. Because there were not enough studies to allow us to factor out these weaknesses statistically, the new analyses addressed this problem by dropping the methodologically weak studies. Additional modifications to the meta-analysis were also made.[19]

Adults and Children Combined. Figure 7.2 presents the average effect sizes for each of the five dependent variables and their 95 percent confidence intervals, for the combined adult-children analyses. The results are very similar to those of the earlier meta-analysis. Once again, exposure to violent video games was found to increase aggressive behavior, aggressive thoughts, aggressive affect, and physiological arousal, and to decrease prosocial behavior.

Children Only. When adult studies were removed from the analyses, there were not enough studies with physiological measures of arousal for

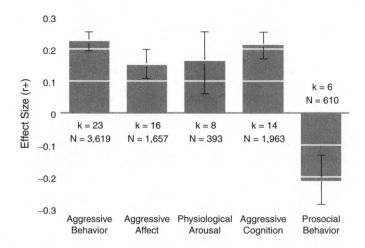

Fig. 7.2. Average Effects of Violent Video Games (r^+), Adults and Children Combined. *Vertical capped bars* indicate 95% confidence intervals. Because the vertical capped bars do not include the zero line for any of the measured effects, all of the effects of violent video games are statistically significant. k = number of independent tests. N = number of participants.

a meta-analytic study, so the variable of physiological arousal was dropped. The remaining four dependent variables have had sufficient numbers of child studies. Figure 7.3 presents the results for children only. The effect size (r+) can range from +1 to −1. Zero would indicate that there is no relation between exposure to violent video games and the outcome being measured. Positive scores indicate that video game violence is associated with increases in the outcome being measured. As can be seen, exposure to violent video games significantly increases aggressive behavior, aggressive affect, and aggressive cognition in children and significantly decreases their prosocial behavior.

To gain a clearer understanding of the magnitude of these results, consider the following comparisons to other research findings: The effect of exposure to violent video games on subsequent aggressive behavior in children, as shown in figure 7.3, is larger than: (a) the effect of exposure to passive tobacco smoke on lung cancer; (b) the effect of calcium intake on bone mass; and (c) the effect of homework on academic achievement.[20] In other words, if you believe that children should not be repeatedly exposed to passive tobacco smoke, that adults should be sure to consume sufficient quantities of calcium, and that children need to do

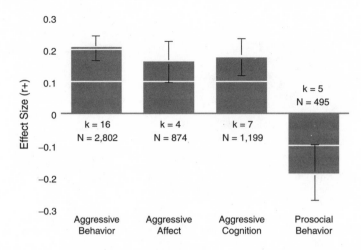

Fig. 7.3. Average Effects of Violent Video Games (r⁺), Children Only. *Vertical capped bars* indicate 95% confidence intervals. Because the vertical capped bars do not include the zero line for any of the measured effects, all of the effects of violent video games are statistically significant. k = number of independent tests. N = number of participants.

homework, you should believe even more strongly that children should not be repeatedly exposed to violent video games.

Manipulation Size and Effect Size. Manipulation size refers to how different the two experimental conditions within a study are. For instance, in a study of the effects of alcohol on driving (in a driving simulator), one might have some people drink 16 ounces of vodka and others drink none. Another study might compare driving performance of people who drank 1 ounce of vodka to that of those who drank none. The first study used a rather large manipulation of alcohol, whereas the second used a small one. The results of the first study are likely to show a huge difference in driving skill whereas the second study will likely find little or none. While examining the video game research literature it became clear that there are vast differences in the types of video games used within the "violent" and "nonviolent" conditions of various studies. This occurs partly because of the changes in video games themselves over the years. In the early days of video games, some parents were concerned about the potential consequences of playing the "violent" video game *Pac-Man*. In recent years, that concern seems laughable to many, and *Pac-Man* could reasonably be used as the nonviolent game in some studies. Games categorized as "high violence" in early studies are very different from the high violence games in more recent studies. It also appears that researchers using younger children often select fairly tame games as their "violent" game, presumably for ethical reasons. In other words, some video game studies have used very small manipulation sizes, comparable to the 1-ounce versus no vodka study described above. Furthermore, several experimental studies have used games with violent content in their "nonviolent" conditions. This is analogous to a driving-skills study comparing those who consumed 1 ounce of vodka with those who consumed .5 ounce. For example, several studies have used *Sonic the Hedgehog* games in the nonviolent condition. But *Sonic* can be hurt by his enemies and can, in turn, kill them (e.g., by throwing fireballs at them). Thus, some studies that appear to show that violent content has little or no effect may do so because their manipulation size is unreasonably small—the violent and nonviolent games being compared may have about the same level of violent content.

To test this idea, Brad Bushman and I rated the violent content of the video games used in the experimental studies of aggressive behavior. This was possible for only eleven of the experimental studies. We rated each game on a feature-anchored scale ranging from 0 to 10. For each of the eleven studies, we then subtracted the violence rating of the "nonviolent" video game from the violence rating of the "violent" video game. In one study, the ratings of the violent and nonviolent games differed by only 2.5 points out of a possible 10. Figure 7.4 shows that experiments in which the violent and nonviolent games differed a lot in how much violence they contained tended to show a larger effect of violent content on later aggressive behavior.

Summary. This updated meta-analysis clearly shows that playing violent video games causes increases in aggressive behavior as well as in several other aggression-related variables and causes decreases in prosocial behavior.[21] Furthermore, the effects of violent video games are significant even if we totally ignore those studies that used adults (mostly college students). The finding that violent video game effects tends to be larger when the violent and nonviolent games differ most in violent content also fits well with other results in the larger media violence research literature.

Given the relatively small number of studies that have been done on video game violence, the strength of these results is somewhat surprising and certainly is evidence that societal concern about violent video games

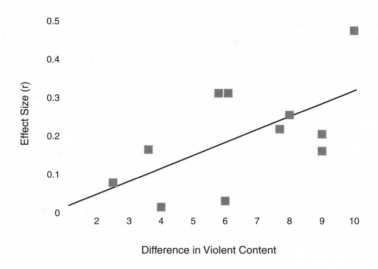

Fig. 7.4. Relation between the Difference in Violent Content of Violent and Nonviolent Video Game Conditions on the Effect of Violent Content on Aggressive Behavior.

is not misplaced. It is likely that as the research literature on violent video games grows larger and more methodologically sophisticated, some differences in size of effect will emerge, most likely along the lines suggested by Jeanne Funk in chapter eight. For example, there are both theoretical and empirical reasons (from the TV and movie violence research tradition) to expect that as more studies are done on violent video games, we will begin to see that the deleterious effects of playing violent video games will be larger on children than on adults. Nonetheless, the current data suggest that assumptions about large segments of the population being immune to the deleterious effects of playing violent video games are unfounded.

There are a host of unanswered questions in need of additional research. Before discussing them, it is important to put the current state of research on violent video games into a broader theoretical perspective. This perspective is obviously important to researchers but should also be helpful to parents, policy makers, and the general public. My colleagues and I have been working for some time on creating a general model of human aggression, with the belief that such a model should help informed citizens make good decisions.

General Aggression Model

The General Aggression Model (GAM) is a useful framework for understanding violent media effects.[22] Aggressive behavior is largely based on the activation and application of aggression-related ideas or knowledge structures that are stored in memory. *Knowledge structure* is a general term that refers to ideas, concepts, beliefs, and other types of knowledge that people learn and use in everyday life. Thus, central to GAM are the social learning processes by which the individual acquires these various knowledge structures as well as the social interaction processes that occur during and shortly after exposure to violent media. There are two parts to GAM: the single-episode portion and the multiple-episode portion.

Figure 7.5 displays the single episode portion of GAM. It illustrates how recent exposure to violent media can cause short-term increases in aggression and other related variables. Playing a violent video game can increase aggressive behavior through its impact on the person's present internal state, represented by cognitive, affective, and arousal variables.

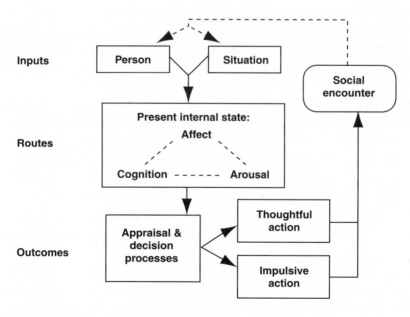

Fig. 7.5. Single Episode General Aggression Model.

In other words, violent media can increase aggression by increasing aggressive cognitions (thoughts), by increasing general physiological arousal, or by creating an aggressive affective (feeling) state. It seems obvious that increasing aggressive thoughts, feelings, and behavioral tendencies must also decrease various prosocial thoughts, feelings, and behavioral tendencies. The effects of a single episode of playing a violent video game are likely to be fairly short-lived, similar to the relatively short-lived effects of smoking one cigarette. However, the effects accumulate over time with repeated exposures, just as the effects of repeatedly smoking cigarettes accumulate and result in serious chronic health problems.

Long-term effects of repeated exposure to media violence involve learning processes, such as learning how to perceive, interpret, judge, and respond to events in the physical and social environment. Such learning develops over time, and is based on day-to-day observations of and interactions with other people, real (as in the family) and imagined (as in the media). Each violent media episode, as outlined in figure 7.5, is essentially one more learning trial. Over time and with repeated exposure these various knowledge structures become more complex, differentiated, and difficult to change. An individual's personality is determined to a large extent by their learning experiences, including their media experiences.

The five types of relevant knowledge structures changed by repeated exposure to violent media are shown in figure 7.6. This figure also links these long-term changes in aggressive personality to aggressive behavior in a given situation through both types of input variables (person and situation) described in the single episode portion of the General Aggression Model. The link to person variables is obvious; the individual is now more prepared to be aggressive in many ways because of aggression-congruent beliefs, attitudes, expectations, and values. Less obvious is how repeated exposure to violent media can change situational variables. What happens is that as people become more aggressive, their social environments change. The people who are willing to interact with them, the types of interactions they have, and the types of situations made available to them all change. Interactions with teachers, parents, and nonaggressive peers are likely to decline in frequency and quality, but interactions with "deviant" peers are likely to increase.

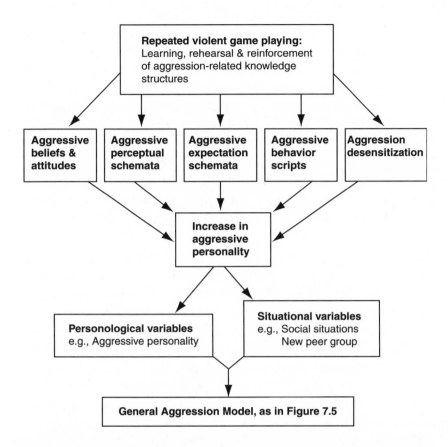

Fig. 7.6. Multiple Episode General Aggression Model: Long-Term Effects of Video Game Violence. Adapted from Craig A. Anderson and Karen E. Dill, "Video Games and Aggressive Thoughts, Feelings, and Behavior in the Laboratory and in Life," *Journal of Personality and Social Psychology* 78, no. 4 (2000): pp. 772–90.

The schema illustrated in figure 7.6 further suggests that the short-term effects of violent media on aggressive cognition are especially important. Temporary mood states and arousal dissipate over time, but the repeated rehearsal of aggressive cognitions can lead to long-term changes in multiple aspects of aggressive personality. The literature on the development of behavioral scripts suggests that even a few rehearsals can change a person's expectations and intentions involving important social behaviors.[23]

Implications for Parents and Public Policy Makers

When considering potential implications of research on violent video games, it is important to keep three factors in mind. The first and most obvious factor is the set of results from studies of violent video games. Though the research literature specifically devoted to violent video games is still relatively small compared to research on the effects of violence in TV and movies, there is now sufficient evidence to state that playing violent video games can cause significant increases in aggression in the short term and that increases in the amount of exposure to violent video games is positively linked to aggression in real world contexts as well as in laboratory-based situations. The second factor is the voluminous research literature on media violence in general. That literature has documented that media violence has significant causal effects on aggression and on interpersonal violence and has successfully withstood a variety of challenges. The processes underlying the effects of TV and movie violence are very similar to those presumed to underlie the effects of violent video games, and therefore findings from the former domain are very relevant to implications for the latter. The third factor concerns advances in understanding the various processes underlying human aggression in general. Numerous advances in understanding human aggression have been achieved in recent years, advances that allowed the formulation of the General Aggression Model. As Kurt Lewin once said, "There is nothing so practical as a good theory."[24] Though no theory is ever complete in all respects, a good one allows accurate predictions about the likely effects of certain actions. Social scientists' understanding of human aggression in general and of media violence effects in particular is now good enough to allow fairly accurate predictions of the likely effects of actions that parents and policy makers might take.

First and foremost, parents need to discover what kinds of media, including video games, their children are ingesting, and then take steps to ensure that their media diet is a healthy one. It can be a daunting task, especially for parents whose computer skills are considerably inferior to those of their children. Nonetheless, it is imperative for parents to control their children's media diets, and the first step in doing this is to discover what they currently are exposed to, where they are exposed to it, and how to take control of that exposure. Some parents lament that it is impossible to totally control what their children see and do and therefore throw up their hands in dismay. It is true that they cannot totally control their children's media diets, but this is no reason to give up all attempts at media diet control. For example, it is difficult to control what games your child plays at a friend's house. However, it is also difficult to control what your child eats when at a friend's house, but the solution is not to abandon your parental responsibility to provide nutritious meals at home. As the General Aggression Model illustrates, the long-term negative effects of exposure to violent video games is related to frequency of exposure. Steps that reduce such exposure in any environment, especially the home, can be beneficial. Such steps might include removing the TV, the video game console, and the computer from the child's room to an area that is more easily monitored by the parent. One can also monitor and control what kinds of computer games are on whatever computers the child uses and can restrict the Web sites that the computer can access while in use by the child. Along these same lines, parents should encourage the parents of their children's friends to provide a healthy media diet rather than a violent one. None of these monitoring and control tasks is easy, but a lot can be accomplished by a committed parent. For example, after completing a TV interview for a San Antonio news show, the interviewing reporter told me that whenever she finds in her house a CD-ROM video game disk that has a violent game on it, she breaks it in half and tosses it in the trash, regardless of whether it belongs to her son or to one of her son's friends. If it belonged to one of her son's friends, she invites that child's parents to discuss the inappropriateness of providing violent games to children, especially to someone else's children.

Second, public policy makers can aid parents in their attempts to provide a healthy media diet to their children by giving them back some of the parental control that has been lost to the media industry and their marketing departments. Legislation that restricts access of minors to violent media, for example, legislation that requires parental permission for minor children to buy, rent, or play violent video games in arcades, is likely to be helpful. Creating a single, unified rating system for various types of entertainment media would also help parents regain some control by simplifying the current confusion of systems. The new rating system should be applied by a group that is truly independent of the entertainment media industries. It should also be based on the best available research. We now know from research, for example, that strictly age-based systems encourage children to seek out media that are "too old" for them.[25] A rating system that more clearly labels the content of the video game might well be more informative to parents and might provide less encouragement to youth to violate age targets. Research also shows that even "cartoon" violence has a negative impact on children, especially on the youngest ones for whom the cartoon violence is supposedly created. In brief, parents need to be on the alert for any video game that encourages or allows the player to harm another creature, human or nonhuman. Such games are very likely teaching the game player subtle but harmful aggression lessons, regardless of how cute the game characters are or how unrealistic the violence appears.

Third, parents can actively teach their children the reasons behind the restrictions they place on certain types of media, why such media can be bad for them. In a sense, this is teaching them to become more media savvy. Similarly, discussing alternative nonviolent solutions to interpersonal conflicts with one's children can help teach more positive values as well as practical guides to life. This can be done in the context of violent media themselves, as well as in numerous everyday situations as conflicts arise.

Finally, reducing the amount of time children spend on electronic media and substituting increased time in social contexts and activities is likely to improve social skills and functioning over time. Chapter 8 describes one such study.

New Directions in Research

We now know that playing violent video games increases aggressive behavior and decreases prosocial behavior in children and in young adults. There are many unanswered questions in need of high quality research. Here are just a few such topics.

1. The short- and long-term effects of realistic gore on desensitization, aggression, and prosocial behavior.
2. Game features that increase or decrease the game player's identification with aggressive characters in video games.
3. The effects of pain cues in the game on short- and long-term desensitization, aggression, and prosocial behavior.
4. The design of exciting games teaching prosocial problem-solving skills.

5. Types of people who are most and least susceptible to the effects of violent video games.

What we've learned so far about the effects of violent video games has taken almost twenty years, in part because of the lack of federal research funding. Given the ubiquity of video games in modern life and the continual increase in the realism and extremity of violence in the games, it is imperative that research on these and related topics be undertaken soon.

NOTES

Epigraph: PC Gamer (February 2001): p. 41.

1. Donald F. Roberts, Ulla G. Foehr, Victoria J. Rideout, and Mollyann Brodie, *Kids & Media @ the New Millennium: A Comprehensive National Analysis of Children's Media Use* (Menlo Park, Calif.: The Henry J. Kaiser Family Foundation, 1999).

2. Douglas A. Gentile and David A. Walsh, "A Normative Study of Family Media Habits," *Journal of Applied Developmental Psychology* 23, no. 2 (2002): pp. 157–78.

3. CIRP, *Cooperative Institutional Research Program Survey Results* (Ames, Ia.: Office of Institutional Research, 1998, 1999).

4. *Video Game Sales Slide 5 Percent in 2000* (Reuters, January 19, 2001).

5. Douglas A. Gentile, Paul J. Lynch, and David A. Walsh, "The Effects of Violent Video Game Habits on Adolescent Aggressive Attitudes and Behaviors" (National Institute on Media and the Family, Minneapolis).

6. Steven L. Kent, *The First Quarter: A 25-year History of Video Games* (Bothell, Wash.: BWD Press, 2000).

7. Craig A. Anderson and Melissa Morrow, "Competitive Aggression without Interaction: Effects of Competitive Versus Cooperative Instructions on Aggressive Behavior in Video Games," *Personality and Social Psychology Bulletin* 21, no. 10 (1995): pp. 1020–30.

8. Craig A. Anderson and Karen E. Dill, "Video Games and Aggressive Thoughts, Feelings, and Behavior in the Laboratory and in Life," *Journal of Personality and Social Psychology* 78, no. 4 (2000): pp. 772–90.

9. FTC, "Marketing Violent Entertainment to Children: A Review of Self-Regulation and Industry Practices in the Motion Picture, Music Recording, & Electronic Game Industries," *Report of the Federal Trade Commission. Federal Trade Commission* (2000), available at www.ftc.gov/reports/violence/; David Walsh, "Fifth Annual Video and Computer Game Report Cards" (National Institute on Media and the Family, Minneapolis, 2001).

10. Debra D. Buchman and Jeanne B. Funk, "Video and Computer Games in the '90s: Children's Time Commitment and Game Preference," *Children Today* 24

(1996): pp. 12–16; Tracy L. Dietz, "An Examination of Violence and Gender Role Portrayals in Video Games: Implications for Gender Socialization and Aggressive Behavior," *Sex-Roles* 38, no. 5/6 (1998): pp. 425–42; Jeanne B. Funk et al., "Rating Electronic Games: Violence Is in the Eye of the Beholder," *Youth and Society* 30, no. 3 (1999): pp. 283–312; Eugene F. Provenzo, *Video Kids: Making Sense of Nintendo* (Cambridge: Harvard University Press, 1991).

11. FTC, "Marketing Violent Entertainment to Children: A Review of Self-Regulation and Industry Practices in the Motion Picture, Music Recording, & Electronic Game Industries," *Report of the Federal Trade Commission. Federal Trade Commission* (2000): available at www.ftc.gov/reports/violence/.

12. Jeanne B. Funk et al., "Rating Electronic Games," pp. 283–312.

13. Brad J. Bushman and L. Rowell Huesmann, "Effects of Televised Violence on Aggression," in *Handbook of Children and the Media*, Dorothy Singer and Jerome Singer, eds., (Thousand Oaks, Calif.: Sage Publications, 2001): pp. 223–54.

14. David Walsh, "Interactive Violence and Children: Testimony Submitted to the Committee on Commerce, Science, and Transportation," downloaded from www.mediaandthefamily.org/senateviolence-full.html on March 24, 2000 (March 21, 2001).

15. Douglas A. Gentile and David A.Walsh, "The Impact of Video Games on Children and Youth" (Arlington, Va.: Educational Research Service, 2001); Singer and Singer, eds., *Handbook of Children and the Media*.

16. Brad J. Bushman and Craig A. Anderson, "Media Violence and the American Public: Scientific Facts Versus Media Misinformation," *American Psychologist* 56, no. 6/7 (2001): pp. 477–89.

17. What is plotted is the lower boundary of the 99.9 percent confidence interval of the average effect size (in terms of $r+$) of studies of media violence effects on -aggressive behavior. This is an unusually conservative criterion for establishing the existence of a true relation between scientific variables. The usual criterion is 95 percent.

18. Craig A. Anderson and Brad J. Bushman, "Effects of Violent Video Games on Aggressive Behavior, Aggressive Cognition, Aggressive Affect, Physiological Arousal, and Prosocial Behavior: A Meta-Analytic Review of the Scientific Literature," *Psychological Science* 12, no. 5 (2001): pp. 353–59.

19. The following newly available studies were added: Michael C. Brooks, "Press Start: Exploring the Effects of Violent Video Games on Boys" (Ph.D. diss., University of Texas at Austin, 1999); Douglas A. Gentile, Paul J. Lynch, and David A. Walsh, "The Effects of Violent Video Game Habits"; Bradley A. Janey, "Masculine Ideology, Television Viewing, and Father Availability As Risk Factors in the Development of Aggression in Preadolescent Males" (Ph.D. diss., Kansas State University, Manhattan, Kans.,1999); Rebecca P. Tews, "The Effect Of Video Games on Anxiety Level and Heart Rate in College Students" (Ph.D. diss., Marquette Univer-

sity, Milwaukee, Wisc., 1999). In addition, the following methodological changes were implemented: (a) effect sizes were collapsed across sex rather than averaged, where possible; (b) for studies in which the "low violence" video game condition actually contained some violent content and the "no game" control condition was not particularly boring or frustrating, the control condition was used as the comparison group, instead of the "low violence" condition; (c) for studies in which the "no game" control condition was particularly boring or frustrating, the "low violence" video game condition was used as the comparison group; (d) studies which reported only combined video game player/observer results were dropped; (e) self and observer reports of aggressive behavior were averaged; (f) studies in which the aggressive behavior was not targeted toward another person were dropped; (g) one experimental study was dropped because the only control condition was rated by participants as significantly less entertaining or exciting than the comparison violent video game.

20. Brad J. Bushman and Craig A. Anderson, "Media Violence and the American Public," pp. 477–89.

21. The ability to draw strong causal conclusions derives from the fact that the true experiments, in which participants are randomly assigned to play either violent or nonviolent video games, produce statistically significant effects by themselves. This characteristic of true experiments is one of the main advantages of this type of study. One main advantage of correlational studies is that they generally assess aggressive behaviors that are more like aggression in the real world. The fact that both types of studies of violent video games yield similar effects provides strong and converging evidence that these effects are substantial and real.

22. Craig A. Anderson and Brad J. Bushman, "Human Aggression," *Annual Review of Psychology* 53 (2002): pp. 27–51.

23. Craig A. Anderson, "Imagination and Expectation: The Effect of Imagining Behavioral Scripts on Personal Intentions," *Journal of Personality and Social Psychology* 45, no. 2 (1983): pp. 293–305; Craig A. Anderson and Sandra Godfrey, "Thoughts about Actions: The Effects of Specificity and Availability of Imagined Behavioral Scripts on Expectations about Oneself and Others," *Social Cognition* 5, no. 3 (1987): pp. 238–58; Richard L. Marsh, Jason L. Hicks, and Martin S. Bink, "Activation of Completed, Uncompleted, and Partially Completed Intentions," *Journal of Experimental Psychology: Learning, Memory, and Cognition* 24, no. 2 (1998): pp. 350–61.

24. Kurt Lewin, "Problems of Research in Social Psychology," in *Field Theory in Social Science*, Darwin Cartwright, ed. (New York: Harper and Row, 1951): p. 169.

25. Brad J. Bushman and Angela D. Stack, "Forbidden Fruit Versus Tainted Fruit: Effects of Warning Labels on Attraction to Television Violence," *Journal of Experimental Psychology: Applied* 2, no. 3 (1996): pp. 207–26.

8

Violent Video Games

Who's at Risk?

Jeanne B. Funk

Many children enjoy playing violent video and computer games. These games are widely available and may be played on dedicated console systems such as a Sony Playstation, on any computer, on the Internet, on a handheld system like the popular Game Boy, and even on some of the newer technology toys. Because similar content is found across these platforms, the terms *electronic game* and *video game* have become interchangeable. The term *video game* is in most common use and will be used throughout this chapter to refer to games played on any of these platforms.

The popularity of violent video games has raised concern for many, and experts have suggested that playing these games may affect children in meaningful, lasting, and harmful ways. A large body of related media research indicates that exposure to media violence contributes to a general desensitization to real-life violence, as well as to an increased likelihood of aggression.[1] Consistent with the Surgeon General's report on youth violence, *aggression* will be defined as disruptive or harmful physical or verbal behavior, and *violence* will be defined as a physical assault that may injure or kill another person.[2] Results of research to examine how playing violent video games may affect children remain preliminary, though important trends are emerging. For example, links have been established between exposure to violent video games and increased aggression.[3]

It has been proposed that some children may be exceptionally vulnerable to negative influence from playing violent video games. This group has been called "high-risk" players.[4] High-risk players may be individuals who are drawn to violent video games because of pre-existing adjustment problems. Game playing may, then, have a causal role in either perpetuating pre-existing problems or in contributing to the development of new problems. For example, some children with academic problems may use video games as either an escape from schoolwork or as an area in which they can excel. Although this could provide a temporary benefit, such as an increase in self-esteem, over the long term academic problems may worsen, leading to a decrease in self-esteem.

Recent research has examined how a preference for violent games may help to identify high-risk players. Surveys of 4th through 8th graders identified no positive, and several negative, correlations between aspects of self-concept, including self-esteem, and a preference for violent video games.[5] In addition, there is research that suggests that children with a preference for violent video games may experience more internalizing problems such as anxiety and depression.[6] Game playing for these children may provide a temporary escape from their emotional pain, but it may also contribute to symptoms by decreasing opportunities for social contact or by creating hypersensitivity to negative messages.

High-risk players could also be those children for whom even a small increase in the relative risk of aggressive behavior triggers aggression. These players would be children who are drawn to violent video games because playing fuels pre-existing violent fantasies. Even if playing violent video games is not the original cause of a child's tendency for aggression, there is no reason to believe that playing violent games will decrease aggressive tendencies. Research clearly indicates that exposure to media violence does not result in catharsis, or emotional release.[7] Indeed, children consistently report that playing violent video games is exciting and arousing. As one 4th grade girl said during a focus group examining children's experience of game playing "So, you gotta be like 'OK, I'm gonna have to win this game, or else I'm dead!' Boom! Kabash!" Another stated, "Yeah. It's like kick! Punch! Yeah. And I do that. And I go 'Come on! Come on! Come on! Come on! Yeah! Yeah! Yeah!'"[8] Obviously, there are more powerful influences on children's behavior than playing violent video games: family life and values are more important; poverty and peer influences are more important. For some vulnerable children, however, playing violent video games could be one modifiable factor that contributes to aggressive or even violent behavior.

A child's early experiences are pivotal to his or her general tendency to be aggressive and particularly to solve conflict in an aggressive manner.[9] As already noted, there is a body of research indicating that exposure to media violence does contribute to the acquisition and expression of aggressive behaviors and to desensitization to violence. For example, television research has demonstrated that people with a heavy exposure to television violence are less likely to take action to help another person who is being victimized.[10] Playing violent video games may affect both cognitive and emotional functioning in vulnerable children. Children who prefer violent games insist that they know that the violent acts they perform are not real. Repeated exposure to unreal game violence, however, may dispose some children to behave as if violence is never real and never has actual negative consequences. Two possible pathways for the negative impact of violent video games on vulnerable children are the development of cognitive scripts for violence and desensitization to violence.

Game Playing and the Development of Cognitive Scripts

The concept of knowledge structure is important in current theories of social development. Memories of past experiences are stored as knowledge structures and these structures determine, in part, how people understand and respond to new experiences.[11] A cognitive script is one type of knowledge structure.[12] A cognitive script is an information-processing shortcut, a general representation of how common events typically unfold. Cognitive scripts are stored in long-term memory and activated automatically, without conscious awareness, given the appropriate experiential triggers. Once activated, scripts tell the individual what to expect and what to do in common, everyday situations. For example, drivers have driving scripts. Once a person decides to drive, their driving script is activated as follows: find the keys, walk to the car, open the door, get in the car, shut the door, put on the seat belt, turn on the ignition, and so forth. A restaurant script is another common example: walk in the door, be seated, order, eat, pay, leave.

Once a script is established, there is a tendency to pay attention to information that is consistent with the script and to overlook or distort information that is not consistent. Remember that script activation occurs automatically, outside of conscious awareness. That is one reason that it takes some time to get used to driving a new car. It seems that every car has a slightly different mechanism for turning on the lights and windshield wipers. The driver may experience frustration when driving a new car on a dark, rainy night until parts of the driving script are revised to accommodate equipment differences.

It is well established that children learn general social rules and specific behaviors from repeated cycles of observation, practice, and reinforcement. Such cycles are integral to playing violent video games, and this makes game playing a potentially powerful learning environment. Unfortunately, many parents are not aware of the actions children must perform in order to be successful playing violent video games. The player first observes repeated demonstrations of violence. Then the player must identify and select the violent strategies built in by the game's designers. Those players who consistently identify and choose the approved violent actions succeed and are exposed to new challenges. Successful players then experience cycles of practice of violent actions coupled with positive reinforcement for choosing these actions. Those players who choose not to apply the approved violent strategies are soon defeated or obliterated. Compromise, cooperation, and prosocial emotions such as empathy are not rewarded in violent video games. It is even possible to personalize the images of game characters, and the technology is available to scan in, for example, a yearbook picture of a peer or teacher onto a potential victim.

Throughout childhood, scripts for recurring situations are constantly being developed and revised in response to many different types of learning experiences. In theory, a child could develop and internalize scripts for situations that trigger aggression based in part on playing violent video games. If such scripts are derived from unreal violence that has no negative consequences, then the child's response to violence in real life will be influenced accordingly: recognition of the true consequences of violent actions will be diminished and violence will be seen as a reasonable alternative in many interpersonal situations. After all, game players know that you can always get more lives simply by pressing a button. Emerging research suggests that playing violent video games has at least a short-term effect on children's knowledge structures. One researcher found that after playing a violent video game, children were more likely to attribute negative intent to the actions of others even when these actions were open to a number of interpretations.[13] If persistent, this attitude would significantly increase the risk for violent behavior.

Desensitization

Desensitization is often cited as one of the primary reasons that media violence has negative impact. Desensitization means that experiences that would normally cause a certain reaction from most individuals do not cause this reaction in a particular individual. Desensitization requires cognitive and emotional changes which may impact both perceptions and responses.[14]

In desensitization, cognitive changes are demonstrated by the acceptance of violent actions committed either by oneself or by others. In other words, because of desensitization the usual belief that violence is horrible and extraordinary is transformed to the belief that violence is ordinary and even inevitable. Therefore, when one is confronted with violence, no action is needed to help the victim. In addition, one may more easily choose violent actions if such actions are perceived to be ordinary behavior and if scripts for aggression are based on fantasy violence.

The emotional component of desensitization is often described as "numbing." When an individual becomes emotionally desensitized to violence there is an actual decrease in physiological reactivity. For most people, the reactions normally associated with exposure to violence are unpleasant. Witnessing violence causes feelings such as shock, disbelief, horror, and dismay. The experience of these emotions contributes to the inhibition of aggressive actions because people prefer to avoid the negative feelings that are normally associated with violence. If an individual no longer experiences these negative reactions in response to violence, however, they will be more accepting of violence in themselves and others. Again, the desensitized individual will be unlikely to take action to oppose violence and more likely to choose a violent response.

There is related media research demonstrating this process. In one classic study, 3rd and 4th graders either watched an aggressive film or did not see any film before being asked to supervise the behavior of younger children, supposedly via a video monitor. In reality, they viewed a videotape that showed the younger children becoming progressively more destructive and aggressive. Children who had previously viewed the aggressive film took significantly longer to seek adult assistance compared to the children who did not see the film. The researchers interpreted this difference in help seeking as evidence that exposure to the violent film led to at least short-term desensitization and higher tolerance of aggression in others.[15] There are also converging data suggesting that, over the long term, heavy exposure to media violence contributes to desensitization.[16]

The Development of Moral Behavior

Because their moral development is a work in progress, children are especially vulnerable to desensitization. Most parents work hard to ensure that children develop strong moral emotions and behaviors, including the ability and inclination to take responsibility for their actions. Moral behavior is motivated by higher-order emotions such as empathy and guilt.[17] These are called "self-conscious emotions" because they require the capacity for the judgment of one's actions in the context of their effect on others.[18] For children, the development of such emotions may be influenced by playing violent video games. These games promote automatic aggression with no room for reflective, other-oriented, responsibility taking reactions. The violent actions required by these games are devoid of moral emotion and moral judgment. For some children, playing violent video games may impair moral development because the normal connection between the performance of violent actions and moral evaluation is missing.

Empathy

Empathy is one of the "self-conscious emotions" that are critical for the development of moral behavior.[19] In common use, the term empathy describes an individual's capacity to understand and, to some extent, experience the feelings of another. Empathy is a complex, multidimensional construct. Defined as an emotional response, empathy is a result of both cognitive and emotional processing.[20] In other words, the process of developing an empathic response requires the individual to take the perspective (cognitive process), and to vicariously experience the emotions of another (emotional process).[21] Children as young as 2 have demonstrated precursors of empathy, and by age 10 to 12 most children have developed what is called "mature empathy."[22] Positive socialization experiences such as the opportunity to view empathic models and to discuss and process emotions are important to the development of mature empathy.[23] In contrast, exposure to situations devoid of empathy could impair the development of mature empathy.

The positive relationship between empathy and prosocial behavior is well established.[24] Lower empathy has been associated with social maladjustment and aggression in youth.[25] More specifically, there is research suggesting that empathy has a role in inhibiting aggression. For example, in one study, aggressive elementary school children showed less empathy than their nonaggressive peers.[26] This suggests that lower empathy may be an important factor in the expression of aggressive behavior in children. It has even been suggested that measures of empathy can be used to directly evaluate an individual's risk of violent behavior.[27]

Empathy is needed to transform internalized moral standards into "hot" or emotionally charged cognitions, which then influence behavior. In the absence of empathy, moral standards may not be sufficiently salient, concrete, and dynamic to activate prosocial and bar antisocial behavior. In one survey, if the adolescent's favorite game was violent, then they were likely to have lower scores on a measure of personality-based empathy.[28] Playing violent video games could impair empathy through the development of competing cognitive scripts or through desensitization to cues which normally elicit empathy. As a result, the activation of internalized moral standards may be impaired. For example, empathy is critical to the experience and expression of guilt.

Empathy and Guilt

Guilt is an emotion that develops in parallel with empathy.[29] The experience of guilt requires empathy for the distress of another and a sense of responsibility for the distress. The process leading to the experience of guilt is complex, first requiring that the individual recognize that he or she has violated internalized moral standards by harming another.[30] But guilt involves more than a recognition that one's behavior causes another's distress; it is also necessary to appreciate that hurting someone is wrong.[31] This is not the message of violent video games. In the absence of corrective messages from family or peers, playing violent video games could increase the relative risk of violent behavior for vulnerable children by decreasing the experience or impact of guilt and by strengthening proviolence attitudes.

Attitudes towards Violence

Many believe that, in American society, daily exposure to multiple sources of violence has contributed to a widespread attitude that violence is an acceptable behavioral alternative.[32] Any expressed attitude is only one of the factors to be considered in the prediction of behavior; however, in several studies, stronger proviolence attitudes in children and adolescents have been associated with violent behavior.[33]

Attitudes are developed through a series of evaluative judgments and, like empathy, have both cognitive and affective components.[34] Attitude formation may occur as a result of effortful information processing (such as in jury deliberations) or automatically without conscious effort (as in the effects of advertising).[35] Individuals tend to process information differently depending on how consistent new information is with pre-existing attitudes.[36] Attitudes and cognitive scripts are congruent in this respect: existing knowledge serves as an interpretive framework for new experiences.

Attitudes towards violence are an integral part of one's moral framework. Proviolence attitudes are likely to develop from a series of life experiences in which violence is experienced as the primary way to express anger and resolve conflict. Such life experiences are common for victims of child abuse and for some inner-city gang members. In these examples, desensitization to violence is also likely to have occurred as part of the process of the development of proviolence attitudes. For example, a survey of urban adolescents revealed that exposure to violence was associated with subsequent use of violence but not with emotional distress. The authors suggested that chronic exposure to violence triggers a desensitization process that limits the emotional impact of subsequent violence exposure and may also strengthen proviolence attitudes.[37] By definition, proviolence attitudes preclude empathy for victims and guilt about the use of aggression, a stance that also must be taken by players of violent video games.

Empathy and Attitudes towards Violence Scale

A survey was conducted to examine relationships among empathy, proviolence attitudes, and a preference for violent video games.[38] Sixth graders completed several questionnaires including the Index of Empathy for Children and Adolescents[39] and the Attitudes Towards Violence Scale.[40] They also sorted their favorite games into one of six predetermined categories based on children's perceptions of game content.[41]

It was expected that a stronger preference for violent games would be associated with lower empathy and stronger proviolence attitudes. This prediction was supported in part: A trend for a significant relationship was found between a preference for violent games and lower scores on a measure of empathy. There was also a trend for a relationship between a preference for violent games, more playing time, and stronger proviolence attitudes. Although these results are intriguing, it must be emphasized that this is a single, preliminary study with many limitations, and the results are far from conclusive. It should also be noted that such a study cannot determine causality: children with stronger proviolence attitudes and lower empathy may simply be drawn to violent video games. As noted previously, however, establishing initial causality may not be critical because there is no reason to believe that frequent exposure to violent video games will decrease proviolence attitudes or increase empathy.

The immediate impact of playing a violent video game was examined in a recent laboratory study that also considered pre-existing characteristics.[42] Children ages 8 through 12 first completed questionnaires measuring empathy and attitudes towards violence and then played either a violent or nonviolent video game on a computer. Then they were asked to describe the likely outcomes of common, everyday situations experienced by many children. Some situations were designed to elicit an empathic response ("You see a child sitting on the side of the playground crying. What happens next?"), while others were expected to elicit thoughts about conflict and aggression ("A child pushes in line at the Discovery Zone. What happens next?").

It was anticipated that children who played the violent video game would give fewer empathic and more proviolence responses than children who played the nonviolent game. However, no significant differences were found. It may not be reasonable to expect that brief periods of game playing will cause a measurable change in relatively stable traits such as empathy and attitudes towards violence, even in relatively young children. When pre-existing characteristics were examined, some interesting relationships were found. Children who reported that their favorite game was violent gave more aggressive responses to the situations. Children who scored higher on the empathy questionnaire were more likely to give empathic responses to the situations. The same relationship held for proviolence attitudes and aggressive responses. The results of this study suggest that it is critical to examine what children bring into an experimental situation as this may be more powerful than the experimental manipulation. These results also suggest a relationship between long-term exposure to violent games and aggressive responses.

Identifying High-Risk Players

Within the framework that has been established, it is possible to begin to identify characteristics that increase the risk for negative impact as a result of playing violent video games. Younger children and bullies and their victims can now be identified as "high-risk" with some degree of certainty. There is also reason for concern about children with defects in emotion regulation. Although the issue of gender will not be specifically addressed, it is worth noting that, in general, girls may be protected by their lower attraction to playing violent games[43] and by their generally stronger empathy, stronger provictim attitudes, and weaker proviolence attitudes.[44]

Younger Children

Because their moral scaffolding is still under construction, younger children are more susceptible to negative impact from violent video games than older children. "Younger" is defined as less than age 11 or 12, or about 5th to 6th grade. As noted previously, the precursors of empathy and guilt emerge early, within the second year of life; however, the development and internalization of moral standards continue until the end of the elementary school years. Somewhere around ages 10 to 12, most children become able to measure their behavior by abstract moral rules and in comparison with the behavior of others.[45] They are then capable of feeling guilty over violating moral rules about how they are supposed to treat other people.

Throughout early childhood, children observe the behavior of others as well as their own behavior. These observations are utilized in the process of internalizing the norm of consideration for others and recognizing when it applies. Feedback is critical to this process. Under typical circumstances, soon after age two, if one child deliberately pushes another child down and the child is hurt, the first child feels guilty. The child who pushes feels empathy for the injured child's pain. This child also feels guilt, in part because of the feedback received from the injured child. In the ideal case, by the end of the elementary school years, children will be able to consistently apply their internalized moral standards to balance their personal needs and desires with their obligation to consider the welfare of others. There is, however, emerging research suggesting that playing violent video games may short-circuit this process. A survey of 4th, 5th, and 6th graders in Japan found that more frequent game players had lower empathy.[46] In a study of 7th and 8th graders, children with a preference for violent games were more aggressive.[47] Violent video games demonstrate violent actions, require that the actions be practiced, and provide no realistic feedback regarding the consequences of violent actions. For younger children, in the absence of counterbalancing influence from parents, other adults, or peers, the messages of violent video games could be internalized as moral imperatives: violence is fun, violence is acceptable, violence is without negative consequences, violence is necessary.

Bullies and Victims

Recent school shootings in the United States have focused attention on the problem of bullying in childhood. Bullying is defined as a recurrent attack by a person with more power on a person with less power.[48] The attack may be physical, verbal, or psychological. Bullying has been recognized in many countries for some time, and remains common: In one recent study of Canadian children, 38 percent of 5- to 14-year-olds reported being bullied that school term.[49] Most other reports place the incidence between 10 percent and 25 percent of children each year.[50] Bullying appears to be especially prevalent and intense during the early adolescent years.[51] Because it is such a common experience, bullying has long been considered to be almost a rite of passage for many if not most children.[52] Today, however, the intensity of victim outbursts has brought considerable public and professional scrutiny to the problem of bullying. It is now recognized that most bullies and victims have current adjustment problems. Bullying experiences also contribute to long-term emotional and behavioral problems.[53]

In research on bullying, three subgroups of participants are typically identified: bullies, victims, and bully-victims (children who are both bullies and victims).[54] Typically, bullies and victims have different personality characteristics. Some researchers report that bullies are generally aggressive and selfconfident.[55] Other researchers report that, compared with children who are neither bullies nor victims, bullies have lower self-esteem.[56] Victims are generally described as being immature and lonely, often experiencing depression and low self-esteem. Many victims have irritating personal habits that seem to activate bullying.[57] A subgroup of victims has been labeled "aggressive-provocative."[58] These children have generally poor ability to regulate their emotional responses and are highly reactive to frustration. When bullying begins, their response is both reinforcing and provocative for the bully. They may actually taunt the bully, provoking successively higher levels of aggression. The interaction typically ends because the victim's behavior deteriorates, ending in helpless displays of frustration. Bully-victims, those who take on both roles, make up a significant proportion of children involved in bullying interactions. In one report, about half the children who reported bullying behavior also reported being bullied by others.[59] Not surprisingly, bully-victims demonstrate characteristics associated with both victims and bullies.[60]

Bullies have various cognitive and emotional deficits. Social problem-solving is one example. Social problem-solving is defined as the individual's ability to successfully deal with everyday interactions.[61] Bullies seem to need to intimidate or take advantage of others in order to cope with the everyday demands of childhood. The role of cognitive scripts is also important in understanding the behavior of bullies. It is well established that children with hostile knowledge structures, those who tend to misinterpret the actions of others as having hostile intent, are more likely to behave in an aggressive manner. Some bullies appear to have developed such tendencies, possibly because they also have deficits in their ability to take the perspective of others.[62] Bullies also have significant deficits in the cognitive and emotional components of empathy. Research has demonstrated that empathy is a component of provictim attitudes.[63] Bullies have low empathy for victims and this prohibits an understanding of the cost of their behavior to victims. Bullies also lack the sense that deliberately victimizing others is morally wrong; their lack of empathy and accompanying lack of guilt prevent any internalized moral principles from influencing their behavior. In addition to having hostile-biased cognitive scripts, low perspective-taking abilities, and impaired capacity for empathy, bullies may have problems with arousal. Some have proposed that bullies have a pervasive problem with emotion regulation.[64] They may be chronically overaroused, perhaps looking for danger, which makes them too self-focused to be sympathetic to victims. Alternately, they may be desensitized and insufficiently aroused by a victim's distress.

Victims also have various cognitive and emotional deficits. Like bullies, victims tend to have poor social problem-solving and, in particular, poor conflict-resolution skills.[65] Their script for aggressive situations does not include successful strategies and responses, only inevitable defeat. Many victims also demonstrate poor emotion regulation as they are highly emotionally reactive.[66] This reactivity may be reinforcing for bullies, initiating a cycle of bullying and maintaining a high level of victim distress. This chronically high distress may further interfere with appropriate responding during an anxiety-provoking bullying experience.

The reason that bullies and victims can be considered high-risk players should now be obvious. Bullies already have many negative characteristics that may be strengthened by playing violent video games: cognitive scripts in which the underlying view is that violence is fun and the right way to solve problems, low empathy, low guilt, and insensitivity to victims. It seems clear that bullies should not be exposed to reinforcement of antivictim attitudes and further arousal that may ignite violent fantasies. As already noted, some measurable relationships have been identified between the development of hostile attribution and playing violent video games in laboratory research.[67] In addition, bullies often defend their actions by saying that the victim provoked them in some way: this justified view of violence is pervasive in violent video games.

In the case of victims, it is very difficult to change roles once you are defined as a victim. The fantasy roles available in violent video games may be appealing to victims as a way to change their identity, at least temporarily, by identifying with aggressive characters they can control. For victims, game play may also provide an escape from unpleasant reality, and a possible way to increase self-esteem through game prowess. However, being overly committed to game playing may preclude corrective social interactions.

Playing violent video games probably will not turn a docile, well-socialized child into a bully. Such play will not turn a strong-minded, self-confident child into a victim. But for children who are already bullies or victims there are no corrective messages or experiences in violent video games.

Children with Problems in Emotion Regulation

Healthy emotion regulation abilities are central to good emotional adjustment. Individuals with healthy emotion regulation skills are able to experience a range of positive and negative emotions, to control the intensity and duration of each emotional experience, and to express emotion in socially appropriate ways.[68] For example, a child with good emotion regulation is able to experience and tolerate frustration and express frustration verbally. This child will not need to deny or suppress feelings of frustration or take them out on others. Emotion regulation is related to moral behavior. Emotionally regulated children have the capacity to experience empathy and to utilize it to guide behavior in prosocial directions.[69] Individuals with good emotion regulation try to avoid the negative arousal associated with anxiety and guilt. Individuals with impaired emotion regulation, however, may not experience negative arousal or may actually seek the arousal associated with causing distress.

Children who constantly seek stimulation have problems with emotion regulation. It has been proposed that some stimulation-seeking children may become addicted to playing video games because playing temporarily satisfies their arousal craving. There are several reports of samples that include small groups of children who actually meet clinical criteria for addiction because game playing interferes with their normal activities, and when they cannot play, they experience a form of withdrawal.[70]

Even when children do not spend an excessive amount of time playing video games, total immersion in game playing is common. A child from the focus group related her experience: "Like say you started at 4:15, you wrote it down, and then it's like 6:17 and you're like 'Oh my God! I spent two hours and something something minutes! I just started.'" Immersion in game playing can be a positive experience when it results in the experiential state called "flow."[71] Flow is a term used to describe the intense feelings of enjoyment that occur when one attains a balance between skill and challenge while engaged in an activity that is rewarding in and of itself.[72] Being in a flow state has been associated with enhanced learning,[73] as well as with enhanced susceptibility to suggestion.[74] In the flow state, there is a separation of thoughts, feelings, and experiences and a suspension of rational thought. One child stated: "When I play video games, everything is like going away and stuff." Another said, "It's actually your mind. It's actually you going there."

In violent games children become immersed in violent actions. This immersion may sometimes provoke a real-life aggressive response from the player. As one girl said about her experience playing a violent game: "I scream at these things. I can't help it." As previously described, children's behavioral repertoires include scripts that engage automatically. When game content is violent, and in the absence of moderating factors such as parental influence, aggressive behavior scripts may develop outside of conscious awareness during flow states. It is theoretically possible that these scripts could later be triggered, resulting in aggressive behavior.

Children with deficits in emotion regulation may also seek immersion in game playing to avoid negative affect such as anxiety and depression. Immersion in violent games may give them a sense of control or power they lack in real life. In one recent study, children with a stronger preference for violent games had more clinically significant elevations on a standardized measure of emotional and behavior problems than those with a lower preference for violent games.[75]

Although some players seek control over arousal, it is clear that prolonged play can also be overarousing and frustrating.[76] For example, in the focus groups of 4th and 5th graders already cited, the following comments were made about what the child described as a nonviolent game: "It's like I get frustrated with it 'cause it's hard. You build like roller coasters and you have this park and you gotta try to like raise money . . . I get frustrated 'cause it's hard." Negative emotional states such as frustration undermine regulatory capacities, already impaired in the stimulation-seeking child.[77] Some children who are devoted to playing violent games seem especially prone to being negatively aroused (frustrated) by this activity. This may result in an escalation of negative affect: As one child said, "When people play games and they sort of lose and you just can't win and you play over and over, some people will get really mad, because I've done it before, you get really mad and you throw a controller or something."

Time Commitment

Time commitment may be a marker for high-risk game playing. Surveys suggest that, for most children, typical time commitment should decrease from grades 4 through 8.[78] In surveys conducted in the mid 90s, 4th grade girls reported playing about 4.5 hours in the home in a typical week, while 8th grade girls reported playing only about 2 hours.[79] Fourth grade boys reported about 7 hours of average weekly home play, while 8th grade boys reported less than 4 hours. There are no absolutes for exactly how much time children of different ages should play. However, when a child has risk factors as described above, when game preference is violent, and when game playing interferes with developmentally appropriate activities, then time commitment should be closely scrutinized.

Conclusions

This chapter has made the argument that some children are especially vulnerable to exposure to violent video games because of pre-existing characteristics. This high-risk group includes young children (ages less than 11 to 12), children who are bullies, victims, or bully-victims, and children with problems in emotion regulation. I have proposed that these groups are especially vulnerable to the disruption of moral development and moral behavior. This disruption may occur via interference with processes regulating empathy and guilt. The development of cognitive scripts based on unreal violence may contribute to proviolence attitudes and behaviors. Children with multiple risk factors are at extremely high risk of being negatively affected by playing violent video games.

The emerging body of research identifying relationships between playing violent video games and increases in aggressive behavior, cognition, and affect is described in chapter 7. In brief, when younger children are studied in laboratory situations, an increase in aggressive behavior occurs immediately after even short periods of playing violent video games.[80] For older children, the results are less consistent, perhaps because it is more difficult to find an accurate behavioral measure of aggression for older children in a laboratory situation.[81] In survey research, only negative findings have been reported: for example, children with a preference for violent video games report lower self-esteem and more aggressive behavior.[82] There is much more work to be done as video games become more realistic with each new iteration of hardware and software. Children's responses to extremely realistic virtual reality games have not even begun to be systematically examined, although it is likely that increased realism will amplify impact. Multiplayer gaming over the Internet is increasingly popular, and the effects of this activity are essentially unknown.

Although a consistent relationship between exposure to violent video games and aggression is emerging, the relationship between violent video games and violent behavior remains to be determined. Some insist that research can never prove that exposure to media violence causes negative social and behavioral outcomes. In a criminal court of law the evidence must be convincing "beyond a reasonable doubt" to prove that a defendant caused or committed the action under question. In civil court, convictions require evidence that the event is "more likely than not." Converging data indicate that playing violent video games, more likely than not, contributes to negative outcomes for vulnerable children.[83]

Steps can be taken to protect vulnerable children. It is critical that parents recognize that game playing can negatively affect some children. Then they must make a decision about what types of games are appropriate for each child. Parents have the most control over the leisure activities of younger children, and some report that children as young as age 3 spend significant time playing video games. Many parents, however, are not aware of either the commercial age-based ratings system or the independent Web sites that describe and evaluate game content.[84] The commercial video-game ratings system should be refined and made more accessible so that parents can use these guidelines to help determine what is appropriate for a particular child, given the child's age and any specific vulnerabilities. At the same time, the gaming industry must keep its promise not to actively market violent games to younger children.[85] Parents have less control over the leisure activities of older children, although they can restrict access to the funds to buy games. Parents can counteract the negative messages of violent video games by discussing their views about the role of violence in conflict resolution with older children.

When children commit acts of violence, this behavior is determined by multiple influences. For example, emerging research on biological factors suggests that it may be possible one day to identify and then treat violence-prone individuals.[86] At the present time, it is clear that three sources of influence must converge in order for a child to commit a violent act: the child must have certain vulnerabilities, the child must have the means to carry out a violent act, and the child must live in an environment that supports violence. Possible sources of vulnerability for children have been addressed; protective factors must also be examined. It is beyond the scope of this chapter to discuss the issue of guns in our culture. But the ready availability of weapons of individual destruction is clearly responsible for the increased lethality of juvenile aggression. Many believe that violent media create a culture that can be toxic for children.[87] Violent video games introduce a unique feature: the individual creates and participates in the violence. However, a child, even a vulnerable child, is not just a sponge that unthinkingly soaks up media messages. Research on media literacy suggests that talking to children about their media experiences can alter the impact of media violence. Children must be given information and support to become critical media consumers, and negative media messages must be countered. Research to identify high-risk as well as protective factors should proceed. The message that violence is necessary, fun, acceptable, and without negative consequences has become the norm in violent media, and particularly in violent video games. This message can be changed.

NOTES

1. Sandra Calvert, *Children's Journeys Through the Information Age* (McGraw-Hill, 1999); L. Rowell Huesmann and Laurie S. Miller, "Long-term Effects of Repeated Exposure to Media Violence in Childhood," in *Aggressive Behavior: Current Perspectives*, ed. L. Rowell Huesmann (Plenum, 1994), pp. 153–86; Haejung Paik and George Comstock, "The Effects of Television Violence on Antisocial Behavior: a Meta-analysis," *Communication Research* 21 (1994): pp. 516–46.

2. *Youth Violence: A Report of the Surgeon General*, available at www.surgeongeneral .gov/library/youthviolence/

3. Craig A. Anderson, and Brad J. Bushman, "Effects of Violent Video Games on Aggressive Behavior, Aggressive Cognition, Aggressive Affect, Physiological Arousal, and Prosocial Behavior: A Meta-analytic Review of the Scientific Literature," *Psychological Science* 12 (2001): pp. 353–59.

4. Jeanne B. Funk and Debra D. Buchman, "Playing Violent Video Games and Adolescent Self-concept," *Journal of Communication* 46 (1996): pp. 19–32; Jeanne B. Funk, Debra D. Buchman, and Julie N. Germann, "Preference for Violent Video Games, Self-concept and Gender Differences in Young Children," *American Journal of Orthopsychiatry* 70 (2000): pp. 233–41.

5. Ibid., pp. 233–41.

6. Jeanne B. Funk et al., "Aggression and Psychopathology in Adolescents with a Preference for Violent Electronic Games," *Aggressive Behavior* 28 (2002): pp. 134–44.

7. Brad J. Bushman, Roy F. Baumeister, and Angela D. Stack, "Catharsis, Aggression, and Persuasive Influence: Self-fulfilling or Self-defeating Prophecies?" *Journal of Personality and Social Psychology* 76 (1999): pp. 367–76; Sandra Calvert, *Children's Journeys Through the Information Age*.

8. Jeanne B. Funk, "What Young Children Experience While Playing Violent Video Games," paper presented at the Fifteenth World Meeting of the International Society for Research on Aggression, Montreal, Canada, July 2002.

9. Nancy G. Guerra, Larry Nucci, and L. Rowell Huesmann, "Moral Cognition and Childhood Aggression." in Huesmann, ed., *Aggressive Behavior*, pp. 153–86.

10. John P. Murray, "Media Violence and Youth," in *Children in a Violent Society*, ed. Joy Osofsky (New York: Guilford, 1997), pp. 72–96.

11. Virgina S. Burks et al., "Knowledge Structures, Social Information Processing, and Children's Aggressive Behavior," *Social Development* 8 (1999): pp. 220–36.

12. Guerra, Nucci, and Huesmann, "Moral Cognition and Childhood Aggression," pp. 153–86.

13. Steven J. Kirsh, "Seeing the World Through Mortal Kombat-Colored Glasses: Violent Video Games and the Development of a Short-Term Hostile Attribution Bias." *Childhood* 5 (1998): pp. 177–84.

14. Brad J. Bushman, and L. Rowell Huesmann, "Effects of Televised Violence on Aggression," in *Handbook of Children and the Media*, ed. Dorothy G. Singer and Jerome L. Singer (Thousand Oaks, Calif.: Sage, 2001), pp. 223–54.

15. Ronald S. Drabman and Margaret H. Thomas, "Does Media Violence Increase Children's Tolerance of Real-life Aggression?" *Developmental Psychology* 10 (1974): pp. 418–21.

16. Marjorie J. Hogan, "Parents and Other Adults: Models and Monitors of Healthy Media Habits," in Singer and Singer, eds., *Handbook of Children and the*

Media, pp. 663–80; Bushman and Huesmann, "Effects of Televised Violence on Aggression," pp. 223–54.

17. Martin L. Hoffman, *Empathy and Moral Development* (New York: Cambridge, 2000); Martin L. Hoffman, "Varieties of Empathy-Based Guilt," in *Guilt and Children*, ed. Jane Bybee (New York: Academic Press, 1998).

18. Nancy Eisenberg, "Emotion Regulation and Moral Development," *Annual Review of Psychology* 51 (2000): pp. 665–97; June P. Tangney and Kurt W. Fischer, eds., *Self-conscious Emotions: The Psychology of Shame, Guilt, Embarrassment, and Pride* (New York: Guilford, 1995).

19. Eisenberg, "Emotion Regulation," pp. 665–97; Hoffman, *Empathy and Moral Development*.

20. Norma Feshbach, "Empathy: The Formative Years. Implications for Clinical Practice," in *Empathy Reconsidered*, ed., Arthur C. Bohart and Leslie S. Greenberg (Washington, D.C.: American Psychological Association, 1997), pp. 33–59.

21. Becky L. Omdahl, *Cognitive Appraisal, Emotion, and Empathy* (Mahwah, N.J.: Erlbaum, 1995).

22. Hoffman, *Empathy and Moral Development*; Feshbach, "Empathy: The Formative Years," pp. 33–59.

23. Douglas Cohen and Janet Strayer, "Empathy in Conduct-disordered and Comparison Youth," *Developmental Psychology* 32 (1996): pp. 988–98.

24. Julia J. Krevans and John C. Gibbs, "Parents' Use of Inductive Discipline: Relations to Children's Empathy and Prosocial Behavior," *Child Development* 67 (1996): pp. 3263–77; Paul A. Miller and Nancy Eisenberg, "The Relation of Empathy to Aggressive and Externalizing/Antisocial Behavior," *Psychological Bulletin* 103 (1988): pp. 324–44; William Roberts and Janet Strayer, "Empathy, Emotional Expressiveness, and Prosocial Behavior," *Child Development* 67 (1996): pp. 449–70.

25. Cohen and Strayer, "Empathy in Conduct-disordered and Comparison Youth," pp. 988–98.

26. Janet P. Boldizar, David G. Perry, and Louise C. Perry, "Outcome Values and Aggression," *Child Development* 60 (1989): pp. 571–79.

27. Albert Mehrabian, "Relations Among Personality Scales of Aggression, Violence, and Empathy: Validational Evidence Bearing on the Risk of Eruptive Violence Scale," *Aggressive Behavior* 23 (1997): pp. 433–45.

28. Mark A. Barnett et al., "Late Adolescents' Experiences with and Attitudes towards Videogames," *Journal of Applied Social Psychology* 27 (1997): pp. 1316–34.

29. Hoffman, *Empathy and Moral Development*.

30. Eisenberg, "Emotion Regulation," pp. 665–97.

31. Karen Caplovitz Barrett, "The Origins of Guilt in Early Childhood," in Bybee, ed., *Guilt and Children*, pp. 75–88; Grossman, Dave, *On Killing* (Boston: Little, Brown, 1995).

32. Edward Donnerstein, Ronald G. Slaby, and Leonard D. Eron, "The Mass

Media and Youth Aggression," in *Reason to Hope: A Psychosocial Perspective on Violence and Youth*, ed. Leonard D. Eron, Jacquelyn H. Gentry, and Peggy Schlegel (Washington, D.C.: American Psychological Association, 1994), pp. 219–50; Mary E. Murray, Nancy Guerra, and Kirk Williams, "Violence Prevention for the 21st Century," in *Healthy Children 2010: Enhancing Children's Wellness*, ed. Roger P. Weissberg et al. (Thousand Oaks, Calif.: Sage, 1997), pp. 105–28.

33. Niki U. Cotton et al., "Aggression and Fighting Behavior Among African-American Adolescents: Individual and Family Factors," *American Journal of Public Health* 84 (1994): pp. 618–22; Ronald Slaby and Nancy Guerra, "Cognitive Mediators of Aggression in Adolescent Offenders: I. Assessment," *Developmental Psychology* 24 (1988): pp. 580–88; Nancy Guerra and Ronald Slaby, "Cognitive Mediators of Aggression in Adolescent Offenders: II. Intervention," *Developmental Psychology* 26 (1990): pp. 269–77; Patrick H. Tolan, Nancy Guerra, and Phillip Kendall, "A Developmental-ecological Perspective on Antisocial Behavior in Children and Adolescents: Toward a Unified Risk and Intervention Framework," *Journal of Consulting and Clinical Psychology* 63 (1995): pp. 579–84.

34. Martin Fishbein and Icek Ajzen, *Belief, Attitude, Intention, and Behavior* (Addison-Wesley, 1975); Daniel J. Mueller, *Measuring Social Attitudes* (New York: Teachers College Press, 1986); Richard E. Petty and Duane T. Wegener, "Attitude Change: Multiple Roles for Persuasion Variables," in *The Handbook of Social Psychology*, ed. Daniel T. Gilbert, Susan T. Fiske, and Gardner Lindzey (New York: Mc Graw-Hill, 1998), pp. 323–90.

35. Daniel M. Wegner and John A. Bargh, "Control and Automaticity in Social Life," in Gilbert, Fiske, Lindzey, eds., *Handbook of Social Psychology*, pp. 446–96.

36. Alice H. Eagly and Shelly Chaiken, "Attitude Structure and Function," in Gilbert, Fiske, and Lindzey, eds., *Handbook of Social Psychology*, pp. 269–322.

37. Albert D. Farrell and Steven E. Bruce, "Impact of Exposure to Community Violence on Violent Behavior and Emotional Distress among Urban Adolescents," *Journal of Clinical Child Psychology* 26 (1997): pp. 2–14.

38. Jeanne B. Funk et al., "Attitudes Towards Violence, Empathy, and Violent Electronic Games," paper presented at the Annual Meeting of the American Psychological Association, San Francisco, Calif., August 1998.

39. Brenda K. Bryant, "An Index of Empathy for Children and Adolescents," *Child Development* 53 (1982): pp. 413–25.

40. Jeanne B. Funk et al., "The Attitudes Towards Violence Scale: A Measure for Adolescents," *Journal of Interpersonal Violence* 14 (1999): pp. 1123–36.

41. Jeanne B. Funk and Debra D. Buchman, "Video Game Controversies," *Pediatric Annals* 24 (1995): pp. 91–94.

42. Jeanne B. Funk et al., "Asking the Right Questions in Research on Violent Electronic Games," paper presented at the Annual Meeting of the American Psychological Association, Washington, D.C., August 2000.

43. Jeanne B. Funk and Debra D. Buchman, "Children's Perceptions of Gender Differences in Social Approval for Playing Video Games," *Sex Roles* 35 (1996): pp. 219–31; Funk, Buchman, and Germann, "Preference for Violent Video Games," pp. 233–41.

44. Ken Rigby and Phillip Slee, "Bullying Among Australian School Children: Reported Behaviour and Attitudes Towards Victims," *Journal of Social Psychology* 131 (1991): pp. 615–27; Ersilia Menesini et al., "Cross-national Comparison of Children's Attitudes Towards Bully/Victim Problems in School," *Aggressive Behavior* 23 (1997): pp. 245–57.

45. Hoffman, *Empathy and Moral Development*; Tamara J. Ferguson and Hedy Stegge, "Emotional States and Traits in Children: The Case of Guilt and Shame," in Tangney and Fischer, eds., *Self-conscious Emotion*, pp. 174–97.

46. Akira Sakamoto, "Video Game Use and the Development of Sociocognitive Abilities in Children: Three Surveys of Elementary School Children," *Journal of Applied Social Psychology* 24 (1994): pp. 21–42.

47. Oene Weigman and Emil G.M. van Schie, "Video Game Playing and Its Relations with Aggressive and Prosocial Behaviour," *British Journal of Social Psychology* 37 (1998): pp. 367–78.

48. Peter K. Smith and Paul Brain, "Bullying in Schools: Lessons from Two Decades of Research," *Aggressive Behavior* 26 (2000): pp. 1–9.

49. Paul O'Connell, Debra Pepler, and Wendy Craig, "Peer Involvement in Bullying: Insights and Challenges for Intervention," *Journal of Adolescence* 22 (1999) pp. 437–52.

50. Rigby and Slee, "Bullying Among Australian School Children," pp. 615–27.

51. Kirsti Kumpulainen, Eila Rasanen, and Irmeli Henttonen, "Children Involved in Bullying: Psychological Disturbance and the Persistence of the Involvement," *Child Abuse and Neglect* 23 (1999): pp. 1253–62.

52. Dan Olweus, *Bullying at School: What We Know and What We Can Do* (London: Blackwell, 1993).

53. Fiona H. Biggam and Kevin G. Power, "Social Problem-solving Skills and Psychological Distress Among Incarcerated Young Offenders: The Issue of Bullying and Victimization," *Cognitive Therapy and Research* 23 (1999): pp. 307–26.

54. Kumpulainen, Rasanen, and Henttonen, "Children Involved in Bullying," pp. 1253–62.

55. Anna C. Baldry and David P. Farrington, "Bullies and Delinquents: Personal Characteristics and Parental Styles," *Journal of Community and Applied Social Psychology* 10 (2000): pp. 17–31; Smith and Brain, "Bullying in Schools," pp. 1–9.

56. Mona M. O' Moore, "Critical Issues for Teacher Training to Counter Bullying and Victimisation in Ireland," *Aggressive Behavior* 26 (2000): pp. 99–111.

57. Baldry and Farrington, "Bullies and Delinquents," pp. 1–9; Kumpulainen, Rasanen, and Henttonen, "Children Involved in Bullying," pp. 1253–62.

58. Melissa M. Mahady Wilton and Wendy M. Craig, "Emotional Regulation and Display in Classroom Victims of Bullying: Characteristic Expressions of Affect, Coping Styles, and Relevant Contextual Factors," *Social Development* 9 (2000): pp. 226–45.

59. Kumpulainen, Rasanen, and Henttonen, "Children Involved in Bullying," pp. 1253–62.

60. Helen Mynard and Stephen Joseph, "Bully/Victim Problems and Their Association with Eysenck's Personality Dimensions in 8 to 13 Year-olds," *British Journal of Educational Psychology* 67 (1997): pp. 51–54; Kumpulainen, Rasanen, and Henttonen, "Children Involved in Bullying," pp. 1253–62.

61. William F. Arsenio and Elizabeth A. Lemerise, "Varieties of Childhood Bullying: Values, Emotion Processes and Social Competence," *Social Development* 10 (2001): pp. 59–73.

62. Burks et al., "Knowledge Structures," pp. 220–36; Nicki R. Crick and Kenneth A. Dodge, "'Superiority' is in the Eye of the Beholder: A Comment on Sutton, Smith, and Swettenham," *Social Development* 8 (1999): pp. 128–31.

63. Jane L. Ireland, "Provictim Attitudes and Empathy in Relation to Bullying Behavior Among Prisoners," *Legal and Criminological Psychology* 4 (1999): pp. 51–66; Rigby and Slee, "Bullying Among Australian School Children," pp. 615–27.

64. Mahady Wilton and Craig, "Emotional Regulation and Display," pp. 226–45.

65. Biggam and Power, "Social Problem-solving Skills and Psychological Distress," pp. 307–26.

66. Mahady Wilton and Craig, "Emotional Regulation and Display," pp. 226–45.

67. Kirsh, "Seeing the World Through Mortal Kombat-Colored Glasses," pp. 177–84.

68. James J. Gross, "Emotion Regulation: Past, Present, and Future," *Cognition and Emotion* 13 (1999): pp. 551–73; Sandra C. Paivio and Christine Laurent, "Empathy and Emotion Regulation: Reprocessing Memories of Childhood Abuse," *Journal of Clinical Psychology* 57 (2001): pp. 213–26.

69. Eisenberg, "Emotion Regulation and Moral Development," pp. 665–97; Roberts and Strayer, "Empathy, Emotional Expressiveness, and Prosocial Behavior," pp. 449–70.

70. Mark Griffiths and Imogen Dancaster, "The Effect of Type A Personality on Physiological Arousal While Playing Computer Games," *Addictive Behaviors* 20 (1995): pp. 543–48; Rina Gupta and Jeffrey L. Derevensky, "The Relationship between Gambling and Video-game Playing Behavior in Children and Adolescents," *Journal of Gambling Studies* 12 (1996): pp. 375–94; Sue Fisher, "The Amusement Arcade as a Social Space for Adolescents: An Empirical Study," *Journal of Adolescence* 18 (1995): pp. 71–86; Carol A. Phillips et al., "Home Video Game Playing in

Schoolchildren: A Study of Incidence and Patterns of Play," *Journal of Adolescence* 18, (1995): pp. 687–91.

71. Jeanne B. Funk, "Electronic Games," in *Children, Adolescents, and the Media*, ed., Victor Strasburger and Barbara Wilson (Thousand Oaks, Calif.: Sage, 2002), pp. 117–44; R.W. Kubey, "Television Dependence, Diagnosis, and Prevention: With Commentary on Video Games, Pornography, and Media Education," in *Tuning in to Young Viewers: Social Science Perspectives*, ed. Tannis M. Macbeth (Thousand Oaks, Calif.: Sage, 1996), pp. 221–60.

72. Giovanni B. Moneta and Mihaly Csikszentmihalyi, "Models of Concentration in Natural Environments: A Comparative Approach Based on Streams of Experiential Data," *Social Behavior and Personality* 27 (1999): pp. 603–38; Mihaly Csikszentmihalyi and Isabella S. Csikszentmihalyi, *Optimal Experience: Psychological Studies of Flow in Consciousness* (London: Cambridge University Press, 1988).

73. Moneta and Csikszentmihalyi, "Models of Concentration," pp. 603–38.

74. Center for Media Education. *Web of Deception: Threats to Children from Online Marketing* (1996), available at www.cme.org.

75. Funk et al., "Aggression and Psychopathology," pp. 134–44.

76. Torben Grodal, "Video Games and the Pleasure of Control," in *Media Entertainment: The Psychology of Its Appeal*, ed. Dolf Zillman and Peter Vorderer (Mahwah, N.J.: Erlbaum, 2000), pp. 197–213.

77. Eisenberg, "Emotion Regulation and Moral Development," pp. 665–97; Alice W. Pope and Karen L. Bierman, "Predicting Adolescent Peer Problems and Antisocial Activities: The Relative Roles of Aggression and Dysregulation," *Developmental Psychology* 35 (1999): pp. 335–46.

78. Debra D. Buchman and Jeanne B. Funk, "Video and Computer Games in the '90s: Children's Time Commitment and Game Preference," *Children Today* 24 (1996): pp. 12–16, 31; Donald F. Roberts, Ulla G. Foehr, Victoria J. Rideout, and Mollyann Brodie, *Kids & Media @ the New Millennium: A Comprehensive National Analysis of Children's Media Use* (Menlo Park, Calif.: The Henry J. Kaiser Family Foundation, 1999); Aletha C. Huston et al., "How Young Children Spend Their Time: Television and Other Activities," *Developmental Psychology* 35 (1999): pp. 912–25.

79. Buchman and Funk, "Video and Computer Games in the '90s," 12–16, 31.

80. Karen E. Dill and Jody C. Dill, "Video Game Violence: A Review of the Empirical Literature," *Aggression and Violent Behavior* 3 (1998): pp. 407–28; Mark Griffiths, "Amusement Machine Playing in Childhood and Adolescence: A Comparative Analysis Of Video Games and Fruit Machines," *Journal of Adolescence* 14 (1991): pp. 53–73.

81. Funk, Buchman, and Germann, "Preference for Violent Video Games," pp. 233–41.

82. Sheila Fling et al., "Videogames, Aggression, and Self-esteem: A Survey," *So-*

cial *Behavior and Personality* 20 (1992): pp. 39–46; Funk, "Electronic Games," pp. 117–44.

83. Anderson and Bushman, "Effects of Violent Video Games on Aggressive Behavior, Aggressive Cognition, Aggressive Affect, Physiological Arousal, and Prosocial Behavior: A Meta-Analytic Review of the Scientific Literature," pp. 353–59; Craig A. Anderson and Karen E. Dill, "Video Games and Aggressive Thoughts, Feelings, and Behavior in the Laboratory and in Life," *Journal of Personality and Social Psychology* 78 (2000): pp. 772–90; Dill and Dill, "Video Game Violence," pp. 407–28; Funk, "Electronic Games," pp. 117–44.

84. See, for example, the Entertainment Software Ratings Board Web site at www.esrb.com and the Web site for the National Institute on Media and the Family at www.mediaandthefamily.org.

85. Federal Trade Commission, *Marketing Violent Entertainment to Children: A Review of Self-Regulation and Industry Practices in the Motion Picture, Music Recording, and Electronic Game Industries*, (2000), available at FTC Consumer Response Center, Room 130, 600 Pennsylvania Avenue, N.W., Washington, D.C. 20580.

86. Marku Linnoila, "On the Psychobiology of Antisocial Behavior," in *Handbook of Antisocial Behavior*, ed. James Breiling and David M. Stoff (New York: Wiley, 1997), pp. 336–40; Adrian Raine, Peter H. Venables, and Sarnoff Mednick, "Low Resting Heart Rate at Age 3 Years Predisposes to Aggression at Age 11 Years: Evidence from the Mauritius Child Health Project," *Journal of the American Academy of Child and Adolescent Psychiatry* 28 (1997): pp. 1457–64.

87. Sisella Bok, *Mayhem: Violence as Public Entertainment* (Boston: Addison-Wesley, 1998); Dave Grossman and Gloria DeGaetano, *Stop Teaching Our Kids to Kill: A Call to Action against TV, Movie and Video Game Violence* (New York: Crown Publishers, 1999).

9

The Effects of Cutting Back on Media Exposure

Thomas N. Robinson

What are some of the things that happen when children learn to reduce their television, videotape, and video game use? In this chapter, I present a new way to think about media effects—the effects of reducing exposure instead of the effects of the exposure itself—and a new approach to studying the effects of real-world media exposure while using rigorous research designs and methods.[1]

Children spend a substantial part of their lives in front of a television set, watching television, videotapes, and DVDs and playing video games. Based on national media use data,[2] and adjusting for the typical sleep times of children at different ages, one finds that 2- to 18-year-old children and adolescents in the United States are spending an average of more than one quarter of their waking hours in front of a television set.[3] The average African American or Latino child and children from lower socioeconomic status families are spending even more of their lives with these media.[4]

Why Study Reducing Media Exposure?

Potential problems associated with excessive media exposure are discussed throughout this volume. Despite a large number of research studies, however, strong evidence of causality — proof that media exposure truly is a cause of the suggested outcome in the real world — has sometimes been difficult to demonstrate. Supporting evidence for suspected effects of media exposure on children has generally come from a mix of ecological studies, retrospective, cross-sectional and prospective observational (epidemiological) studies, natural experiments, laboratory experiments, and field experiments. Each of these research designs has strengths and weaknesses.

Ecological studies look for associations between community-level or large-group exposures and the behaviors of those communities or large groups; comparing rates of drinking and driving in countries with and without bans on alcohol advertising, for example. Although ecological studies may suggest an association between an exposure and a behavior, they cannot prove that the exposure "causes" the behavior (causality), however, and also cannot demonstrate a link between an individual's exposure and that same individual's behavior. Are the individuals who drink and drive also those individuals who have seen the alcohol advertising? A mistaken conclusion from this kind of research (attributing community or group attributes to individuals) is considered an "ecological fallacy."

Epidemiological studies usually link individual-level exposures (e.g., an individual's amount of television viewing) with individual-level behaviors but are often limited by errors in measuring media exposure. The accurate measurement of media exposure is particularly difficult; and increasingly so as media technologies have advanced and multiplied. Even measuring people's media use by videotaping them (direct observation), has its limitations.[5] Measurement error may result in reduced statistical power to identify significant relationships between media exposure and behavior, making it more difficult to find associations that are truly present or accurately gauge their magnitude. In addition, if measurement errors are nonrandom and a systematic bias is introduced (e.g., different types of people either overestimate or underestimate their actual media use), the bias may either produce false relationships between media exposure and behavior that truly do not exist or obscure one's ability to find a relationship that truly does exist. In either case, the result will be an incorrect conclusion. In addition, studies where data are collected at only one point in time (cross-sectional studies) are unable to determine which factors come first. For example, does lots of television watching lead to weight gain or does weight gain lead to lots of television watching?[6]

Prospective epidemiological studies, those that measure media exposure first and then follow children forward over time to assess subsequent changes in behavior, are able to discern which comes first (a temporal relationship). However, because observed statistical associations between media exposure and children's behaviors may be due to a third factor that is related to both media exposure and the behavior(s) of interest (a confounding factor), even prospective studies are unable to discriminate correlates or associations from true causes. For example, preschool children who watch more educational television when they are young may have better vocabularies when they enter school than children who watch less educational television. However, preschool children with parents who read to them may also watch more educational television than preschool children whose parents do not read to them. Does watching educational television as a preschooler lead to a better vocabulary at school entry, or is the better vocabulary really due to being read to by one's parents?

Natural experiments occur when a "natural" event or manipulation occurs in the real world that allows one to observe subsequent changes: comparing changes in behavior before and after television is first introduced into isolated areas, for example. Natural experiments provide valuable information from real-world settings but other significant social changes are often occurring at the same time, making it difficult to conclude that the specific event or exposure of interest (in this case, the introduction of television) is the true cause of the observed changes in behavior. In addition, natural experiments often occur in small or isolated communities, so the observations may not fully apply to the current multimedia, multichannel media environment that most of today's children experience.

A causal relationship can only be truly demonstrated in an experimental trial in which a manipulation of the exposure (e.g., a manipulated change in television viewing) results in a change in the outcome of interest.[7] A randomized controlled trial, an experiment in which participants are randomly assigned to either the exposure of interest or a control group and then observed for subsequent changes, is the gold-standard study design for demonstrating cause and effect relationships.

Laboratory experiments in which children are exposed to specific media content and then observed for changes in their behaviors and compared to a control group of children exposed to different content are often most helpful for identifying specific causes and mechanisms: when children are randomly selected to be exposed to videotapes that model aggressive play or non-aggressive play and then observed during a subsequent play period, for example. In addition, in contrast to epidemiological studies, where it is very difficult to accurately measure media exposure (measurement error), the amount of exposure is manipulated by the experimenter. This allows for a more accurate estimate of the true magnitude of the relationship between the exposure and the behavior. Unfortunately, because laboratory conditions are contrived and often limited to measuring short-term exposures and behavior changes, the results of laboratory experiments may be difficult to generalize to real-world settings.

By contrast, field experiments, randomized controlled trials in which media exposure is provided in natural settings, offer the most accurate assessments of the causal effects of media exposure in the real world. For example, children could be randomly assigned to either watch a specific amount of violent television or to watch the same amount of nonviolent television but to make no other changes from their usual routine. Differences in the subsequent behaviors of the two groups of children could then be attributed to the differences in their television viewing. In the current environment, however, in which children are already exposed to such high levels of television and other mass media, those studies would be difficult to perform using realistic "doses" of media exposure.

To address some of the limitations of the above study designs, we have recently introduced a variation on the typical field experiment: randomized controlled trials of behavior changes after *reducing* media exposure. In the current environment, where heavy media use is the norm, the question of greatest health, social, practical, and policy importance is: will reducing television, videotape, and video game use decrease hypothesized media effects? By reducing exposure to these media (the presumed causal risk factor) in a randomized controlled trial, observed effects on health and behaviors can be attributed to the intervention to reduce media exposure. In this way, cause and effect relationships between media exposure and the behaviors are demonstrated by examining the effects of reduced exposure to media use, in contrast to the standard controlled trial approach in which exposure to the presumed risk factor is increased. The results from such studies complement the results from the other types of studies. In addition, the results have much more immediate relevance. Instead of just learning that media exposure causes a particular outcome, one also now has something that one can do about it (a tested solution).

Reducing Children's Television Viewing

The rest of this chapter describes some of the results of a randomized controlled trial of reducing children's television, videotape, and video game use. These results have been previously reported in detail in scientific publications.[8] The study involved third and fourth grade students in two public elementary schools in a single school district in San Jose, California. The two schools were selected by school district personnel and school principals because they were demographically and scholastically comparable. Both school principals and all 3rd and 4th grade teachers agreed to participate in the study prior to random assignment. One school was then randomly chosen to implement an eighteen-lesson curriculum to reduce television, videotape, and video game use. The other school served as an assessments-only control school, participating in the same before and after assessments but receiving no curriculum. Assessments were performed in the fall and spring of the school year, an interval of approximately six to seven months. All children enrolled in the two schools were eligible to participate in the study.

Although the two schools agreed to participate as a whole, and all children in the media-reduction school received the lessons as part of their standard classroom curriculum, only children with permission could participate in the evaluation measurements. Parents or guardians had to provide signed written informed consent for their children to participate in measures and surveys at the beginning and end of the study. Parents also had to provide informed consent before they, themselves, were interviewed at the beginning and end of the study. Finally, children were asked to give their assent to participate before each measurement.

More than 95 percent of children in both schools contributed at least some data to the study, and about 72 percent of parents in both schools completed phone interviews at the beginning and end of the school year. Children in the intervention and control schools were comparable in age (average about 8.9 years), sex (about 50% girls), number of televisions in the home (average about 2.7), number of video game players hooked to televisions (average about 1.5), and the percent of children with a TV in their bedroom (average about 43%).[9]

The Conceptual Model

Before we designed the curriculum, we identified three possible approaches for reducing media use: (1) nonselectively reducing television, videotape, and video game use—reducing total screen time without concern for content or context; (2) selectively reducing use—reducing total screen time by becoming more selective about content or context; and (3) displacing television and videotape viewing and video game use with other activities. Although the third mechanism was thought to have the greatest potential for reducing media use, we chose not to use it in this study. This is because one of the underlying purposes of the study was to test the hypothesized causal association between reduced media use and specific health and behavioral outcomes. To keep the experimental model "clean," it was important that the curriculum specifically targeted only reducing television, videotape, and video game use and did not directly promote other behaviors as replacements (physical activity, reading and homework, after school activities). Otherwise, one would not be able to tell whether any differences observed between the two groups were the effects of reducing media use, the effects of the replacement activities, or the combination of the two. In order to isolate the effects of reducing media use alone, the curriculum was limited to nonselective and selective methods to reduce television, videotape, and video game use without promoting or providing specific alternative activities as substitutes.

The Curriculum

We designed the SMART curriculum (Student Media Awareness to Reduce Television) within the conceptual framework of Bandura's social cognitive theory, addressing the reciprocal interactions between personal, behavioral, and environmental factors.[10] It primarily consisted of eighteen classroom lessons that were delivered by the regular 3rd and 4th grade classroom teachers. Initial lessons included self-monitoring activities and motivated children to want to reduce their television use. By counting up their viewing hours, children were made aware of how much time they were spending watching television and videotapes and playing video games and how that time might be used instead for activities that they volunteered that they liked even more than television, videotapes, and video games. These lessons were followed by a TV Turnoff[11] where children were challenged to watch no television or videotapes and play no video games for ten full days. Ninety percent of children participated in at least some of the turnoff and two-thirds completed the entire ten days without television, videotapes, or video games.[12]

After the turnoff, classrooms of children agreed on a more modest 7-hour-per-week budget. Children who handed in weekly parent signature slips documenting their compliance received public recognition in the classroom and credits toward achieving awards upon reaching 5, 10, 15, and 20 cumulative weeks of staying within their budgets. About 55 percent of the students turned in at least one "under budget" slip signed by a parent. To assist with budgeting, each household also received a TV Allowance, a set-top electronic time manager that budgets, monitors, and controls viewing through use of a Personal Identification Number (PIN) for each member of the family. Because this device controls power to the television, it also controls VCR and video game use. Children and parents were informed they could receive additional TV Allowance units, at no cost, for every television in their home. About 42 percent of parents returned response slips reporting they had installed the TV Allowance. Although we know that the average family had 2.7 television sets in their household, only about one-quarter of the families requested one or more additional TV Allowances. This may have been an indicator of the mixed feelings many parents have about the role of television in their households. Parents often tell us that they would like their children to watch less television but that they also find it useful for keeping their children occupied.

Additional lessons taught children skills for budgeting viewing time more selectively (what we call "intelligent viewing"), planning ahead to watch what they really wanted to watch instead of whatever happens to be on. Teachers also sent home "SMART Kids, SMART Families" newsletters that were designed to keep parents informed about the concurrent classroom activities, to motivate them to help their children stay within their budgets, and to suggest some possible behavioral and environmental strategies for limiting television, videotape, and video game use for the entire family.

Effects on Media Use

Children in the intervention school significantly reduced their television viewing by an average of about one-third compared to children in the control school, as measured by both child self-reports and parent reports about their children. Children in the intervention school also reported reducing their video game use significantly more than children in the control school. Parent reports of children's video game use, parent and child reports of videotape viewing, and parent reports of overall household television viewing also showed trends toward decreased use compared to the control school, but these were not statistically significant.[13] Changes in self-reported television, videotape, and video game use are illustrated in figure 9.1.

Effects on Aggressive Behavior

Violence is pervasive in television, movies, and video games. It has been estimated that by the age of 18 years, U.S. children witness 200,000 acts of violence on television alone.[14] The relationship between media violence and aggressive behavior has been the focus of more than a thousand studies. Reviews of the research literature have concluded that exposure to television violence increases children's aggressive attitudes and behaviors.[15] There have been fewer studies of the specific effects of violent video games on children. The increased arousal associated with playing video games, however, has led to speculation that their effects may be even stronger than those of violent television and movies. Therefore, it was appropriate to see if our school-based intervention to reduce children's television, videotape, and video game use would result in decreased aggressive behavior.

To test the effects of our intervention on aggressive behavior, we per-

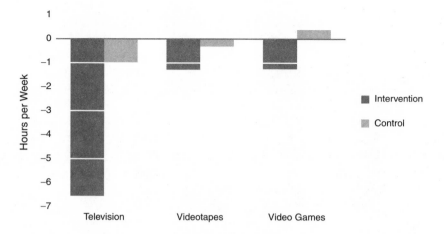

Fig. 9.1. Changes in Television, Videotapes, and Video Game Use. Mean changes in self-reported hours per week of media use among children in the intervention and control schools. Data from: Thomas N. Robinson, "Reducing Children's Television Viewing to Prevent Obesity: A Randomized Controlled Trial," *Journal of the American Medical Association* 282, no. 16 (1999): pp. 1561–67.

formed a number of different assessments: peer ratings of aggression, direct observations of aggression on the school playground, and parent ratings of their child's aggression.[16] All aggression measures were made on the same days in both schools at the beginning and end of the school year, before and after the curriculum was delivered in the intervention school. We hypothesized that, compared to children in the control school, children in the intervention school would become less aggressive, as judged by their peers, by direct observation on the school playground, and by their parents.

Our primary measure of aggression was peer ratings of aggression. To assess peer perceptions we modeled our survey on the peer nomination method developed by Eron, Walder, and colleagues.[17] Children were asked to place a check beside the names of their classmates in response to fifteen questions: one warm-up question, ten questions about aggressive behavior (e.g., Who often says "Give me that"? Who starts a fight over nothing? Who pushes or shoves children?), mixed in with two popularity questions and two prosocial behavior questions. Children were instructed to place checkmarks by the names of as many students as they wanted in answer to each question but not to pick themselves. Each

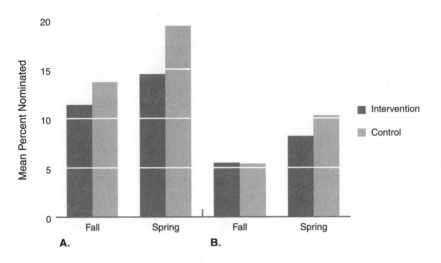

Fig. 9.2. Changes in Peer Ratings of Aggression among Boys (A) and Girls (B). Mean peer ratings of aggression at the beginning (fall) and end (spring) of the school year among children in the intervention school and the control school. Data from: Thomas N. Robinson et al., "Effects of Reducing Children's Television and Video Game Use on Aggressive Behavior: A Randomized Controlled Trial," *Archives of Pediatrics and Adolescent Medicine* 155, no. 1 (2001): pp. 17–23.

question also contained an option for "no boy" or "no girl." A score for each question was computed as the number of times a student was chosen divided by the number of other students completing the survey. Scores on the ten aggression questions were then combined to calculate a total peer rating of aggression for each child. Aggressive behavior scores were inversely correlated with popularity and prosocial behavior scores.[18] Consistent with our hypothesis, over the course of the school year, peer ratings of aggression increased significantly less for children in the intervention school versus those for children in the control school, a relative reduction of about 16 percent. These changes are illustrated separately for boys and girls in figure 9.2.

To directly observe aggression on the school playground, we based our protocol on the procedure previously used by Joy et al.[19] A 60 percent random sample of participating children as selected from class lists were observed in free play during recess on the school playgrounds. For ten days at the beginning and end of the school year, eight trained observers, who were blinded to the experimental design, were randomly assigned to one of the two schools on a daily basis. Each observer watched the selected children in a different random order and categorized all aggressive acts during a one-minute period. Observers were trained to use very specific classification criteria for different types of verbal and physical aggression. Each child was observed from three to thirteen different times at the beginning of the school year and from five to seventeen different times at the end of the school year. When two observers watched the same child simultaneously, agreement of their ratings was high. Over the course of the school year, children in the intervention school reduced their verbal aggression on the playground by about 47 percent (an average of about one fewer verbally aggressive act every 10 minutes) and reduced their physical aggression on the playground by about 37 percent (an average of about one fewer physically aggressive act every 11 minutes) compared to children in the control school. The difference in verbal aggression was statistically significant, but, with this small sample size, the difference in physical aggression did not reach statistical significance.[20] Changes in observed verbal aggression for boys and for girls are shown in figure 9.3.

We were also able to complete phone interviews at the beginning and end of the school year with about 72 percent of the parents or guardians of the participating children. To assess parent perceptions of their child's aggressiveness, we used the aggression subscale of the parent report form of the Child Behavior Checklist,[21] a widely used measure of behavioral problems of children 4–16 years of age. The differences between groups were not statistically significant, but the intervention resulted in parent ratings of their children's aggressiveness that were about 8 percent lower than parent ratings in the control school, after adjusting for their baseline ratings. The lack of statistically significant differences for parent reports of aggression may suggest that the intervention—and the influences of media exposure—are more specific to, or more likely to be expressed as, aggression at school than at home. Because changes in parent reports of aggression did favor the intervention group, this finding could also be explained by insufficient statistical power, due to the smaller sample size and/or lower reliability and validity of parent report measures. Parents may have fewer opportunities, as compared to peers, to see their children act aggressively, and parent ratings may therefore be less sensitive to

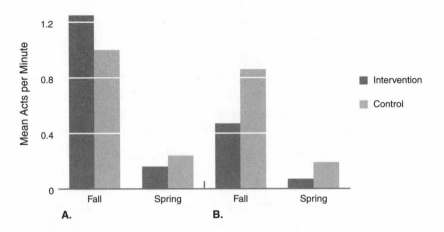

Fig. 9.3. Changes in Observed Verbal Aggression among Boys (A) and Girls (B). Mean acts of verbal aggression per minute observed on the playground during recess at the beginning (fall) and end (spring) of the school year among children in the intervention school and the control school. Data from Thomas N Robinson et al., "Effects of Reducing Children's Television and Video Game Use on Aggressive Behavior: A Randomized Controlled Trial," *Archives of Pediatrics and Adolescent Medicine* 155, no. 1 (2001): pp. 17–23.

change. Similarly, because only one parent or guardian was interviewed for each child, it is possible that parent reports are less sensitive because they capture only a subset of aggressive behavior in the home.[22]

It has also been suggested that exposure to media violence leads to children perceiving the world as a more mean and scary place.[23] Therefore, we tested whether reducing media exposure would reduce these perceptions. We used a twelve-item questionnaire (e.g., Do you think most people are mean or most people are friendly? How important is it to know how to fight? Are you scared of being hurt by a criminal?). These items were adapted from instruments previously demonstrated to correlate with amount of television viewing among young adolescents and children.[24] In our sample of children, internal consistency was only moderately high. The intervention resulted in children's ratings of a mean and scary world that were about 5 percent lower than those of children in the control school, but this difference was not statistically significant.[25]

Effects on Consumeristic Behavior

Another oft-cited concern about television is the frequent advertising directed at children.[26] A recent content analysis found that advertisements make up approximately 16 percent of children's television viewing.[27] This figure does not include entertainment programming that is based on specific toys or shows with their own accompanying line of toys and other products. Experimental studies have demonstrated that television commercials successfully inflate children's perceptions of the value of advertised toys.[28] Moreover, because exposure to commercials is a part of television viewing, it is not surprising that time spent watching television is positively correlated with children's requests for toys[29] and that parents report that television is the most common source of children's purchase requests.[30] To date, attempts to prevent commercials from influencing child behavior have had little success. Therefore, we were interested to observe whether our media reduction intervention might also result in decreases in children's consumeristic behavior.

To assess consumeristic behavior, we designed a question about toy requests. At the beginning and end of the school year, children in both schools were asked, "In the past week, have you asked your mother or father to buy any toys that you have seen on TV?" During phone interviews, we asked the parents and guardians of participating children a similar question: "In the past week, has your child requested that you purchase any toys that he/she has seen on TV?" We hypothesized that children in the intervention school would reduce the frequency of their purchase requests versus children in the control school.

Changes in children's reports of their toy requests are illustrated in figure 9.4. As hypothesized, the intervention produced a statistically significant reduction in children's reported toy purchase requests. By the end of the school year, the average odds of a child requesting a toy purchase in the prior week was about 70 percent lower among intervention school children than among control school children, adjusting for baseline purchase requests, sex, and age. The effects as reported by parents were similar, reflecting a nearly 60 percent lower odds of toy requests among children in the intervention school. In the smaller sample of participating parents, however, this latter difference was not statistically significant.[31]

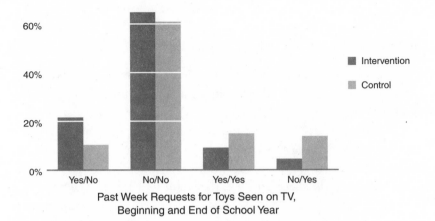

Fig. 9.4. Changes in Children's Self-Reported Toy Purchase Requests. Percent of children in the intervention school and the control school, at the beginning of the school year and the end of the school year, who asked (Yes) and did not ask (No) a parent during the previous week to buy a toy or toys he or she saw on TV. Children who reported asking for a toy purchase at the beginning of the school year but not at the end of the school year are labeled "Yes/No," children who reported not asking for a toy purchase both at the beginning and the end of the school year are labeled "No/No," and so on. Data from Thomas N. Robinson et al, "Effects of Reducing Television Viewing on Children's Requests for Toys: A Randomized Controlled Trial," *Journal of Developmental and Behavioral Pediatrics* 22, no. 3 (2001): pp. 179–84.

Although it is possible that parent reports are a more accurate picture of children's toy purchase requests than children's self-reports, that appears unlikely. The direction and effect size of the parents' reports were quite similar to those of the children's self-reports. One likely explanation for the lack of statistical significance may be the smaller sample of parents who participated in interviews. In addition, because only one parent or guardian was interviewed for each child, they may not know of all purchase requests. This is suggested by the finding that parent reports in both groups indicated an overall lower prevalence of purchase requests and fewer changes over the school year than child self-reports. In contrast, children may be more likely to report all the requests they made to all parents or guardians. Finally, parents or guardians may not be as aware as their children are that television was the source of a specific toy request.[32]

To further explore the link between reduced television viewing and reduced toy purchase requests, we also examined these associations

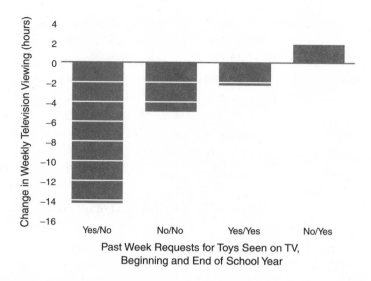

Fig. 9.5. Changes in Toy Purchase Requests and Changes in Television Viewing (Intervention School Only). Change, from the beginning of the school year to the end of the school year, in self-reported television viewing hours per week among intervention school children who reported asking for a toy purchase at the beginning of the school year but not at the end of the school year (Yes/No), children who reported not asking for a toy purchase both at the beginning and the end of the school year (No/No), and so on. Data from: Thomas N. Robinson et al., "Effects of Reducing Television Viewing on Children's Requests for Toys: A Randomized Controlled Trial," *Journal of Developmental and Behavioral Pediatrics* 22, no. 3 (2001): pp. 179–84.

among the children in the intervention school alone. These results showed an obvious, and statistically significant, graded response in the expected direction (figure 9.5).[33] Children who requested toy purchases at the beginning of the school year but not at the end of the school year were also those children who, on average, decreased their television viewing the most. In contrast, those children who requested toy purchases at the end of the school year but not at the beginning of the school year were those who, on average, increased their viewing.

Future Implications

There has been widespread advice from health, psychological, and educational organizations to limit children's television viewing. The American Medical Association and the American Academy of Pediatrics both recommend that parents limit their children's viewing to no more than 1 to 2 hours per day.[34] There has, however, been little previous research into how to accomplish reductions in television, videotape, and video game use and whether such reductions are even possible. Our studies demonstrate that it is, in fact, possible to reduce children's television, videotape, and video game use with a social cognitive theory-based, classroom curriculum. In addition, such an intervention appears to have particularly broad beneficial effects—many of those that are predicted by the prior experimental and epidemiological research on the effects and correlates, respectively, of television viewing on children's health and behavior. To date we have already witnessed reductions in body fatness, and as described above, decreased aggressive behavior and decreased consumeristic behavior, in response to this intervention.[35]

In addition, we found that children in the intervention school significantly reduced the number of meals they ate while watching television.[36] This change was the source of many of unsolicited testimonials from parents. A number of parents told us how much they enjoyed their new habit of talking with their children at the breakfast and dinner tables now that they had stopped eating their family meals in front of the television set. Other parents told us that by limiting television, videotapes, and video games during the afternoons, their children found new friends in the neighborhood and were spending more time playing outside with them.

The studies described above have a number of limitations and represent only the first step in this line of research. First, because the studies involved children in only two elementary schools, it is impossible to completely rule out the possibility that the results seen were due to unknown differences in the intervention and control schools that were unrelated to the intervention itself. This possibility is made less likely, however, because the schools were in a single school district, school district officials considered the schools to be demographically and scholastically matched, and baseline measures of many different parameters, across a number of different domains, were comparable between the two schools.[37] In addition, the cross-over patterns of a number of the results lessen the likelihood of scaling or "ceiling effects" (where changes in one group are limited by having insufficient room to improve or worsen), regression to the mean (where differences between groups are due to one group starting at an extreme), and selection-maturation biases (where pre-existing differences between the two groups lead to different rates of change or "maturation") as alternative interpretations of the results.[38]

Second, the intervention targeted all television, videotape, and video game use, instead of just television viewing alone, violent media alone, or advertising alone. In addition, we did not assess specific exposure to different types of content, so we do not know whether violent media exposure or advertising exposure, for example, were reduced. It may be argued, as a result, that we have not sufficiently tested the causal relationship between exposure to violent media content and aggression or exposure to advertising for toys and children's toy purchase requests. However, the present design was chosen for both practical and scientific reasons. In the current multimedia, multichannel, remote-control environment, actual exposure to specific content is extremely difficult, if not impossible, to assess accurately in a real-world setting. The definition of what constitutes violent media or advertising, for example, is not necessarily straightforward or uniformly agreed upon. Should some cartoons be included as violent media but not others? Should a cartoon about a toy product be considered an advertisement? Requiring parents and children to differentiate violent media from other types of content, advertising from entertainment and educational programming would make the intervention much more difficult to implement, requiring extensive training of teachers, parents, and children, and, thus, less likely to be adopted and less generalizable.

This potential limitation of not targeting reduced exposure to specific content, however, may also be considered a strength. Because the intervention did not target just specific types of content, therefore potentially diluting intervention effects (e.g., some children in the intervention school may not have reduced their violent media exposure at all, they may even have increased it), it may also be argued that the findings described above are even stronger evidence of the benefits of reducing media exposure on aggressive behavior and consumeristic behavior.[39]

Virtually all of the contributors to this volume have noted that there is much yet to be learned about the effects of mass media exposure on children's health and behavior. As a result, additional well-designed and rigorously implemented laboratory experiments, field experiments, and epidemiological studies are needed to fill gaps in our knowledge, to guide child, parent, family, and social behavior and decision-making, and to inform public policy. This chapter has described one new approach to studying the effects of media exposure: reducing this exposure. In the current environment of heavy media use, the question of greatest health, social, practical, and policy importance is: Will reducing television, videotape, and video game use decrease hypothesized media effects? The answer to this question has immediate relevance. It will now be important to replicate this study with larger and more demographically diverse samples in other geographic areas and with longer follow-up to confirm these findings. We also need to extend the model to study other hypothesized effects of media exposure and to evaluate the generalizability of this approach to other settings. For example, future studies should assess the effects of reducing media use on academic performance, body image and weight concerns, tobacco, alcohol, and other drug-related attitudes and behaviors as well as racial, ethnic, and gender stereotypes.[40] Studies of the mechanisms by which this intervention influences individual behavioral outcomes will also improve our understandings of the relationships between exposure to specific media content and subsequent behavior. In addition, to inform public policy, future studies should be designed to identify subgroups of children who are more or less likely to respond to the intervention and to distinguish the elements of the curriculum and implementation most closely linked to beneficial outcomes. The answers to these questions will help parents, educators, and policy-makers more widely disseminate successful approaches to address excessive media use in the most efficient and effective manner.

NOTES

1. This work was funded by grants from the American Heart Association, California Affiliate, the National Heart, Lung and Blood Institute (RO1 HL54102), the Children's Health Research Fund at Lucile Packard Children's Hospital at Stanford, and a Robert Wood Johnson Foundation Generalist Physician Faculty Scholar Award.

I thank Joel D. Killen, Ph.D., Helena C. Kraemer, Ph.D., Melissa Nichols Saphir, Ph.D., Marta L. Wilde, M.A., K. Farish Haydel, Ann Varady, M.S., Lisa C. Navracruz, M.D., Dina L.G. Borzekowski, Ed.D., Sally McCarthy, Connie Watanabe, M.A., and the students, parents, teachers, and school administrators who participated in the project.

2. Donald F. Roberts, Ulla G. Foehr, Victoria J. Rideout, and Mollyann Brodie, *Kids & Media @ the New Millennium: A Comprehensive National Analysis of Children's Media Use* (Menlo Park, Calif.: The Henry J. Kaiser Family Foundation, 1999).

3. Thomas N. Robinson, "Television Viewing and Childhood Obesity," *Pediatric Clinics of North America* 48, no. 4 (2001): pp. 1017–25.

4. Roberts et al., *Kids & Media*; Thomas N. Robinson and Joel D. Killen, "Ethnic and Gender Differences in the Relationships between Television Viewing and Obesity, Physical Activity and Dietary Fat Intake," *Journal of Health Education* 26, (1995): pp. S91–S98; Ross E. Andersen et al., "Relationship of Physical Activity and Television Watching With Body Weight and Level of Fatness among Children: Results from the Third National Health and Nutrition Examination Survey," *Journal of the American Medical Association* 279, no. 12 (1998): pp. 938–42.

5. Dina L.G. Borzekowski and Thomas N. Robinson, "Viewing the Viewers: 10 Video Case Studies of Children's Television Viewing Behaviors," *Journal of Broadcasting and Electronic Media* 43, no. 4 (1999): pp. 506–28.

6. Thomas N. Robinson, "Does Television Cause Childhood Obesity?" *Journal of the American Medical Association* 279, no. 12 (1998): pp. 959–60; Thomas N. Robinson, "Reducing Children's Television Viewing to Prevent Obesity: A Randomized Controlled Trial," *Journal of the American Medical Association* 282, no. 16 (1999): pp. 1561–67.

7. Helena C. Kraemer et al., "Coming to Terms with the Terms of Risk," *Archives of General Psychiatry* 54, no. 4 (1997): pp. 337–43.

8. Robinson, "Reducing Children's Television Viewing to Prevent Obesity"; Thomas N. Robinson et al., "Effects of Reducing Children's Television and Video Game Use on Aggressive Behavior: A Randomized Controlled Trial," *Archives of Pediatrics and Adolescent Medicine* 155, no. 1 (2001): pp. 17–23; Thomas N. Robinson et al., "Effects of Reducing Television Viewing on Children's Requests for Toys: A Randomized Controlled Trial," *Journal of Developmental and Behavioral Pediatrics* 22, no.3 (2001): pp. 179–84.

9. Robinson, "Reducing Children's Television Viewing to Prevent Obesity."

10. Albert Bandura, *Social Foundations of Thought and Action* (Englewood Cliffs, N.J.: Prentice-Hall, 1986).

11. Marie Winn, *Unplugging the Plug-in Drug* (New York: Penguin Books, 1987).

12. Robinson, "Reducing Children's Television Viewing to Prevent Obesity."

13. Ibid.

14. Aletha C. Huston et al., *Big World, Small Screen: The Role of Television in American Society* (Lincoln: University of Nebraska Press, 1992).

15. Ibid.; Surgeon General's Scientific Advisory Committee on Television and Social Behavior, *Television and Growing Up: The Impact of Televised Violence* (Washington, D.C.: U.S. Department of Health, Education, and Welfare, 1972); David Pearl, Lorraine Bouthilet, and Joyce Lazar, eds. *Television and Behavior: Ten Years of Scientific Progress and Implications for the Eighties* (Rockville, Md.: National Institute of Mental Health, U.S. Department of Health and Human Services, DHHS Publication no. [ADM] 82–1196, 1982).

16. Robinson et al., "Effects on Aggressive Behavior."

17. Leonard D. Eron, Leopold Walder, and Monroe Lefkowitz, *Learning of Aggression in Children* (Boston: Little, Brown and Company, 1971); Leopold O Walder, Robert P. Abelson, Leonard D. Eron, Thomas J. Banta, and Jerome H. Laulicht, "Development of a Peer-Rating Measure of Aggression," *Psychological Reports* 9 (1961): pp. 497–556.

18. Robinson et al., "Effects on Aggressive Behavior."

19. Leslie A. Joy, Meredith M. Kimball, and Merle L. Zabrack, "Television and Children's Aggressive Behavior," in *The Impact of Television: A Natural Experiment in Three Communities*, ed. Tannis MacBeth Williams (New York: Academic Press, 1986), pp. 303–60.

20. Robinson et al., "Effects on Aggressive Behavior."

21. Thomas M. Achenbach, *Manual for the Child Behavior Checklist/4–18 and 1991 Profile* (Burlington, Vt.: University of Vermont Department of Psychiatry, 1991).

22. Robinson et al., "Effects on Aggressive Behavior."

23. George Gerbner et al., "The Demonstration of Power: Violence Profile No. 10," *Journal of Communication* 29, no. 3 (1979): pp. 177–96.

24. Ibid.; Suzanne Pingree and Robert Hawkins, "U.S. Programs on Australian Television: The Cultivation Effect," *Journal of Communication* 31, no. 1 (1981): pp. 97–105; Jerome L. Singer, Dorothy G. Singer, and W. Rapaczynski, "Family Patterns and Television Viewing As Predictors of Children's Beliefs and Aggression," *Journal of Communication* 34, no. 2 (Spring, 1984): pp. 73–89.

25. Robinson et al., "Effects on Aggressive Behavior."

26. American Academy of Pediatrics Committee on Communications, "The Commercialization of Children's Television," *Pediatrics* 89, no.2 (1992): pp. 343–44; Shel Feldman, Abraham Wolf, and Doris Warmouth, "Parental Concerns about Child-Directed Commercials," *Journal of Communication* 21, no.1 (1977): pp. 125–37; Thomas B. Ward, "Opinions on Television Advertising to Children: A Content Analysis of Letters to the Federal Trade Commission," *Merrill-Palmer Quarterly* 30, no. 3 (1984): pp. 247–59.

27. Howard L. Taras and Miriam Gage, "Advertised Foods on Children's Television," *Archives of Pediatrics and Adolescent Medicine* 149, no. 9 (1995): pp. 649–52.

28. Anees Sheikh and Martin Moleski, "Children's Perception of The Value of an Advertised Product," *Journal of Broadcasting* 21, no. 3 (1977): pp. 347–54.

29. Ibid.; Thomas S. Robertson and John R. Rossiter, "Children's Responsiveness To Commercials," *Journal of Communication* 27, no. 1 (1977): pp. 101–6.

30. Pat L. Burr and Richard M. Burr, "Product Recognition and Premium Appeal," *Journal of Communication* 27, no. 1 (1977): pp. 115–17; Pat L. Burr and Richard M. Burr, "Parental Responses to Child Marketing," *Journal of Advertising*

Research 17, no. 6 (1977): pp. 17–20; Thomas R. Donohue, "Effect of Commercials on Black Children," *Journal of Advertising Research* 15, no. 6 (1975): pp. 41–47.

31. Robinson et al., "Effects on Children's Requests for Toys."

32. Ibid.

33. Ibid.

34. American Medical Association, *Physician Guide to Media Violence* (Chicago, Ill.: American Medical Association, 1996); American Academy of Pediatrics Committee on Communications, "Media violence," *Pediatrics* 95, no. 6 (1995): pp. 949–51.

35. Robinson, "Reducing Children's Television Viewing to Prevent Obesity"; Robinson et al., "Effects on Aggressive Behavior"; Robinson et al., "Effects on Children's Requests for Toys."

36. Robinson, "Reducing Children's Television Viewing to Prevent Obesity."

37. Ibid.; Robinson et al., "Effects on Aggressive Behavior"; Robinson et al., "Effects on Children's Requests for Toys."

38. Glenn H. Bracht and Gene V. Glass, "The External Validity of Experiments," *American Educational Research Journal* 5 (1968): pp. 437–74; Thomas D. Cook and Donald T. Campbell, *Quasi-Experimentation. Design and Analysis Issues for Field Settings* (Boston: Houghton Mifflin, 1979).

39. Strengths of these studies include the randomized controlled trial design, blinding students, parents, and teachers to the specific study hypotheses, blinding data collectors to which school received the curriculum, the consistency of effects across multiple measures within and across topic domains and from different sources (children, parents, and observers), the use of a potentially generalizable intervention delivered by the regular classroom teachers in the participating public elementary schools, and an analysis approach which appropriately accounted for the design with the school as the unit of randomization.

40. Dina L.G. Borzekowski, Thomas N. Robinson, and Joel D. Killen, "Does the Camera Add Ten Pounds? Media Use, Perceived Importance of Appearance, and Weight Concerns Among Teenage Girls," *Journal of Adolescent Health* 26, no. 1 (2000): pp. 36–41; Thomas N. Robinson, Helen L. Chen, and Joel D. Killen, "Television and Music Video Exposure and Risk of Adolescent Alcohol Use," *Pediatrics* 102, no. 5 (1998): p. e54, available at www.pediatrics.org/cgi/content/full/102/5/e54.

10

The Contradictions of Parenting
in a Media Age

Kay S. Hymowitz

A merican parents are deeply troubled about popular culture and its effect on their children. Or so we have often heard. Certainly, parents say they fear that the violence and sexual obsessions of television, rap music, video games, and the Internet will harm their kids. They show their concern by buying books like Tipper Gore's *Raising PG Kids in an X-rated Society* and by creating and joining advocacy groups like Action for Children's Television. Some advertisers are convinced that parental worries are powerful enough to modify their business decisions; recently the Los Angeles–based Parents Television Council successfully pressured a number of corporate sponsors to shun sexually suggestive prime-time programs including both the World Wrestling Federation's infamous *SmackDown!* and the critical success *Boston Public*. Politicians appear to believe that taking a stand against the excesses of popular culture is a way to attract parent-voters. During the hotly contested 2000 presidential campaign, candidates, who doubtless had the poll numbers to support their indignation, seized upon an FTC report showing that entertainment companies routinely market their violent products to children as a perfect symbol of their abiding concern about "the nation's children."

What They Say and What They Do

Despite these professions of concern, however, actual evidence that parents are all that distressed by popular culture is, at best, ambiguous. True, in surveys a large majority of parents say that they restrict their children's television viewing, which, despite the implication of heavy metal music and the Internet in several school shootings, remains the medium of greatest concern.[1] But although a relationship between heavy television viewing and both poor school performance and obesity has been widely reported,[2] by most estimates kids are watching an average of more than 2.5 hours of television a day. Many parents allow—the better word might even be "encourage"—their children to begin the television habit early; children between 2 and 4 years old are already watching 2 hours a day. Fifty-eight percent of families with children have the television on during dinner; 42 percent are "constant television households," that is, they have the television running throughout much of the day regardless of whether or not anyone is actively watching.[3] Although kids with sets in their bedrooms watch considerably more hours of television, receive less monitoring of what they do watch, and do worse in school, the percentage of children with their own sets has risen steadily over time. A Kaiser report shows that thirty-two percent of 2- to 7-year-olds and 65 percent of 8- to 18-year-olds have bedroom sets. The more recent Annenberg report claims a slightly more modest 57 percent of 8- to 16-year-olds have personal televisions. The Annenberg researchers also cite one downward trend—a decrease from 31 percent to 24 percent over the past five years in the number of preschoolers with personal sets—but they point out that this decline has been more than made up for by a significant rise in the number of elementary-school-age children and a smaller but still notable increase among adolescents with bedroom televisions.[4] Looking at the total picture, the Annenberg survey concludes; "Parental concerns about the media are not statistically related to the time their children spend with television."[5] Taking into account all other media, including video, computer games, and CD's, which according to most surveys parents are even less likely to supervise, *Kids & Media @ the New Millennium* estimates that kids between 2 and 7 consume over 4.25 hours of media a day, and those between 8 and 18 nearly 8 hours a day.

Do parents at least monitor the content of the shows their children are watching? Again, the evidence suggests, not very much. Yes, the large majority say they are concerned about the materialism, explicit sexuality, gender and racial stereotyping, and—to a lesser extent—violence in the media.[6] And there is some indication that they forbid their children to watch television before they have finished their homework, or to view porn channels or R-rated movies with nudity and cursing.[7] Still, even young children don't get much supervision from parents. "Despite signs of increased concern," writes one scholar in a survey of the literature on the television habits of children between kindergarten and 3rd grade, "parental involvement in the television viewing of their children, on the whole, is at most moderate, and at the least nonexistent."[8] An Annenberg study based on focus groups of 3rd, 6th, and 9th graders and their mothers says that the parents "do feel it is important to mediate their children's viewing." Mothers describe seeing their children become agitated, disrespectful, and sleepless either from watching too much television or from watching "problematic" shows. Yet the author summarizes her findings: "Parents don't actively seek out information about programming," and "children make viewing decisions without their parents' help."[9]

The emergence of new technologies such as cable, pay movie channels, and VCRs, with their capacity for bringing ever more sensational material into the living room—or child's bedroom, as the case may be—has not made parents any more proactive.[10] "Cable's more adult content," one study concluded, "does not invite greater parental restriction."[11] Parents are even less involved in attending to what music their children are listening, though it is arguably the most influential—and depending on the genre, the most vicious and crude—of all the media forms used by adolescents.[12] Nor have new television ratings systems increased parental involvement. In a review of several studies on the subject, Bradley S. Greenberg and Lynn Ramboldi-Hnilo found that the few parents making use of the ratings system were among the minority already actively supervising their children's viewing and had children who were "low to moderate consumers of television [and] high academic achievers," ratings or no. Most parents failed to take much interest in the new system. "Violent and sexual content and coarse language are significant concerns, these parents claim. In general, their attitude toward the ratings is supportive, indeed quite positive," the authors write, "but behaviors that would correspond with this attitude are largely absent."[13] *Media in the Home 2000* even showed a marked decline from a year earlier in the number of parents aware that these ratings even exist.[14]

A number of researchers have speculated that many parents who do have rules fail to enforce them.[15] Kids "watch it anyway," either just turning it on knowing that parents aren't going to do anything about it or sneaking a look when parents aren't paying attention. "They turn it off and I turn it on," one 3rd grade suburban boy told interviewers. "They turn it off. Then I turn it on. But then they turn it off. Then I go upstairs. We don't have cable upstairs."[16]

Certainly, many of the shows children commonly watch are not the sort that bring to mind the phrase "parental supervision." During the 1999–2000 season, according to Nielsen Media Research, the number four show among 2- to 5-year-olds was *Friends*. *The Simpsons* was number five, although in focus groups parents often criticize the cartoon for what they view as its gratuitously nasty portrayal of family relations.[17] Indeed, when parents are asked about the last show they viewed with their children, *The Simpsons* and *Friends* are among the ten most frequently mentioned.[18] Nielsen has found that the top twenty picks among children 6 to 11 include such distinctly child-unfriendly shows as *Beverly Hills 90210*, *Frasier*, and *E.R.* (which one would have thought had the added problem of being broadcast between 10 and 11 P.M.); in previous years *Roseanne*, *Baywatch*, and *Married with Children* were among the top-rated syndicated programs among children between 2 and 11.[19] A more careful reading of the FTC report that unleashed such a storm of protest from Washington politicians would have put the whole issue of entertainment companies marketing to young children in a different light. It seems that children were not coming across ads for R-rated movies and games when they were watching Nickelodeon, but when they were reading *Cosmo Girl*, a junior version of *Cosmopolitan*, or watching *SmackDown!*, MTV, or *Dawson's Creek*. All of these venues, the report noted without irony, are "especially popular among 11- to 18-year-olds." The FTC report also revealed that movie studios include 9- and 10-year-olds in focus groups to test market some of their violent films. All of the children who attended these groups had permission from their parents.

So how do we explain the dissonance between what parents say about popular culture and what they actually do about it? Some of it can be chalked up to parental peer pressure. Everyone knows that alarm about popular culture is part of what goes under the rubric "being a good parent" in America today, hence parents' tendency to underreport the number of hours their children spend watching television and to overreport the control they exercise over their children's viewing habits.[20] They read what experts have to say about the subject in newspapers and watch them on talk shows; perhaps they have heard warnings from teachers and conversations about household rules among neighbors and parents of their children's classmates. If their doctor is following the 1999 guidelines of the American Academy of Pediatrics, they have even been questioned about family television routines in the pediatrician's office during their child's last annual checkup. It's not hard to figure out what you are supposed to say. But deep down, many might wonder just how serious a problem popular culture is. After all, they were television and rock 'n' roll babies themselves; when they were children in the sixties and seventies, they were watching over 2 hours of television a day.[21] They probably remember what some skeptics call the "moral panics" of yesteryear that surrounded figures like Elvis Presley or the Rolling Stones and that were the source of considerable anxiety among their own parents. They naturally believe despite the sound and fury that greeted the pop culture furors of their own youth, they "came out fine."[22]

Still, there is more to parental waffling over whether a child can watch *Friends* than a memory of listening to "Let's Spend the Night Together." Decisions about what children watch on a television, movie, or computer screen or about what games they are allowed to play ultimately rely on assumptions about the nature of childhood and, by extension, about adult obligations towards the young. These assumptions shifted considerably during the decades during which today's parents matured into their child-rearing years. Those decades brought about a significant change in attitudes towards children, changes that in no small measure have been reflected and promoted in popular culture itself. During this era Americans grew out of old-fashioned notions of childhood innocence and vulnerability and increasingly placed their bets on children's competence, autonomy, and savvy. In other words, as the dangers of popular culture have taken on the aspect of conventional wisdom, a subject of media headlines and parenting magazines, Americans were already committed to an ethos of child empowerment that made any clear response to those dangers highly problematic. The revolution in the view of childhood does not mean that parents never feel queasy about a popular culture that they know makes its profits by representing blood, body parts, and sex and that beckons to their youngest children on a daily basis; but it does mean that they find the moral grounds that would allow them to forbid their 12-year-old from buying an Eminem CD or a *Duke Nukem* video game, or to prohibit their 10-year-old from watching the slasher movie *I Know What You Did Last Summer* or MTV seriously eroded.

The New View of Childhood

The transformation in childhood was a long time in coming, but it was the immediate post–World War II period, the same period that, not coincidentally, saw the emergence of television, that marked the real beginnings of a shift in parental attitudes towards child rearing. This shift was especially noticeable in the swelling ranks of the middle class.[23] Advice literature of the time urged parents to throw off the old-fashioned, Calvinist-tinged training in self-denial and impulse-control that had served as the favored approach of their own parents and encouraged them to allow their children more pleasure, more play, and more opportunities for self-expression. Alarms about the child's character gave way to warnings about his self-confidence. Most Americans associate these new ideas, which are often crudely summed up by the word *permissiveness*, with Dr. Spock, but he was merely the most celebrated of the numerous experts who helped to usher in a new era of parent-child relations that one commentator of the time described as "fun morality."[24] "Parents are likely to succeed best if their attitude is that of friend and helper, rather than that of director or punisher," was the advice from a 1959 pamphlet from the Child Study Association.[25] Adding an aura of sophistication to these ideas were the works of anthropologists such as Margaret Mead, which depicted exotic cultures where children enjoyed an easier, more relaxed approach in everything from weaning to toilet training to sexual activity than in the United States and where presumably neuroses were fewer.[26] Apparently many parents heeded much of this advice. Surveys of the period show that while blue-collar parents continued to cite "obedience" as their chief goal in child rearing, middle class parents prized their children's independence and the warm relations that accompanied the new approaches.[27]

Some observers were not so favorably disposed towards the new parent-child relations. A number of social scientists, most notably David

Riesman, were struck not so much by the more competent and expressive children evoked by experts and advocates as by the weakness and confusion of adults. Riesman's highly influential *The Lonely Crowd* criticized contemporary parents who took their cues from a youth-oriented peer group instead of the authority of their own traditions or their own individual common sense. Increasingly in doubt as to how to bring up their children, "parents turn to other contemporaries for advice; they also look to the mass media; and ... they turn, in effect, to the children themselves."[28] Jules Henry, an anthropologist and even fiercer critic of the midcentury middle class, was especially alarmed at the loss of traditional masculine authority: modern fathers, he argued, were more inclined to participate in their son's activities than to bring their sons into adult interests.[29] As we will see, their critiques bore noticeable similarities to the image of family life as it was coming to be portrayed on television and in the movies.

Highly praised as Riesman's book was, his cautions ultimately failed to influence the future of child rearing. In fact, the already noticeable change in attitudes that had occurred in the 1950s turned out to be only a barely remembered prologue for the revolution in childhood that took place in the late 1960s and 1970s. In all elite sectors of American society—the law, public policy, academia, public health—such a radically new notion of children was taking hold that the 1950s came to seem not the era of a kinder, gentler childhood but a repressive gulag. Parents were now attacked as part of the problem. Parental love was a "force of violence" bent on "destroying most of [children's] potentialities,"[30] in the words of one of the more radical theorists of the time. Soon stories of hidden middle-class cruelties towards children became a staple of magazine cover stories and best sellers and seemed to confirm this critic's view. Teachers also came under fire. A school was a "Blackboard Penitentiary" according to one article in *Psychology Today*.[31] Experts began questioning the long-held distinction between child incompetence and adult competence and, by extension, the assumption that adults had much to pass on to children.[32] For Lawrence Kohlberg, the most influential theorist of moral development at the time, for example, children did not learn right and wrong from adults but through their own thinking. "Children think for themselves," he wrote in an essay, suggestively titled "The Young Child as Philosopher." "The basic ideas of children do not come directly from adults or other children and will be maintained in spite of adult teaching." Believing that children needed to reason their way to moral enlightenment, Kohlberg derided any attempt by adults to transmit social norms and religious codes to children. This, he believed, was as simplistic as trying to hand a child a "bag of virtues."[33]

Legal thinking of the time echos these themes. Child advocates, who were now increasingly likely to be lawyers themselves, urged that the new assumptions about children's competence and independence be given the authority of law. In a 1973 essay made famous during the 1992 presidential election, Hillary Rodham sought to blur the traditional bright-line boundaries between adults and children when she called for a redefinition of childhood in the eyes of the law; "The legal status of infancy, or minority, should be abolished and the presumption of incompetence reversed," she wrote, in matters that "significantly affect the child's future."[34] Around that time, the chairman of the American Bar Association's section on Rights and Responsibilities proposed that "all legal distinctions between children and adults be abolished."[35] These advocates were surprisingly successful. By the late 1960s the Supreme Court had made a number of decisions relating to children and adolescents that, if they didn't entirely do away with "legal distinctions between children and adults," took major steps in that direction. The first and most important, *In re Gault*, granted minors for the first time since the founding of the juvenile court seventy years earlier, the right to counsel, the right to remain silent, and the right to confront witnesses.[36] In 1969 *Tinker v. Des Moines School District* the Court extended to students the "constitutional right to freedom of speech or expression" inside schools.[37] Over the next decade several other major decisions granted female minors the right to seek an abortion without getting permission from or even notifying their parents. The logic behind these decisions shows how much the American Bar Association and the Court were in sync with prevailing opinions of social scientists and public health officials. "There is no factual justification for treating fourteen-year-old women differently, in this regard, from eighteen-year-old women," the American Psychological Association wrote in an amicus brief in one parental notification case that came later on in the 1980s, "there is no basis for the differentiation of adolescents from adults on the ground of competence alone."[38]

The phrase *fourteen-year-old women* speaks volumes about the profound change in thinking about children that was occurring during these years. "Since 1960 the socialization of children has undergone more radical changes than at any time in 150 years," wrote one historian in 1981.[39] Indeed, by the late 1970s blue-collar parents had joined the middle class in rejecting obedience and conformity and claiming "thinking for themselves" as a major goal of their childrearing.[40] Parents in 1976 stressed the "relational interpersonal aspects of parenthood" far more than those in 1957.[41] Adults became less likely to define themselves according to social roles,[42] not just male and female, but parent and child.

When you compare American children to their counterparts in other cultures, it becomes clear that these were not simply abstract ideals. Far more than in other cultures and regardless of age, American children are treated as autonomous, self-directing actors and they think of themselves that way as well. In their attempts to promote independence, American parents are more likely to let their infants determine their own sleeping and eating schedules, to place them in separate cribs in their own rooms, and to "baby-proof" their homes so as to give them freedom to explore their surroundings rather than to be confined on laps, in back slings, or in play pens.[43] By the time they are five years old, American children have a lively sense of individual rights and personal liberty.[44] And when they are teenagers, they are given far more freedom to pursue their own pleasures than adolescents in many other societies. A study of 10th and 11th graders in Hong Kong, Melbourne, and San Francisco found that American kids had "markedly earlier timetables for attending boy-girl parties, dating, choosing [their] own friends, even if parents disapproved, and choosing to do things with friends rather than with family."[45] Other recent surveys show that contemporary American children are much more likely to say that parents treat them like adults than Japanese children and to say that parents treat older and younger children equally.[46] A chapter entitled "Make Her the Authority" in a contemporary guidebook on raising girls captures American thinking in its boldest form. The author approvingly cites the example of a father who encourages his daughter "to be comfortable arguing or being mad at me. I figure if she has lots of practice getting mad at a six-foot-two male, she'll be able to say what she thinks to anyone."[47] It's hard to imagine a parent in Bombay or even Berlin thinking this way, much less finding expert support for their position.

The moral conundrum that faces American parents when they encounter *I Know What You Did Last Summer* or *Dawson's Creek* should be clear enough. On the one hand, they know their child is still a child in the sense of being financially and emotionally dependent on them. They might well see evidence of their child's inexperience and immaturity on a regular basis. They hear a growing public clamor about the dangers of popular culture. Still, they believe that good parents do not simply "turn it off." Rather they encourage and respect their child's autonomy. A while ago, in response to an article about popular culture, I got a letter from a father of two daughters, 5 and 8 years old, that captured the dilemma perfectly. The man was troubled by his girls' fascination with Britney Spears and the Backstreet Boys. "I didn't expect the open sexuality of the music industry to invade my house until my oldest daughter became a teenager," he wrote ". . . How do I get [her] to shy away from the sex-oriented material on her own, the way she does with scary movies or shows?" Consider his dilemma, doubtless a common one in American homes: He may dislike the "open sexuality" of the music his daughter listens to; yet, though his daughter is only 8, he cannot conceive of simply banning the offending music, not because such an effort is hopeless, but because he believes the right thing is for her to choose to do so "on her own." The comments of a 4th grade girl interviewed during an Annenberg focus group reflect a similar commitment to children's independent decision making: "My parents tell me that I will have to suffer the consequences of making bad choices about what I watch."[48]

A moral commitment to autonomous decision making is only one part of the contradiction today's parents find themselves mired in. With children being recast as competent, independent actors, it was inevitable that Americans would also question lingering Victorian sentiments about childhood innocence. Up until the midcentury, children were largely cast as naïfs in need of solicitous protection by adults. In fact, this notion, though inspired by Romantic poets and philosophers, most notably Rousseau, had been central to the bourgeois enterprise. The doctrine of childhood innocence lent weight to both the ideal of "separate spheres," where men went off to their place of work every day and women tended domestic life, and ultimately to the suburbanization of America. Since children needed space (with any luck, green space) and freedom to pursue their fantasies and play as well as to be protected from the seductions and vulgarities of the market, it made sense for mothers to be at home near lawns and playgrounds. The city bred savvy, wise-acre urchins; small towns and suburbs produced simple, suitably naive children who could enjoy their "magic years," in the phrase of one popular advice book of the 1950s.[49] Away from the corruptions of the city, the young child's magic years could then give way to latency, when according to the Freudian theory that greatly influenced psychological thinking at that time, sexual urges remained quiescent and cognitive growth accelerated. Children in a magical, fantasy world or busy exploring and gaining mastery over their new environment needed to be protected from sex, violence, death, and other complex realities of adult life. For their part, adolescents in this pre-pill era had to be discouraged not only from sexual exploration but also from unnecessary titillation.

By 1970, these views, especially as they pertained to teenagers, were under attack. One of the first official salvos came from Justice William O. Douglas in his 1967 dissent in *Ginsberg v. New York*, a case that concerned the legality of a state statute prohibiting the selling of obscene materials to minors. Douglas did not merely reject the constitutionality of such statutes. He scoffed at the very idea that children needed such meddling from adults, condemning the very word *protecting* to mocking quotation marks.[50] Radical feminists of the period and children's liberation advocates also joined in scorning the idea of protection. Protectiveness, they argued, was "an ideology of control," a means of disguising the rule of the powerful over the weak.[51]

It wasn't long before these sentiments moved into the mainstream. By the early 1980s, Marie Winn in her much-discussed book *Children Without Childhood* observed that "something has changed" in the nature of childhood. Instead of a period of protection, it had become "a time of preparation." Winn noted evidence for these new attitudes not just in "a steady stream of barely pubescent girls" in sexually suggestive poses on television, in the movies, and on billboards but in the rejection on the part of many parents of the doctrine of children's innocence and impressionability.[52] Indeed, with memories of government secrecy as well as their own protected 1950s childhoods still fresh in their minds, many seemed to see little difference between protectiveness and censorship and vowed to tell it to their own kids "like it is." "I was determined that there were going to be no more scary secrets, no more J. Edgar Hoover. When I got to be a parent, everything was going to be upfront," one mother put it in a *New York Times* article entitled "Little Big People."[53]

Children's book publishers were quick to adapt to the new era of childhood experience. *Nancy Drew*, *The Hardy Boys*, and even *Little Women* and *Robinson Crusoe* with their cozy, small town family life and fantasy adventures were for magic-years children, not the competent, independent children of the post–Vietnam years who lived in the same world as adults and were tough enough to confront its gritty truths. The New Realists, including Judy Blume and Norma Klein, were among the first to challenge the persona of the old-fashioned, tender, child-reader. Blume's 1970 novel *Are You There God? It's Me Margaret* introduced a gossipy, suburban 6th grade heroine obsessed with "God, bras, and boys," in no particular order. By the end of the decade, children's literature was following the model of the new after-school television specials, which in the guise of public service, "educated" children in such real-life problems as divorce, drugs, alcoholism, and child abuse.[54] In a survey of children's literature over these years, Anne Scott Macleod found not only a reluctance on the part of adults to define a moral world for children, but an eagerness to reveal the most sordid human possibilities. One 1976 book cited by Macleod, *The Late Great Me* by Sandra Scoppettone, begins; "We were the all-American family because at the core, like every other typical family, there was rot."[55] More recent works not listed by Macleod continue the trend. Michael Dorris's 1997 posthumous novel for 8- to 12-year-olds, *The Window*, portrays a world where adults are forever disappearing. The main character's mother is in a detox program, her thoughtless and incompetent father shuffles her from place to place. Brock Coles's *The Facts Speak for Themselves* concerns a 13-year-old girl whose love—the middle-aged father of one of her friends—is shot by her mother's ex-boyfriend. The list could go on.[56]

In a world with children but no childhood, even the youngest tots no longer needed protection from scary secrets. Judy Blume, whose prose style, if not her pubertal themes, was more suited for 2nd graders than 6th, had already attracted early readers who were just starting to struggle through chapter books. But by the 1980s even picture books for nonreaders were joining the trend. The first of this new genre, *Hiroshima No Pika*, published in 1980 and recommended for 5- to 8-year-olds, included graphic descriptions of atom bombs and burning flesh. Five years later came *Rose Blanche* by Roberto Innocenti, billed as a story of the Holocaust through a child's eyes. "It is our duty to tell children some terrible truths," wrote a reviewer of *Rose Blanche* in the *New York Times* in words that would have been greeted with incomprehension by parents just two decades earlier. "If the telling causes horror and sorrow, these are appropriate emotions for certain historical events."[57] The next year brought the publication of *The Children We Remember* by Chana Byers Abell, a book of photos about children of the Holocaust. It was followed in the early nineties by *The House That Crack Built*, a book tracing in pictures the illegal drug business from the exploitation of South American cocoa farmers to inner-city gangs to rich drug lords and *Smoky Night*, a picture book describing the looting, fires, and ethnic tensions of the Los Angeles riots, which earned the prestigious Caldecott award.

Meanwhile, educators were also enlisting in the "new realism." The most remarked-upon shift appeared in sex education. Instead of the old-fashioned sex-segregated classes whose red-faced facts were assumed to be largely irrelevant until the students being taught them were ready to marry, educators increasingly redefined their role as disinterested dispensers of practical information for emotionally and presumably sexually mature decision makers. In many districts, students learned not just the facts of reproduction, but also about methods of birth control and in some controversial instances, about abortion and homosexuality.[58] Already by 1981, according to the Guttmacher Institute, 94 percent of school districts agreed that the major goal of sex education should be "informed decision making,"[59] that is, simply giving kids information necessary for them to make their own decisions. With the emergence of AIDS, the new realism took on new urgency and spread to younger grades, in some cases as early as kindergarten. But sex education was not the only area where the schools were abandoning ideals of childhood innocence. Attempts to fight prejudice led educators to introduce the subjects of slavery, ethnic cleansing, and the Holocaust to children as young as kindergarten.[60]

Of course, the trend towards unflinching frankness in adult dealings with children did not go entirely unopposed. As sex education became increasingly explicit, some parent groups rose up in opposition. Partly in response to this opposition, Congress passed a 1996 bill linking the teaching of sexual abstinence to federal funds, though it is still hard to know precisely how this has played itself out in actual classrooms. In several decisions in the mid- and late 1980s the Supreme Court increased the power of school authorities to control student speech. In one case involving a principal who tried to prevent students from publishing articles on teen pregnancy and their parents' divorce in the school newspaper, the Court affirmed the right of educators to supervise the content of "school-sponsored expressive activities,"[61] that is, to censor student newspapers. But significantly, a number of state legislatures passed their own bills effectively nullifying the Court's decision and reaffirming students' right to free speech in their newspapers. Indeed, at least when it came to printed material, for many, the idea of protecting children had become difficult to distinguish from political censorship and was deemed a position palatable only to the radical right. It is precisely on these grounds that as of today the American Civil Liberties Union and the American Library Association are protesting the Children's Protection Act that would link federal funds to filtering devices on computers accessible to children in the nation's libraries.

Children in the Media Age

Clearly, a transformation of this magnitude in attitudes towards children did not occur in a social or technological vacuum. Changes in family structure played an enormous role in advancing notions of children's competence and in equalizing the status of parents and children. For one thing, during these last thirty years, parents have had fewer children, a factor that social scientists have long recognized encourages more egalitarian modes of childrearing.[62] As of 1964, the lifetime average was three children per woman. By the mid-1970s, the average had fallen below two where it remains today.[63] The movement of mothers into the workforce has had a similar impact on American beliefs. Working mothers tend to hand over more responsibilities to their children at younger ages. Perhaps even more important has been the growth of single-parent families. If only for practical reasons, single parents also tend to give their children more responsibilities and more autonomy in decision making than married parents do. This may go some way toward explaining why children of divorced, separated, or never-married parents are more likely to have televisions in their bedrooms and to watch significantly more television than children in married-couple families.[64]

And that takes us to the profound influence of television itself. Television has made it increasingly difficult to maintain the persona of the innocent, magic-years child. Understanding print required a fairly long apprenticeship in decoding and abstract thinking, but as Neil Postman has observed, television has the capacity to expose the adult world to even the youngest children. "The maintenance of childhood depended on the principles of managed information and sequential learning," Postman has written. By making it impossible for adults to control the release of information, television ensured the "disappearance of childhood."[65]

While it is unarguably true, however, that television helped to break down the boundaries between the adult and child worlds by equalizing access to information, Postman's emphasis on the childhood-destructive effects of the small screen tends to downplay how much the medium, and popular culture in general, simply reflected rather than instigated the broad shift in attitudes about the nature of children. In their published opinions about children, the men and women who write for and decide what is produced for television, movies, records, or computer games don't sound all that different from the experts, advocates, judges, and novelists we have already met. Like them, they are inclined to hold to the view that children are more competent and "sophisticated" than they have been given credit for. Take the example of Cy Schneider, one of the founding intelligences behind the children's network, Nickelodeon. "We must stop treating children as helpless, gullible sheep who need to be carefully watched and protected," Schneider has written in words that are repeated endlessly in trade publications. "Children are not that easy to entertain and persuade. In reality children are intelligent and discriminating and skeptical."[66] The marketers who sponsor children's television shows are equally impressed by youthful competence and sophistication. "The smart, active child viewer is the image behind much of the advertising industry's own research," one scholar has noted. Advertisers present themselves as "friend and equal to the child who, in this scenario is a streetwise, robust kid with abilities that [developmental psychologists] have underestimated."[67]

Still, whatever the moral foundation of this modern respect for children's capacities, the media's interest in the subject has hardly been selfless. Advertisers knew that empowered children could make better consumers than dependent, compliant ones, and they were naturally attracted to media content that could advance that cause. One way that the media could hasten the empowerment of children was by reducing authorities, and parents especially, in the child-consumer's eyes. This was a project media "creatives" undertook with a vengeance. Throughout popular culture, parents attempting to wield authority over their children were—as they still are—often portrayed as uptight anachronisms, clueless dopes, selfish narcissists, or, at best, in programs such as *The*

Cosby Show, playful benignities. And parents get off easy compared to teachers, principals, neighbors, and other adults in children's lives.

The kids on TV are another breed entirely. Savvy and knowing, they are the clever voices of experience. They know the way the world works in a way their parents, being old and stuck in an irrelevant past, never can. In other words, popular culture did not corrupt traditional childhood simply by exposing the young to information formerly reserved for adults. It also undermined childhood by telling and retelling the story of children's abundant capabilities and need for self-expression, which adults were either despotically trying to squelch—usually unsuccessfully—or smiling at in helpless resignation. For children, the appeal was obvious. Popular culture, particularly television, offered them a fantasyland where authority did not stand in the way of pleasure and adventure. For parents, whose role as we have seen was already being redefined in contradictory ways, the effect was even further demoralization. In addition to worrying about violating their autonomy if they tried to get Johnny to eat his peas or Debby to stop seeing the juvenile delinquent from the next town—or, for that matter, getting either of them to turn off the set or turn down the music—they also had to worry about looking like idiots.

The popular theme of uncertain parental authority deferring to youthful self-expression took hold in the 1950s, precisely the same cultural moment that experts were first advising parents to loosen up. Most contemporary commentators view the 1950s as the height of the American patriarchy, epitomized by notorious television shows like *Father Knows Best* and *Ozzie and Harriet*. These shows actually represented not the triumph of old-fashioned parents and childhood, but their swan song.[68] On early situation comedies like *I Remember Mama* and *The Goldbergs*, Dad, stuck in the past, had to learn the ways of the modern world from his children. Indeed by the 1950s, the man of the television house was as likely to resemble the cartoon character Dagwood Bumstead ("a joke which his children thoroughly understand" according to one critic[69]) or the dim Chester Riley in *The Life of Riley* as the serenely smug Robert Young of *Father Knows Best*. During the early 1950s, articles began to appear decrying TV's "male boob" with titles like "What is TV Doing to MEN?" and "Who Remembers Papa?"[70] Ozzie of notorious *Ozzie and Harriet* fame, was reduced from Father to Pop in his children's eyes. Smiling blandly as, apparently jobless, he wandered around in his cardigan sweater, clapping mildly in time to his son's guitar riffs, Ozzie was a portrait of the grinning ineffectuality so despised by social critics like David Riesman and the harbinger of the future of popular culture's pater familias.

The theme of the authenticity of youthful self-expression triumphing over outdated or unsupportable adult authority was not limited to television. At the movies, also, viewers saw the drama of the dense, old-fashioned, authoritarian father or father-figure cut down to size by his enlightened modern children, especially in some of the "teen-pics" geared for adolescent audiences. Consider the plot line of one teen movie entitled *Rock, Pretty Baby*. Jimmy Daley wants to be a rock 'n' roll star. His problem is that his father wants him to be a doctor. Trouble brews when Jim pawns his medical books to buy a guitar, but finally with prodding from Mrs. Daley—it's frequently the mother who acts as mediator between the stodgy father and the younger generation—Mr. Daley comes to see he's been too strict. He demonstrates his conversion by getting five traffic citations rushing Jimmy to his band's live TV performance in an amateur show. The father congratulates Jim after the performance in words whose sentiments the purveyors of popular culture would mine repeatedly over the next forty years; "Sometimes it takes a father longer to grow up than his son."[71]

During the following decades, while the image of the young soared, screen adults took a steady beating. In movies like *Vice Versa, Freaky Friday, Like Father, Like Son,* the three *Back to the Future* movies and, in a slightly different vein, *Big,* children become their parents and parents, their children. Screen prodigies like the hero of the aptly titled *Little Man Tate,* the 16-year-old doctor in the TV series *Doogie Howser,* the 14-year-old "modern pre-woman" in Nickelodeon's early 1990s series *Clarissa Explains It All,* and the 9-year-old lawyer on *Ally McBeal* repeat the theme. On television, carping, droning old-timers who would deny the young their pleasure or fun, adults are the butts of the child-world joke. They are, as the *New York Times*'s Charles McGrath noted after surveying Saturday morning cartoons, "either idiots, like the crazed geek who does comic spots on 'Disney's 1 Saturday Morning,' or meanies, like the crotchety, incompetent teachers and principals on the cartoons 'Recess' and 'Pepper Ann.'"[72]

Feckless parents belatedly recognizing the abilities of their children remains a staple of situation comedy. In the late 1970s hit series *One Day at A Time*, we have the lead character musing of her 15-year-old daughter; "I didn't get to be her age until I was thirty-four." "I remember when I realized I could beat my dad at most things," observes Homer Simpson, Ozzie's cartoon grandson; "Bart could beat me at most things when he was four." But increasingly screen parents were growing so irrelevant, they just about disappeared. The teen films of director John Hughes, which were highly popular in the 1980s, were such an adult-free zone. As one observer described the films, "teenagers rule in a world where youth culture is the only one that matters. Parents in these films are notoriously absent . . . their advice is antiquated, consisting generally of pompous pronouncements about subjects they obviously know nothing about."[73] Teen television—which, judging from Nielsen ratings, often has a large pre-adolescent audience—is much the same: *Beverly Hills 90210, Dawson's Creek*, and to a lesser extent *Buffy the Vampire Slayer*. In one notable episode of *Dawson's Creek*, the lead character stumbles in on his parents in a compromising position on the living room couch. Of course, this being television, the son is entirely cool about this embarrassing moment; it is the parents who turn beet red. The scene is reminiscent of a recent ad for *Time* showing a confused looking middle-aged man and an irritable teen-age boy. "It's time we had a talk about sex," goes the text. "Fine, Dad, what do you want to know?"

The critically acclaimed series *Gilmore Girls* is the most recent take on the theme of parent-child reversal, one that manages to have its cake and eat it too; the parent really is nothing more than a kid. *Gilmore Girls* concerns a thirty-two-year-old single mother, Lorelai Gilmore, and her sixteen-year-old daughter, Rory. *Gilmore Girls* has been praised for eschewing the usual sex-obsessions and sultry knowingness of television teenagers. But what the show lacks in hormones, it more than makes up for in television's staple age-reversals. With her apple-round cheeks, and line-free face, the hyper-active, motor-mouthed girl-woman mother picks fights with her daughter over borrowed sweaters and the size of their "boobs," makes pop culture allusions as obsessively as any fan club teeny-bopper, and mugs and pouts during her weekly adolescent-style tiffs with her own parents. Rory, on the other hand—no surprise here— is the real adult. Sober, hard-working, and thoughtful, she is forever having to rein in her mother's teen antics. That the series was the first show to receive funding during its development from the Family Friendly

Programming Initiative, a conglomeration of advertisers seeking more family friendly shows, suggests that television's age-androgyny is not only no longer subversive, it's utterly wholesome. In an interview with *USA Today* Lauren Graham, who plays Lorelai, unknowingly reveals how deeply the mother-daughter peer relationship resonates today. A viewer told of a fight she had with her daughter that ended up with her saying; "Why can't we just have witty banter like Rory and Lorelai?" "It's a model, in a way," the actress explains about her screen parenting, "for how you wish you could talk to your kid. And for kids, it's the kind of friendship you wish you had with a parent."[74]

In a different society, this popular narrative that adults do not have to be adults who wield authority over the young at all, might be nothing more than escapist fantasy. But as we have seen, in today's America this fantasy is not all that distant from the reality, or at least the officially recommended one. Whether imagined or real, it's a model that in a media-saturated age has become increasingly dysfunctional. There is a disconnect between the way we think about children and the actual conditions of contemporary childhood.

The Flaw in the Philosophy

What advocates of the autonomous, self-choosing, thoroughly informed child have not understood is that their vision is a myth that depends on a considerable degree of social coherence, order, and clarity. Arguably, adults can afford to give kids a good deal of autonomy and information when the range of youthful actions and choices are circumscribed by entrenched custom, the highly developed superegos that tend to breed in closely knit bourgeois homes, and a shared moral order. If for no other reason than the ubiquity and fragmentation of popular culture itself, kids no longer grow up in such a well-ordered landscape.

As much as many of today's parents remember watching hours of television a day and listening to music their parents feared, the truth is that their own children's experience of popular culture is something new in the history of childhood. Children today are utterly immersed in media images and themes. At the same time that the media has become more prominent in their lives, they have less time at home with their parents. The upshot is, as one child psychiatrist has noted, "the rise of media has coincided with a decline in the family as the primary socializing agent."[75]

The problem is bigger than that. The rise of media has coincided—and surely had something to do with—a weakening of both other cultural institutions and alternate forms of pleasure and release. Writing in 1954 about his son's fascination with horror comics, the movie critic Robert Warshow well understood that their plots provided a titillating fantasy of anarchic freedom, probably not so different than children today experience playing *Duke Nukem*. But he could also count on those fantasies being balanced not only by a culture with unambiguous taboos but also by the restraints and complexities inherent in the activities to which the boy devoted most of his time: reading real books, drawing, painting, playing with toads, writing stories and poems, and looking at objects through a microscope.[76] Parents today can't rely on a culture with the same sources of self-restraint. An adolescent today who spends 6 or more hours a day seeped in the anarchic, vengeful fantasies of rap music, violent movies, computer games, and Internet chat rooms has little in common with the boy who loved horror comics in 1954. The boy who loved horror comics lived during a time when he continually bumped against a culture that refused to endorse the reality they represented. But the adolescent today watches the brutal revenge flick *The Basketball Diaries* and hears its themes repeated in the lyrics of his favorite rap song, its images echoed in the music videos he watches, its sentiments repeated by his friends in half-joking conversations, its plot repeated in a creative writing class without teachers or students making much of it (at least before Columbine). He can even read about other kids his age who have already chosen to act on them. No wonder that for some kids, *The Basketball Diaries* begins to seem more than fantasy.

This new landscape of childhood means that at a time when work hours are more demanding and when somewhere around a third of all adults rearing children don't have the helping hand of a spouse, parents need to do something they've never been required to do before perhaps at any time in history: deliberately and consciously counter many of the dominant messages of their own culture. To seriously engage the predicament of their children in a media-saturated and youth-worshipping age means nothing less than this. To get parents to see their role as providing children with a meaningful counter-culture would require a cultural shift of proportions that are, admittedly, difficult to imagine. It would mean nothing less than recovering an understanding of childhood vulnerability; finding ways to distinguish intellectual censorship and needed attempts at shaping youthful imagination; and discovering a palatable, modernized image of authority. It might also mean turning the television off and the music down.

NOTES

1. Emory H. Woodard IV and Natalia Gridina, *Media in the Home 2000: The Fifth Annual Survey of Parents and Children* (Philadelphia: Annenberg Public Policy Center, 2000), p. 41. This survey reports 88 percent of parents saying they supervise their children's use of television. See also Karen Kapland, "California: News and Insight," *Los Angeles Times*, 1 October 1997, p. D2, for the results of a survey of a thousand parents showing 80 percent monitoring TV programs and 72 percent restricting Internet sites.

2. A correlation between heavy television viewing and poor school performance can be found in many surveys, including Woodard and Gridina, *Media in the Home 2000*, and Donald F. Roberts, Ulla G. Foehr, Victoria J. Rideout, and Mollyann Brodie, *Kids & Media @ the New Millennium: A Comprehensive National Analysis of Children's Media Use* (Menlo Park, Calif.: The Henry J. Kaiser Family Foundation, 1999). On obesity see Ross E. Anderson et. al., "Relationship of Physical Activity and Television Watching with Body Weight and Level of Fatness Among Children," *Journal of the American Medical Association* 280 (March 1998), pp. 938–42.

3. Roberts et al., *Kids & Media*, pp. 19–20, 15.

4. Roberts et al., *Kids & Media*, p. 13; Woodard and Gridina, *Media in the Home 2000*, p. 16; Douglas A. Gentile and David A. Walsh, *MediaQuotient: National Survey of Family Media Habits, Knowledge and Attitudes* (Minneapolis: National Institute on Media and the Family, 1999). This survey cites lower numbers—56 percent of 13- to 17-year-olds with televisions in their bedroom, 46 percent of 8- to 12-year-olds, and 20 percent of 2- to 7-year-olds, for an average of 38 percent—which may be partly explained by the fact that his research was conducted a year earlier than Roberts's (personal communication with the author).

5. Woodard and Gridina, *Media in the Home 2000*, p. 3. Roberts et al., *Kids and Media*, also finds that families whose 8- to 18-year-olds are heavy viewers are just as likely to say there are family rules about watching television as families whose 8- to 18-year-olds are light viewers, p. 73.

6. Woodard and Gridina, *Media in the Home 2000*, p. 31. Gentile and Walsh, (*MediaQuotient*) are the exception in finding a greater number of parents citing violence over sexual content as their chief concern about media, p.3.

7. Kelly L. Schmitt, *Public Policy, Family Rules, and Children's Media Use in the Home*, (Philadelphia: Annenberg Public Policy Center, 2000), p. 28.

8. George Comstock, with Haejung Paik, *Television and the American Child* (New York: Academic Press, 1991), p. 51.

9. Schmitt, *Public Policy*, p. 23.

10. David Atkin, Carrie Heeter, and Thomas Baldwin, "How the Presence of Cable Affects Parental Mediation of TV Viewing," *Journalism Quarterly* (Autumn, 1989): pp. 557–63.

11. David J. Atkin, Bradley S. Greenberg, and Thomas F. Baldwin, "The Home Ecology of Children's Television Viewing and the New Video Environment," *Journal of Communication* 41, no. 3 (1991): p. 49.

12. Peter G. Christenson and Douglas F. Roberts, *It's Not Only Rock & Roll: Popular Music in the Lives of Adolescents* (Cresskill, N.J.: Hampton Press, 1998).

13. Bradley S. Greenberg and Lynn Rampoldi-Hnilo, "Child and Parent Responses to the Age-Based and Content-Based Television Ratings," in *Handbook of Children and the Media*, ed. Dorothy G. Singer and Jerome L. Singer (Thousand Oaks, Calif.: Sage, 2001), p. 626–27.

14. Woodard and Gridina, *Media in the Home 2000*, p. 32.

15. See, for instance, Josephine Holz, *Measuring the Child Audience: Issues and Implications for Educational Programming* (Philadelphia: Annenberg Public Policy Center, 1999), p. 21.

16. Schmitt, *Public Policy*, p. 31.

17. Ibid., p. 28. See also Kelly Fudge Albada, "The Public and Private Dialogue about the American Family on Television," *Journal of Communication* 50 pp: 79–110.

18. Woodard and Gridina, *Media in the Home 2000*, p. 39–40.

19. Larry McGill, "By the Numbers—What Kids Watch," *Media Studies Journal* (Fall, 1994): p. 101.

20. Bradley Greenberg, Philip M. Erikson, and Mantha Vlahos, "Children's Television Viewing Behavior as Perceived By Mother and Child," in *Television and Social Behavior*, vol. 4, ed. E.A. Rubinstein, George Comstock, and J.P. Murray (Washington, D.C.: U.S. Government Printing Office, 1972). See also Schmitt, *Public Policy*.

21. Comstock and Paik, *Television and the American Child*, p. 30.

22. Schmitt, *Public Policy*, p. 24, and Comstock and Paik, *Television and the American Child*, p. 62.

23. Actually, though they became especially heated in the 1950s, concerns about the proper use of parental authority are inherent in the American project and go back to the beginnings of the republic. For a discussion of this point and for a more complete account of the history that follows, see Kay S. Hymowitz, *Ready or Not: Why Treating Children as Small Adults Endangers Their Future and Ours* (New York: Free Press, 1999), especially chapter 1.

24. Martha Wolfenstein, "Fun Morality: An Analysis of Recent Child-Rearing Literature," in *Childhood in Contemporary Cultures*, ed. Margaret Mead and Martha Wolfenstein (Chicago: University of Chicago Press, 1955), pp. 168–77.

25. Aline B. Auerbach, *The How and Why of Discipline* (New York: Child Study

Association, 1959), p. 10. See also Dorothy Walter Baruch, *New Ways in Discipline: You and Your Child Today* (New York: McGraw Hill, 1949).

26. Mead's most famous work, *Coming of Age in Somoa*, was actually published several decades earlier, but it was widely discussed in the fifties. See also John W. Whiting and Irvin L. Child, *Child-Training and Personality: A Cross-Cultural Study* (New Haven: Yale University Press, 1953).

27. Duane F. Alwin, "Trends in Parental Socialization Values: Detroit, 1958–1983," *American Journal of Sociology* 90 (1984): 359–82. See also Daniel R. Miller and Guy E. Swanson, *Changing American Parent: A Study in the Detroit Area* (New York: John Wiley and Sons, 1958).

28. David Riesman, *The Lonely Crowd* (New Haven: Yale University Press, 1950), p. 47.

29. Jules Henry, *Culture Against Man* (New York: Random House, 1963), p. 143.

30. R.D. Laing, *The Politics of Experience* (New York: Ballantine Books, 1967), p. 58.

31. Craig Haney and Philip G. Zimbardo, "The Blackboard Penitentiary: It's Tough to Tell a High School from a Prison," *Psychology Today*, June 1975, pp. 26ff.

32. Arlene Skonick, "The Limits of Childhood: Conceptions of Childhood Development and Social Context," *Law and Contemporary Problems* 39, no. 3 (1975): pp. 38–77.

33. Lawrence Kohlberg, "The Young Child as Philosopher" and "Development as the Aim of Education," in *Child Psychology and Childhood Education: A Cognitive-Developmental View* (New York: Longman, 1987). pp. 18, 46.

34. Hillary Rodham, "Children Under the Law," *Harvard Educational Review* 43 (November 1973): p. 507.

35. Quoted in Bruce C. Hafen, "Exploring Test Cases in Child Advocacy," *Harvard Law Review* 100 (1986): p. 447.

36. *In re Gault*, 387 U.S., 1.

37. *Tinker v. Des Moines School District*, 393 U.S., 506.

38. *Thornburgh et al. v. American College of Obstetricians Gynecologists et al.*, 106 S.Ct. 2169 (1986). The amicus brief is reprinted in *American Psychologist* 40, no. 1 (1987), pp. 77–78.

39. Steven Mintz, "The Family as Educator: Historical Trends in Socialization and the Transmission of Content Within the Home," in *Education and the Family: A Research Synthesis*, ed. William J. Weston (New York: New York University Press, 1989), pp. 96–121.

40. Alwin, "Trends in Parental Socialization Values," pp. 359–82.

41. Joseph Veroff, Elizabeth Douvan, and Richard A. Kulka, *The Inner American: A Self-Portrait from 1967 to 1976* (New York: Basic Books, 1981), p. 240.

42. Mark Mellman, Edward Lazarus, Allan Rivlin, "Family Time, Family Val-

ues," in *Rebuilding the Nest*, ed. by David Blankenhorn, Steven Bayme, and Jean Bethke Elshtain (Milwaukee: FSA Publications, 1991), pp. 82–8.

43. Rebecca Staples New, "Parental Goals and Italian Infant Care," Amy L. Richman, Patrice M. Miller, and Margaret Johnson Solomon, "Socialization of Infants in Suburban Boston," and Lois Wladis Hoffman, "Cross-Cultural Differences in Childrearing Goals," in *Parental Behavior in Diverse Societies*, ed. Robert A. LeVine, Patrice M. Miller, and Mary Maxwell West (San Francisco: Jossey-Bass, 1988), pp. 51–64, 65–74, 99–122.

44. Richard A. Shweder, Manamohan Mahapatra, and Joan G. Miller, "Culture and Moral Development," in *Cultural Psychology: Essays on Comparative Human Development*, ed. James W. Stigler, Richard A. Shweder, and Gilbert Herdt (Cambridge: Cambridge University Press, 1990), pp. 130–204.

45. Shirley Feldman and Doreen A. Rosenthal, "Culture Makes a Difference . . . or Does It? A Comparison of Adolescents in Hong Kong, Australia, and the United States," in *Adolescence in Context: The Interplay of Family, School, Peers and Work in Adjustment*, ed. Rainer K. Silbereisen and Eberhard Todt (New York: Springer-Verlag, 1994), p. 107.

46. Cited in Seymour Martin Lipset, *American Exceptionalism: A Double-Edged Sword* (New York: W.W. Norton, 1996), p. 219.

47. Barbara Mackoff, *Growing a Girl*, (New York, Dell Publishing, 1999), p. 44.

48. Holz, *Measuring the Child Audience*, p. 20.

49. Selma Fraiberg, *The Magic Years: Understanding and Handling the Problems of Early Childhood* (New York: Scribner's, 1959).

50. *Ginsberg v. New York*, 390 U.S., 654.

51. Howard Cohen, *Equal Rights for Children* (New York: Littlefield, Adams, 1980), p. 151. In feminist literature, see, for instance, Jenny Kitzinger, "Defending Innocence: Ideologies of Childhood," *Feminist Review* 28 (January 1988): pp. 77–87.

52. Marie Winn, *Children Without Childhood* (New York: Pantheon, 1983), p. 56.

53. Lucinda Franks, "Little Big People," *New York Times*, 10 October 1993, section 6, p. 28.

54. Evidently, this was the same reasoning television executives used about the teen soap opera, *Beverly Hills 90210*. According to Merry White, *The Material Child: Coming of Age in Japan and America* (New York: Free Press, 1993), p. 135, producers of the show view it "as a public service show and a recent episode concerning condom distribution in high school was referred to by sex-education experts and politicians as a watershed moment in television education."

55. Anne Macleod, *American Childhood: Essays on Children's Literature of the Nineteenth and Twentieth Century* (Athens: University of Georgia Press, 1994), pp. 207–8.

56. Deborah Haitzig, *Why Are You So Mean to Me?* (New York: Random House/Children's Television Workshop, 1986); Lynne Jonell, *Mommy, Go Away!* (New

York: G.P. Putnam, 1997); Rodman Philbrick, *Freak the Mighty* (Blue Sky Press, 1993); Michael Dorris, *The Window* (New York: Hyperion Books for Children, 1997); Brock Coles, *The Facts Speak for Themselves* (Arden, N.C.: Front Street, 1997). See also Sara Mosle, "The Outlook's Bleak," *The New York Times Magazine*, 2 August 1998, p. 34.

57. Patty Campbell, "Children's Books," *The New York Times Book Review*, 21 July 1985.

58. Jeffrey P. Moran, *Teaching Sex: The Shaping of Adolescence in the 20th Century* (Cambridge: Harvard University Press, 2000), chapter 6.

59. "Teenage Pregnancy: The Problem That Hasn't Gone Away" (New York: Alan Guttmacher Institute, 1987).

60. Laura R. Petovello, *The Spirit That Moves Us: A Literature-Based Resource Guide: Teaching About Diversity, Prejudice, Human Rights, and the Holocaust* (Gardner, Maine: Tilbury House, 1998). Volume 1 recommends literature, including illustrated picture books, about the Holocaust for kindergarten through grade 4.

61. *Hazelwood School District v Kulmeier*, 484 U.S., 260 (1988).

62. Mintz, "The Family as Educator," p. 104, and Glen H. Elder Jr. and Charles E. Bowerman, "Family Structure and Child-Rearing Patterns: The Effect of Family Size and Sex Composition," *American Sociological Review* 28 (1963): pp. 891–905.

63. "American Families: A Changing Economy and Society," *Population Bulletin* 55, no. 4 (2000).

64. On parental supervision in single parent families, see Sara McLanahan and Gary Sandefur, *Growing Up with a Single Parent: What Hurts, What Helps* (Cambridge: Harvard University Press, 1994), esp. 103ff, and Jeffrey T. Cookston, "Parental Supervision and Family Structure: Effects on Adolescent Problem Behaviors," *Journal of Divorce and Remarriage* 32, nos. 1–2 (1999): pp. 107–22. On television in children's bedrooms see Woodard and Gridina, *Media in the Home 2000*, p. 15, among others.

65. Neil Postman, *The Disappearance of Childhood* (New York: Random House, 1982), p. 80.

66. Cy Schneider, *Children's Television, The Art, the Business, and How it Works.* (Chicago: NTC Business Books, 1989), p. 2.

67. Ellen Seiter, *Sold Separately: Parents and Children in Consumer Culture* (New Brunswick, N.J.: Rutgers University Press, 1993), p. 107.

68. Lynn Spigel, *Make Room for TV: Television and the Family Ideal in Postwar America* (Chicago: University of Chicago Press, 1992), Gerard Jones, *Honey I'm Home: Sitcoms Selling the American Dream* (New York: Grove Wiedenfeld, 1992), and Mark Crispin Miller, "Deride and Conquer," in *Watching Television*, ed. Todd Gitlin (New York: Pantheon Books, 1986), pp. 196ff.

69. Arthur Asa Berger, *The Comic Stripped American: What Dick Tracy, Blondie,*

Daddy Warbucks and Charlie Brown Tell Us about Ourselves (New York: Walker, 1973), p. 103.

70. Spigel, *Make Room for TV*, p. 60.

71. Thomas Doherty, *Teenagers and Teenpics: The Juvenilization of American Movies in the 1950's* (Boston: Unwin Hyman, 1988), especially pp.89–90. Of course, some of the movies geared to teenagers, such as those starring Pat Boone, were far more conventional.

72. Charles McGrath, "Giving Saturday Morning Some Slack," *New York Times Magazine*, 9 November 1997, p. 54.

73. Joe L. Kincheloe, "The Advent of a Postmodern Childhood," in *Kinderculture: The Corporate Construction of Childhood*, ed. Shirley R. Steinberg and Joe L. Kincheloe (Boulder, Colo.: Westview, 1997), p. 36.

74. Robert Bianco, "The Three Gilmore Girls Redefine Family Ties," *USA Today*, 1 March 2001, p. 1D.

75. Jeffrey Jensen Arnett, "Adolescents' Use of Media for Self-Socialization," *Journal of Youth and Adolescence* 24, no. 5 (1995): pp. 519–33.

76. Robert Warshow, "Paul, the Horror Comics, and Dr. Wertham," *Commentary*, (June 1954).

11

The Role of Government in a Free Society

Newton Minow and Nell Minow

This disclaimer appeared before and after a popular program on MTV in which the host, Johnny Knoxville, behaves like an adolescent Evel Knievel. "*Jackass* features stunts performed by professionals and/or total idiots. In either case, MTV insists that neither you nor any of your dumb little buddies attempt the dangerous crap on this show." Instead of riding a motorcycle over a canyon, Knoxville rides a shopping cart downhill or locks himself inside a port-a-potty while it is turned upside down. For teenagers, this is considered fun to watch. Adults probably get more amusement from imagining the delicate negotiations that must have been necessary to come up with a disclaimer that made the lawyers happy without making the show seem un-cool.

The lawyers were presumably happy because the language allowed them to say that they did their best to persuade young viewers not to imitate what they saw, thus preventing liability for damages. But if their goal was to prevent not just liability but actual damages or to communicate the danger of these stunts to impressionable kids, they failed. On January 28, 2001, three young boys were so impressed with an episode of *Jackass* in which the star covered himself with steaks and then barbecued himself that they decided to try it themselves. Jason Lind, age 13, poured gasoline on his arms and legs and lit himself on fire. He was hospitalized in critical condition, and his friend, age 14, was charged with reckless endangerment.

Even *Broadcasting & Cable* magazine, which usually can find no wrong with television programs of any kind, thought *Jackass* had gone too far. The magazine editorialized: "What disturbs us is that the antics have apparently inspired a lot of kids to go out and copy their JACKASS heroes, even to the extent of videotaping their stunts. The result has been serious injuries. It seems only a matter of time before someone kills himself or herself ... MTV can hide behind the First Amendment, and maybe avoid trouble from the government. But the fact that the First Amendment affords protection to panderers is nothing to brag about. And nothing to applaud" (30 April 2001).

The very "coolness" of the disclaimer was attacked by at least one well-known source as the reason it was so easily disregarded. Lind's father contacted his senator, former Vice Presidential candidate Joe Lieberman, to ask him if he could get *Jackass* off the air. In his letter to Viacom, the owner of MTV, Lieberman said that the disclaimer is "self-mocking and trivializes the seriousness of the stunts' potential consequences." He suggested that there was no disclaimer that would be effective for the show's target audience: "I recognize that the program is rated for adults and that it comes with general disclaimers. But there are some things that are so potentially dangerous and inciting, particularly to vulnerable children, that they simply should not be put on TV, and this is clearly one that crosses that line." MTV admitted in a letter to Senator Lieberman that while the show is directed at 18- to 24-year-olds, a third of the audience is 17 or younger. The show later adopted a less self-mocking disclaimer.[1]

World Wrestling Entertainment also has a less-cool disclaimer, directed at parents, on its Web site (parents.wwe.com/). Alongside photos of WWE stars encouraging viewers to register to vote and a testimonial from a mother who says she uses the WWE's *SmackDown!* show to teach her four-year-old colors and pattern recognition, the site says:

> We at WWE have families of our own, so we understand how important it is for parents to take an active role in their children's free time. We encourage all parents to help their children select suitable entertainment, and to understand the differences between fantasy and real life.

Our programs are tailored for teens and young adults, who comprise 50 percent of our audience. About 64 percent of our audience is 18 years of age or older. Some of our viewers are younger children. If parents make the decision to allow their children to watch our programming, we encourage those parents to watch with their children. We urge parents who allow younger children to watch programming to explain that what [WWE] Superstars do on television should not be emulated or attempted in real life.

We do not know if Lionel Tate's mother had that conversation with him. We do know that she was taking a nap when the then-12-year-old killed a 6-year-old girl. The same week that Jason Lind decided to imitate *Jackass*, Tate became the youngest person ever convicted of murder in the United States. Lionel Tate, now 13 years old, is too young to be executed, but he faces life in prison without the possibility of parole for killing Tiffany Eunick.

Tate acknowledges that he is responsible for the massive injuries that killed the girl. His defense was that he did not mean to hurt her. Tate's lawyer said that he was imitating the moves he had seen on television. According to testimony at the trial, Tate did not understand that professional wrestlers were trained to make it look as though they were hurting each other when they really weren't. His lawyer said, "He wanted to emulate them. Like Batman and Superman, they were his heroes. He loved to play."[2]

Like Lind's father, we may be tempted by this story to call for government intervention. The government usually responds promptly and effectively when children are in danger. The government recalls hazardous toys and sets standards for cribs. It requires seatbelts and airbags for drivers and special car seats for infants and small children. Federal and local laws prevent children from buying alcohol and cigarettes.

But when we try to protect children from media we run into a conflict with one of the core principles of American society, the principle of freedom of speech. This is not just a priority. It is the First Amendment to the Constitution, the leading statement of the Bill of Rights, the very definition of a free society. The Supreme Court will uphold limits on freedom of speech only when they are necessary to protect us from a clear and immediate danger. The Court might allow the government to prevent Knoxville or the WWE stars from going on camera to urge viewers to imitate them. But what are the Court's options when television programs include disclaimers—even highly ineffective ones—urging viewers not to imitate the activities they show?

Parents have some control over their children's access to movies, because children have to be taken to the theater and have to have money to pay for tickets. When movies come to video and cable, though, there is almost no way to prevent children from watching them. A 12-year-old has about a 50–50 chance of being able to sneak into a theater to see the raunchy and explicit *There's Something About Mary*. But she or he has a 100 percent chance of being able to see it—or the nonrated "director's cut" of the equally raunchy and explicit *American Pie*—on video, DVD, or cable. And there is nothing short of 24-hour parental supervision to keep a child away from *Jackass*.

How did this happen, and what can we do about it?

Control of the Airwaves

When radio broadcasting began, early in the last century, most democratic countries chose to establish strong, publicly financed broadcasting systems first, followed by commercial systems. Their assumption was that the airwaves were too valuable a resource—for education, for culture, for citizenship—to entrust exclusively to private, profit-seeking companies. Later, when television came in, they stayed with this approach. Japan's NHK and the United Kingdom's BBC were early examples.

The United States went in the opposite direction. For-profit broadcasters were the foundation of the system. The commercial stations got the airwaves to use as they wished, accountable primarily to their shareholders. They did, however, have to make a commitment to "the public interest, convenience, and necessity" in order to get their licenses. The meaning of the term *the public interest* and the nature of the commitment to it has been the topic of heated debate ever since.

One aspect of public interest is a negative, Hippocratic-oath-style commitment to "first do no harm." The other aspect is an affirmative obligation to do some good. Both have been controversial. At one extreme, there are free-market extremists who believe that there should be no public interest obligation of any kind. They point to other media, such as newspapers. Anyone can start a newspaper without any kind of license from the government. The publication is not required to serve the public interest or meet any other standard of behavior. Indeed it is as clear as it can be that any attempt to require such a license would be a violation of the First Amendment. The same applies to movies and recordings of music and production of live theater. Why is television different?

The answer is "scarcity." In theory, at least, anyone who wants to can set up a printing press (or stop by Kinko's) and crank out a newspaper. Nothing except a lack of financing can stop anyone who wants to make a movie, put on a play, or record some music. But the airwaves are limited, and the government has to make sure that the broadcast band is allocated in such a way that people can send and receive clear signals. If we just let everyone broadcast anything, every television and radio would be a Tower of Babel.

When the spectrum is limited, there will always be more applicants than channels. The allocation has to be made on some basis. It could be by lottery. It could be by auction. Either of those would be the choice of the libertarians and the free-market economists. But our system has taken a third option: the decision is based on some subjective and qualitative judgment of the commitment and ability of individual applicants to serve the public. Still, putting the government in the position of evaluating the intellectual and artistic merits of competing applicants would be a legal, political, and logistical nightmare. So the uneasy compromise was some vague promise to act in the public interest, language lifted from a century-earlier statute regulating the first major technological advance in modern communications—the train. The first time the issue of allocating radio bands was presented to the Supreme Court, Justice Frankfurter wrote, "Unlike other modes of expression, radio is inherently not available to all. That is its unique characteristic, and that is why, unlike other modes of expression, it is subject to governmental regulation. Because it cannot be used by all, some who wish to use it must be denied."[3] Thus, the necessity of selecting from among applicants did not violate the First Amendment, even though the selection might be based on a qualitative evaluation of the merits of the applications and the result was that some people would not have the access to television that others did.

The scarcity argument had more force when there were three broadcast networks and hundreds of newspapers. Now we have cable television and look forward to a world of broadband in which it may actually be cheaper to start your own broadcast station through a Web page than it is to pay the costs of copying a newspaper at Kinko's. The scarcity argument is still valid as long as there are not enough channels available for everyone who wants to use one. But it is increasingly difficult to apply an affirmative obligation for each broadcaster to provide programming that meets some standard of "fairness" and addresses the needs of every element of the audience.

The commercial broadcast networks are like old-fashioned department stores, designed for one-stop shopping, providing everything from furniture to notions. Just as department stores languish in huge shopping malls while customers buy what they want from specialty boutiques, the networks are finding that their news programming is being taken over by all-news stations and their children's programming taken over by such boutique stations as PBS and Nickelodeon. So we must now think about whether a policy justified by scarcity of the spectrum should be reconsidered for what might become a post-scarcity world.

The first issue to address is when scarcity will, in fact, disappear from the calculus. The answer is pretty clear: it will be a long time before it does. At this point, around 20 percent of Americans do not have cable and are not expected to get it. Within that 20 percent is a disproportionate number of poor and disadvantaged viewers who do not have a wide range of other options for information and entertainment. That means that the broadcast channels — which will always be limited in number — will continue to occupy a singular and critical position and cannot be treated as though they were no different from cable channels and other outlets.

Even if we assume that the scarcity argument will disappear, there is a second issue: can a complete absence of content-based regulation give us the television we want or need? What would happen if the FCC got out of the business entirely, allocating channels to the highest bidder? No one regulates the Internet, and that seems to have produced plenty of content for every taste. But the highest quality Internet content still comes from outside commercial sources. The *New York Times*'s Web page is sponsored by the *New York Times*. There is minor marginal expense in taking the articles prepared for the subscriber-and-advertiser-supported print publication and posting them online. So far, at least, the online content-providers who have been able to make a profit — pornographers and casinos — support the worst fears of the race-to-the-bottom theorists.

Though the congressmen who created the legal framework for broadcast regulation believed fervently in the power of the marketplace to create and sustain the good life, their enthusiasm was tempered by the bitter and often bloody lessons of the industrial revolution and infused with the spirit of progressivism. They believed that capitalism's rough edges could be smoothed and its strengths magnified through the government's efforts to make sure that the citizens were educated and the children protected. For the foreseeable future, then, we can expect to see some role for the government in allocating and overseeing the broadcast spectrum. That role, however, will continue to be recalibrated. One reason is the changing technologies, but the other reason goes back to a fundamental contradiction between two of the core principles of American politics and culture.

Balancing Free Speech and the Interests of Children

Two passionate convictions collide when we face the challenge of children and popular culture. The first is our commitment to freedom of speech, guaranteed to us by the First Amendment. No right is more cherished or more emblematic of the American ideal than the right to say whatever we want to, whenever we want to, without limits. With some exceptions, our view has been that the cure for inaccurate, outrageous, or even hateful speech is more speech, not less. The second conviction is our commitment to protecting our children. Innumerable laws protect children by requiring that they be immunized, that they ride in special car seats, that they work only very limited hours, even that they be removed from their parents if they are not adequately cared for. While many of these protections are less than a hundred years old, the law has recognized for centuries that children do not have the necessary experience and judgment to be able to make important decisions. We do not allow them to enter contracts, own real estate, drive a car, get married, or vote. They cannot even consent to having sex—it is considered statutory rape if they are under age, no matter what they agree to or even seek.

The collision of these two convictions leaves us with a world in which a 15-year-old is considered too young to consent to sex but not too young to be subjected to an onslaught of sexual situations and imagery in the media. Parents who study food labels in the grocery store to protect their children from chemical additives are unable to apply the same scrutiny to movies, television, music, and video games to protect their children from toxic images and messages. Parents carefully screen babysitters, teachers, and friends and caution their children about not talking to strangers to make sure that the people their children spend time with are caring and responsible. But they are unable to protect their children from the strangers that studies tell us they spend more time with than they spend in school, with family, or with friends—the strangers who come into their living rooms through the television, radio, and stereo to show them a world of irresponsible violence, indiscriminate sex, substance abuse, disrespectful behavior, almost always without consequences.

Can we do better than this? Even if we could return to the era of the Hayes Code in which movies were subject to strict rules that covered everything from the length of a kiss to the mildest of four-letter words and the appropriate portrayal of a clergyman, we would not want to. Adults want to tell and be told stories that require a wider range of complexity than that era permitted. Fights over whether *I Love Lucy* could use the word *pregnant* or *I Dream of Jeannie* could show her belly button seem silly to us now. Nor can we expect self-regulation by the television networks in an era where they compete with cable, videos, and the Internet. If we are going to protect children from Howard Stern's "Lesbian Dating Game" and Jerry Springer's "My Dad Got My Babysitter Pregnant" we have to find some way, consistent with the First Amendment, to set some limits.

Radio

Previous efforts to achieve that balance have met with little success. The first radio regulation law, in 1912, did not even try. Congress at that time anticipated that the primary market for radios would be point-to-point communication, as between ships at sea. Congress assumed that the demand for licenses would be small and imposed no discretionary standard; whoever asked for a license got one. Thousands of Americans, enchanted with the new technology, started broadcasting out of their homes, creating a jumble of signals that ended only when the War Department ordered all amateurs off the air during World War I.

After the war, the U.S. Navy and General Electric created the Radio Corporation of America (RCA), where they were soon joined by Westinghouse, AT&T, and the United Fruit Company. Again, the intention was to focus on international message service, and again, they utterly underanticipated the demand for broadcasting. Westinghouse began the first radio network, KDKA in Pittsburgh in 1920. There was a lot of debate about how to finance this new technology. Some urged that they be underwritten by private philanthropists, as Andrew Carnegie had done with libraries. Some wanted them to be financed by the government, like schools. RCA President David Sarnoff supported a tax on radio sets, as the British had done. AT&T suggested "toll broadcasting," by which the broadcasters would simply be the highway, and providers of programs would be like the truck drivers who pay a toll in exchange for using them.

After the 1912 radio act was thrown out as unconstitutional in 1926, the Radio Act of 1927 established the airways as public property and included the famous language directing that broadcasters serve "the public interest, convenience, and necessity." The new Federal Radio Commission (FRC, later the Federal Communications Commission) began to sort through the broadcasters to decide who could stay on the air. The big losers were the educational and nonprofit stations, deemed "propaganda" or "special interest." Although they asked to have a part of the spectrum set aside for them, the FRC turned them down when the commercial broadcasters objected, promising that they would provide educational programs. The FRC asked the commercial broadcasters to provide "well-rounded" programs that included "religion, education, and instruction, important public events, discussions of public questions, weather, market reports and news, and matters of interest to all members of the family."[4]

They did not. Many programs were created, packaged, staffed, and cast not by broadcasters but by advertisers. In 1922, Herbert Hoover warned that "so great a possibility" as radio should not "be drowned in advertising chatter," but a decade later, his worst fears had come to pass. Franklin Roosevelt was characteristically committed to reform, and by the time he took office in 1933, educators and others were calling for change. Intellectual and political leaders from John Dewey to Alexander Meiklejohn to H.L. Mencken argued that commercial broadcasting was inherently adverse to controversy and dissenting opinion and that it became intractably so by the nature of advertiser-supported programming. They wanted the airwaves regulated like a public utility. Some even pushed for nationalization of the broadcast system. Newspaper publishers, who saw radio as competition for advertisers, initially supported this idea. But then they began to buy radio stations, and changed their minds. Senators Robert Wagner and Henry Hatfield proposed setting aside 25 percent of the spectrum for educational and nonprofit use. The broadcasters, however, proved powerful advocates for the status quo and the reformers were unable to present a united proposal. All efforts at reform failed. The 1934 Communications Act was almost identical to the predecessor Radio Act, except that it added telephony and all other communications technologies to the now—Federal Communications Commission's jurisdiction.

It is worth looking at the arguments raised in this debate, almost seventy years ago, because many of them still resonate in today's discussion of these issues. Just as in recent arguments over the V-chip and the allocation of the digital spectrum, the broadcasters argued in 1934 that it was not necessary to set aside part of the spectrum because they were already obligated to serve—and in fact were serving—the public interest. Indeed, CBS Chairman William Paley promised the Senate Commerce Committee in 1930 that no more than 30 percent of his network's broadcasting time would ever be sold and that the rest would be available for unsponsored educational and noncommercial programs.

The big difference in the rhetoric of that era was that no one made the argument that is always the first one raised by broadcasters today—they never said that efforts to influence the subject matter of their broadcasts violated the First Amendment. It is even harder than imagining a time before television to think back that far and remember that in those days the Supreme Court had made very few First Amendment rulings and the idea of an absolute right to freedom of speech, especially in a context outside political debate, was very far in the future. Even the American Bar Association, back in 1929, did not consider the First Amendment when they weighed into this debate. Incredibly, the ABA supported government censorship, which it found "unavoidable and in the best interests of the public."[5]

Radio raised some important issues that were resolved on the basis of politics and expedience, not public policy. All of those factors would be multiplied many times with the introduction of the next new communications technology, television.

Television

Even with radio's potential to capture an audience and make a great deal of money already established, no one anticipated the impact of television when it was first introduced at the 1939 World's Fair in New York. Some observers dreamed, like E.B. White, that it would create a "saving radiance in the sky," or, like FCC Chairman Paul Porter, that it would "drive out the ghosts that haunt the dark corners of our minds—ignorance, bigotry, fear. It will be able to inform, educate, and entertain an entire nation with magical speed and vividness."

Television remained on hold during World War II. After the war, it grew slowly. In 1949, there were only forty-eight stations. In 1950, only 7 percent of homes had televisions, and only large urban areas received signals. Programming now lovingly remembered as "the golden age" of television reached very few people, and almost all of them were affluent and well educated.

In 1949, during a freeze on new spectrum assignments, FCC Commissioner Freida Hennock, a Truman appointee, again raised the proposal of allocating 25 percent of the spectrum to educational, noncommercial broadcasting. Again, the broadcasters objected. In 1952, the FCC lifted the freeze and 12 percent of the channels were set aside as Hennock proposed, though these channels were mostly at the ultra-high-frequency end of the spectrum that could not be received by most televisions. Four years later, the number of commercial stations had increased by 500 percent, signals reached just about every neighborhood, and televisions were in 73 percent of American homes. With the potential for reaching large numbers of people, programming again became advertiser-driven.

William Paley's promise to keep 70 percent of his network available for noncommercial programs was quickly forgotten. Broadcasters began to soften their claims that they were already serving the public interest by providing educational and public service programming. They did not forget them entirely though. In one memorable case, a station included in its application for renewal of its license the broadcast of *The Flintstones* cartoon series as educational programming for children. Television's failure to live up to its promise was universally decried, but not much was done. The FCC cancelled a few licenses based on fraud or slander but never seriously questioned the license of any major commercial station. The FCC Commissioners were so cozy with the broadcasters they regulated that they regularly went to work for them after leaving the Commission. Some were even cozier than that, and allegations of conflicts of interest led to scandals in the 1950s.

Newton Minow became the Chairman of the FCC in 1961, and when he was asked to address the National Association of Broadcasters, he told them that television was a "vast wasteland," and he expected them to be able to do better. Even then, though, the FCC focused on opening the doors to new sources of programming, not on strengthening oversight through the licensing process. While Minow was at the FCC, they issued rules requiring all new televisions to be able to get UHF stations, so that viewers could see what was then called educational television (now public television). They supported the development of cable channels, too. The idea was that choices and competition would do more to promote better programming than trying to develop content regulation that would withstand a Constitutional challenge.

Surprisingly, the first real public-interest-based challenge to a station's license came not from the FCC, but from an outside group. The United Church of Christ asked the FCC not to renew the licenses of two broadcasters in Jackson, Mississippi, because they had ignored news of local desegregation efforts and censored network news reports that mentioned those efforts. The FCC ruled, four to two, that the church did not have standing; and they approved the renewal. The church challenged the FCC in court and won. The public had a right to say something about the public interest, and when they wanted to challenge a license, they should be heard. In light of the court's decision, the FCC heard the case again and reaffirmed its earlier decision to renew the licenses. The Church of Christ challenged it again, and this time the court told the FCC to consider alternative applicants for the licenses. Eventually, one of the stations did lose its license, as did one in Boston, but those cases remain anomalous, and license renewal has remained all but automatic.

In the next decade, the 1970s, children became the primary concern of reformers. In 1975, the FCC chairman persuaded the networks to set aside the first two hours of prime-time broadcasts as "family-viewing time." The Writers Guild sued the FCC, charging that the rule violated the First Amendment. They won. That was the end of family time. Then the government, in a moment of disastrous stupidity, decided that the

Code of Standards and Practices voluntarily adopted by the broadcast networks was a violation of antitrust law, and they actually sued to get it rescinded. Once these guidelines were gone, the pressure from cable stations and videos led to a further collapse of traditions that had, only years before, required married couples to have twin beds. Suddenly, we had *The Jerry Springer Show, Beavis and Butthead, Married with Children.*

The FCC's authority over content was very limited. Allocation of a limited spectrum could be justified on scarcity grounds; but any attempt to limit content would be challenged on First Amendment grounds, as the Writers Guild had done with the family-viewing-time rules. Any questioning of sexual material or violent material that might be shown to children resulted in immediate screams of government censorship. *Broadcasting & Cable* magazine compared it to book burning.

If we accept the notion that the First Amendment prohibits us from trying to protect our children from the mass media, we have committed the perverse error of divorcing our commitment to free speech—the gift by which the Founding Fathers intended us to deliberate on the public interest—from our commitment to the public interest itself. The First Amendment prohibits limits on the expression of ideas. It does not make all ideas equal. On the one hand, we do not take the "marketplace of ideas" idea far enough. We forget that markets are characterized by failures that they cannot themselves correct. On the other hand, we take the metaphor too literally: very often all that interests us about an idea is the dollar value that the market attaches to it.

Thus it is, for example, that the chief executive officer of Time Warner, one of the largest and most powerful entertainment and media companies in the world, responds to criticism of a rap song advocating that policemen be executed by saying that the critics are infringing on the singer's freedom of speech. Thus it is that when PBS cancels the showing of a documentary that it believes has been doctored to support its conclusion, the producer claims that his freedom of speech has been violated. A dentist organized a letter-writing campaign to raise concerns about afternoon talk shows featuring strippers and serial killers, asking whether this was appropriate at a time of day when children were watching. He was accused of censorship and violating the First Amendment. A rap star whose album was not carried by a large chain of department stores because of its language released a second version, with the offending words bleeped out. Critics called that censorship.

Once and for all, the First Amendment prohibits the government from interfering with freedom of speech. No one but the government can violate that provision of the Bill of Rights. Can the government direct Time Warner not to release the "cop-killer" song? No. They never tried. It was shareholders, including the policemen's retirement fund, who criticized Time Warner for releasing the song. And what happened to their freedom of speech to express that view? Who was protecting that? As Justice Potter Stewart said, there is a difference between the right to do something and the right thing to do. It's time to give the censorship charge a rest and force the people who produce outrageously violent and sexually explicit material to admit that it is not about freedom; it is about money, and as long as they think they can make some, they will continue to produce it.

Encouraging New Developments

There is nowhere that this issue has been as badly mangled as with the debate over the V-chip. The FCC issued a rule providing that new televisions must include a V-chip, a violence-censorship chip that (in theory) allows parents to filter out programs they don't want their children to see. What was the broadcasters' response? Yes, they cried "censorship" and violation of their First Amendment rights. If a V-chip violates their freedom of expression, so does a remote control, so does an off button, so does a parent! What violation occurs when a parent decides that a child may not see, for example, *Pulp Fiction*?

Would we say that it was censorship to require child-guard caps on medications? That is just what a V-chip is. The broadcasters' responses varied from "our programming is so suitable that no V-chip is needed" (eliciting the response: then you should want the V-chip because it will eliminate your competition and send all the viewers to your station) to "it will be so complicated that children will know how to use it better than their parents" (eliciting the response: then you should want the V-chip because you want the kids to watch your programs). The broadcasters are happy to argue to regulators that people are not influenced by what they see on television and then turn around and argue to the advertisers that they should buy ads because people are influenced by what they see on television.

As has happened over and over in this area, the technology has leapt ahead of the regulators. Newton Minow was a supporter of the V-chip and hoped that it would be possible for parents to easily elect the V-chip configurations suggested by the group of their choice, whether the local PTA or a national group such as Kids First! or an organization of churches or synagogues or mosques. Something much better and more workable has come along, ironically, through another technology fought by the broadcasters.

The Telecommunications Act of 1996 required the broadcasters to provide closed-captioning for all of their programs, so that they would be accessible to deaf and hearing-impaired viewers. The broadcasters protested loudly, insisting that it was impossible to achieve and much too expensive. But it turned out to be possible and affordable, and no one really thinks about it any more. In addition, it has turned out to be of enormous value in two ways that were entirely unexpected. First, the largest category of users of closed captioning turns out not to be deaf and hearing-impaired people but immigrants trying to learn English. So the audience is much larger and more devoted than anyone expected. Second, the by-product of closed-captioning is that, in effect, there is a transcript available of every word said on television.

This has made possible a new technology that will be of tremendous value to broadcasters and viewers. Hard-drive-based recorders like TIVO can be programmed to figure out what you like and record it for you. You can tell it to record every episode of *Friends* regardless of channel or time, so that you can get the older episodes in syndication and the new ones broadcast by the network. You can tell it to record every golf tournament on television, or only the ones in which Tiger Woods is playing. You can tell it to record every movie featuring Meg Ryan or every documentary about classical music. And parents can record all programs that do not use certain words that signal that they may be inappropriate for children. All of that is possible because the machines "read" the transcripts to find out what is in the programs.

The FCC would never have been allowed to require the broadcasters to publish transcripts of their programs. But by requiring closed-captioning, they have created a data bank that will help viewers find the programs they want, even in a 100-channel world. With so much coming into our homes, people will rely more and more on this technology to program their televisions for them. And parents will be able to feel more confident than they have in twenty years about what their children see.

We are even more heartened, however, by another development that relies not on new technology but upon the two intellectual pillars of the broadcasters' favorite line of defense—the marketplace and the First Amendment. An advocacy group called the Parents Television Council monitors television that it considers harmful to children and reports its findings to its members, urging them to take action. Instead of complaining to the networks or the government, they go where the money is and complain to the advertisers. The PTC publishes the names and contact information of the networks and advertisers for programs it considers especially bad (and those it considers especially good), so that its members can contact them to express their views.[6]

The PTC selected the WWE's *SmackDown!* show as its primary target, calling it "the most ultra-violent, foul-mouthed, and sexually explicit show on prime-time television."[7] So, they contacted the advertisers, companies such as AT&T, Coca-Cola, Domino's, and Burger King, and asked them not to support *SmackDown!* with advertising dollars. Many agreed. Some responded, as General Motors did: "As soon as we became aware of the content of the program, GM instructed the station contacts that our advertising should never run on this show again."[8] When executives at MCI Worldcom were not responsive, representatives of the PTC, including the late Steve Allen, attended the annual shareholders' meeting to read statements and provide footage from the program.

One of the WWE's trademarks is the "trash talk" of its combatants. So it is not surprising that WWE Chairman (and star wrestler) Vince McMahon wrote to the PTC in October 1999 urging the PTC to "lighten up," reminding them that the WWE's "action-adventure soap opera with comedy central elements" does not use guns or knives and, of course, suggesting that the PTC was attempting to interfere with the WWE's Constitutional rights. In a moment of sublime irony surpassing the broadcasters' claim that expressing criticism of their products violates their First Amendment rights, the WWE responded to the PTC with a lawsuit filed in November 2000, charging "tortuous interference" with business relationships, defamation, and product disparagement. Whether due to the influence of the PTC or not, the WWE's advertising and licensing revenues are down, and so is its stock.

It seems that the role for the government will continue to be limited. It can encourage and support choices, but it cannot push for content regulation beyond demanding that programmers provide accurate enough disclosure of what the content is for parents to exercise some discretion. That is still a very complex area. The Motion Picture Association of America, which rates feature motion pictures released to theaters, has hundreds of movies to screen and plenty of time before release to review them. Even so, most people do not think it does a very good job, despite the recent addition of the basis for the rating. Television produces tens of thousands of hours of programs, many with some of the most troubling content, such as the news, with no time for prior review. And there is also the problem of human nature—children will always want whatever we tell them is too old for them. Predictably, the primary impact of the television rating system was a cacophony of howls across America, "I don't want to watch that! It's rated TV-Y, and that means it's for babies!"

But we draw some hopeful conclusions from the recent impact of such nongovernmental entities as the PTC and from evidence of a growing consumer backlash. In 2001, family movies *Monsters, Inc., Shrek,* and *Harry Potter* led at the box office. The appetite for raunchy material seems to be waning, even from the core teenage audience. Movies such as *Little Nicky, The Animal,* and *The Adventures of Pluto Nash* have all flopped recently. On television, *Sesame Street* has been going strong for thirty years and has been followed by outstanding programs such as *Arthur, Puzzle Place, Blue's Clues,* and *Between the Lions.* There is more, both in quantity and quality, for young children on television now than ever before, although we still criminally ignore children from 9 to 16. We do not think we will ever return to the innocent days of *Father Knows Best* and *Happy Days,* but we are confident that good programs will be there for people who want to watch them.

NOTES

1. It now reads: "WARNING: The following show features stunts performed by professionals under very strict control and supervision. MTV and the producers insist that neither you or [sic] anyone else attempt to recreate or perform anything you have seen on this show. MTV insists that our viewers do not send in any home footage of themselves or others being jackasses. We will not open or view any submissions, so don't waste your time." Nevertheless, even with this amended warning, teenagers continue to injure themselves in an attempt to imitate or inspire the *Jackass* show. An 11-year-old boy injured himself when he soaked a rag in degreaser, wrapped it around his leg, and lit it on fire. A 16-year-old boy filmed himself being hit by a car. A 19-year-old ran through the rain in a hospital gown, brandishing a

chain saw. According to an Associated Press story in the 25 April 2001 edition of *USA Today* entitled "MTV Shuns Responsibility for Stunts," an MTV spokeswoman, Jeannie Kedas, said it's "incredibly upsetting" when young people hurt themselves, but MTV is not responsible.

2. A libel action brought by the WWE was settled when Tate's lawyer issued a statement apologizing for this defense. He now says that he does not believe that watching the WWE's television show was the reason Tate killed.

3. *National Broadcasting Co., Inc., et al. v. United States*, 319 U.S. 190 (1943).

4. *In the Matter of the Application of Great Lakes Broadcasting Co.*, FRC Docket No. 4900, 3 FRC Ann Rep. 32 (1929).

5. Cited in Newton Minow and Craig LaMay, *Abandoned in the Wasteland: Children, Television, and the First Amendment* (New York: Hill and Wang, 1995): p. 78.

6. See, for example, www.parentstv.org/takeaction/advertise.html.

7. www.parentstv.org/advertisinginfo/WWESmackdown1.html.

8. Then there was the reply from Federated Department Stores: "Let me assure you that the day any of our stores sign on to sponsor world wrestling [the WWE] is a day to expect blizzard conditions in hell." See www.parentstv.org/advertisinginfo/WWEsGoodGuys.html.

Index

Note: Page numbers in *italics* indicate figures and tables.

Communications Decency Act (1998), 86

community, self-created autonomous, of adolescents, 7

competition and aggression, 144

computers: in classrooms, 31–32; number of in households, 23; video games and, 146

Conker's Bad Fur Day (Nintendo), 28–29

consumerism: contradictions of, 56–57; objectification of body and, 50–52; reduced media exposure and, 205–7, *206, 207*; time spent on activities of, 55. *See also* advertising

Cooper, Lee, 112

"copycat violence," 49

The Cosby Show, 228–29

Cosmo Girl, 217

courts, evidence requirements for, 184

cultural uses and music preferences, 105–6

The Culture of Narcissism (Lasch), 55–56

culture of obscenity, 42–45, 60–62

curriculum: content and values, 25–30; formal *vs.* informal, 19–25; for reducing media exposure, 198–200

dancing to music, 128–29, 130–31

Dawson's Creek, 217, 222–23, 231

depression: high-risk players and, 169, 182; music listening and, 102–3; prevalence of, 4

desensitization to violence: effects of, 172–73; instrumentalism and, 49, 50; as outcome of viewing violence, 74–75, 175–76

Dewey, John, 248

Dickinson, Roy, 51

disengagement: of adolescents, 4; of people from neighbors, 9

Dole, Robert, 98

Doom, 149

Dorris, Michael, *The Window,* 225

Douglas, William O., 224

downward social comparison, 102–3

driving/racing games, 147

drugs. *See* alcohol; substance use

Duke Nukem, 147, 219

eating disorders, 52–53

ecological study, 194

educational approaches to media: accommodation, 30–32; civic reasoning, 36; civil society and, 36–37; good, promoting acquaintanceship with, 35–36. *See also* media literacy

Elshtain, Jean Bethke, 54, 56, 58, 61

Eminem, 4–5, 219

emotion regulation, problems in, 181–83

emotions. *See* feelings

empathy: attitudes toward violence and, 176–77; bullying and, 180; guilt and, 174–75; moral conscience and, 50; overview of, 173–74

engaged resistance, 60–61

epidemiological study, 194–95

ethnicity: jazz and, 129; music video use and, 107–8; rap music and, 136; time of interaction and, 193

Etzioni, Amitai, 42

Eunick, Tiffany, 242

Evans, Dylan, 20

Ewen, Stuart, 50–52

exposure, cult of, 45, 46

The Facts Speak for Themselves (Coles), 225

family environment: attitudes toward children and, 227; media exposure and, 232–34; sexual content exposure and, 78–79. *See also* parents; raising children

Family Friendly Programming Initiative, 231–32

fandom, obsessions of, 22

Father Knows Best, 229

fear and violence on television, 75

Federal Communications Commission, 249, 251, 252, 253, 254

Federal Radio Commission, 248

feelings: catharsis and, 139–40, 169–70; fandom and, 22; guilt, 174–75; media and, 21; music and, 101–4, 139; scorn as social cement, 23; self-conscious, 173. *See also* empathy

field experiment, 196

filters, 86–87

First Amendment of Constitution, 2–3, 242–43, 249, 251–52, 253

first-person shooter game, 145–47

flight simulation games, 148

Flight Unlimited, 148

freedom of expression, 140

freedom of speech: commitment to public interest and, 252; protection of children and, 242–43, 246–47; in schools, 226–27. *See also* First Amendment of Constitution

frisson, 127

Funk, Jeanne, 158

gambling, 85

Game Boy, 144, 168

"gangsta" rap, 4–5, 98, 137, 141

gender: affective uses of music and, 102; music depicting sex and, 110; music listening and, 100; music video use and, 107–8; social uses of music and, 105; television exposure and, 67; video game playing and, 145

General Aggression Model, *159*, 159–61, *161*, 162

Gilmore Girls, 231–32

Ginsberg v. New York, 224

girls: as objects, 52–53; violent video games and, 177. *See also* gender

Gleason, Jackie, 130

The Goldbergs, 229

good, promoting acquaintanceship with, 35–36

Gore, Tipper, 58, 98, 214

government regulation: of airwaves, 243–46; of Internet, 86; of radio, 247–49; of television, 250–53, 255–56

Graham, Lauren, 232

Greenberg, Bradley S., 216

Greeson, Larry, 116

Grossberg, Lawrence, 105

guilt, 174–75

Gurstein, Rochelle, 45–46, 47

Hansen, Christine and Ranald, 116

Harris, Eric, 149

hate speech / hate groups, 85

Hatfield, Henry, 249

Hayakawa, S. I., 100

heavy metal music: fans of, 115, 138–39; lyrics of, 109, 111; message of, 98, 116; as transgressive, 134–36

Hendrix, Jimi, 131

Hennock, Freida, 250

Henriksen, Lisa, 97, 99

Henry, Jules, 220

Henry J. Kaiser Family Foundation studies: mass media exposure, 66; music listening, 98–99; sexual behavior on television, 9, 69–70; sources of adolescent information, 67–68

Hewlett, Sylvia Ann, 48–49, 53

high-risk players: bullies and victims, 178–81; children with emotion regulation problems, 181–83; cognitive scripts and, 170–72; desensitization and, 172–73; identifying, 177; multiple risk factors and, 183; overview of, 169; protection of, 184–85; time commitment and, 183; younger children, 177–78

Himmelfarb, Gertrude, 42

hip-hop. *See* rap music

Hiroshima No Pika, 225

Hispanic youth and music listening, 100

HIV infection, 76

Hollywood, 29–30

homicide, 73

Hoover, Herbert, 248

The House That Crack Built, 226

Hughes, John, 231

hyperindividualism, 54–56

Ice Cube, 137

I Know What You Did Last Summer, 219, 222–23

incoherence of world, 56–57

income: disposable, of children, 1–2, 10, 52; media use and, 24. *See also* consumerism

independence, image of, 106

industrial revolution, 6

Innocenti, Roberto, *Rose Blanche*, 225

In re Gault, 221

institutions, community, 5, 6–7, 233

instrumentalism, 48–54

interdicts, 126–28, 141

interest, 20–21

Internet: blocking technology for, 86–87; in classrooms, 31–32; content on, 3, 81–82, 245; dangers of, 11, 83–85; downloading video games from, 146; government regulation of, 86; interactivity and, 81, 84; media literacy and, 87; pornography on, 84; use of, 24–25, 82–83

interruption, 21–22

intimacy: degraded version of, 48; ideology of, 45–46

I Remember Mama, 229

Jackass, 240–41

jazz, 128–29

Joe Camel, 10

John Paul II (pope), 56, 61

Joplin, Janis, 131

Katz, Jack L., 127

KDKA, 248

Kilbourne, Jean, 52–53

Kinder, Marsha, 107

Kinkel, Kip, 85

Kiss, 132

Klebold, Dylan, 149

Klein, Norma, 225

knowledge: feeling and, 20–21; increasing with television and Internet time, 3

knowledge structure, 159, 160, *161*, 170–72

Knoxville, Johnny, 240

Kohlberg, Lawrence, 220–21

Kubey, Robert, 33

Kunkel, Dale, 69–70

laboratory experiment, 196

Lasch, Christopher, 55–56

The Late Great Me (Scoppettone), 225

learning process and exposure to media violence, 160, 161, 170–72

legal status of children, 221

Lewin, Kurt, 162

libertarianism, 58–59

Lieberman, Joe, 241

Lind, Jason, 240–41

The Lonely Crowd (Riesman), 220

Lowenstein, Doug, 149–50

Lull, James, 105

Macleod, Anne Scott, 225

Madonna, 4–5

mainstream culture. *See* popular culture

Marilyn Manson, 54, 98

McGrath, Charles, 230

McMahon, Vince, 255

Mead, Margaret, 219

media: empowerment of children by, 228–29; level of use, age, and, 24; pervasiveness of, 25; reform program for, 36–37; rewards of, 21–22, 25–26

media literacy: benefits of, 185; Internet activity and, 87; parents teaching, 164; positives and negatives of, 35–36; risks of, 61; as teaching strategy, 32–34

Meiklejohn, Alexander, 248

Mencken, H. L., 248

Merrow, John, 34

messages in music: heavy metal, 135–36; love and sex, 109–11; overview of, 108–9; punk, 133; rap, 136–37; substance use, 112–14; violence, 111–12

Metallica, 135

meta-mood, 103

Minow, Newton, 251, 254

moral behavior, development of: age and, 177–78; attitudes toward violence and, 175–77; emotion regulation and, 181; empathy and, 173–74; guilt and, 174–75; overview, 173

moral sense: development of, 8, 50; impact of exposure to sexuality on television on, 77; parents and, 222–23; politics and crisis in, 57–59; reasoning and, 220–21; as relative and subjective, 42–44

Morrison, Jim, 131

Mortal Kombat, 144–45, 146

Motherhood Project, 40, 54, 57, 60–61

Motion Picture Association of America, 256

movies: antiparent theme in, 230; slasher films, 77–78, 219, 222–23; teaching, 35–36; on television, 69, 71; tobacco and alcohol use in, 72–73

MTV, 217, 219, 240, 241

music: affective uses of, 101–4; content-related effects of, 114–19; cultural uses and preferences, 105–6; history of, 141; jazz, 128–29; messages in, 108–9; mood and, 97, 102–3, 139; popular, at the edge, concerns over, 125–26; punk, 132–34; rock 'n' roll, 129–31; socialization and, 98, 104–5; time spent with, 97, 98–100; as transgressive, 126–28, 137–41; uses and gratifications of listening to, 100–101; views of, 96–97. *See also* heavy metal music; messages in music; rap music; rock music

musician: reputation of, 114; style of, 130, 131

music videos: alcohol in, 113; attitudes toward premarital sex and, 76–77; content-related effects of, 116–19; love and sex themes in, 110–11; substance use in, 73; time spent watching, 100; uses of, 107–8; violence in, 69, 111

Nader, Ralph, 52

narcissism, 55–56

National Longitudinal Study of Adolescent Health, 4

National Television Violence Study, 68

Ndibe, Okey, 41–42

news media, misinformation in, 150–52, *151*

newspaper, 243–44

Nickelodeon, 228

Nintendo console video games, 144–46

North Carolina language/communication-arts guidelines, 33

obscenity: culture of, 42–45, 60–62; definition of, 46–47, 48; effects of viewing, 9–10; instrumentalism and, 48–54; legal debate over, 46; sale of to minors, 224. *See also* pornography

Obscenity and Public Morality (Clor), 46–47, 48

Oldenberg, Don, 40

Oliver, Mary Beth, 102–3

One Day at A Time, 231

Ozbourne, Ozzy, 135

Ozzie and Harriet, 229–30

Paley, William, 249, 250

parallel processing, 22–23

paranoia and consumerism, 51–52

parents: antiparent theme, 229–32; as children's friends, 12; concerns of, 11–12; contradictions between what is said and what is done by, 215–19; emotional bond between children and, 5–6; interests of children and, 13; level of education of and children's exposure to television, 67; peer pressure on, 217–18; supervision of media diet by, 41, 162–64, 184–85, 216–17, 233–34; values and, 1, 2. *See also* raising children

Parents Music Resource Center, 134

Parents Television Council, 214, 255

parties, "theme" birthday, 41
Pattison, Robert, 128
Pleasant-Jones, Loretta, 40
politics: moral crisis and, 57–59; in music, 132, 134, 137
Pong, 143
popular culture: antisocial messages in, 53–54; as appalling, 39–40; childhood and, 229; curriculum of, 19–20, 21–22; degradation of, 13; expressive repertoire of, 28–29; focus on, 22–23; Hollywood and, 29–30; inescapability of, 40–42; interest in, 20–21; oppositional use of music and, 105–6; opting out of, 59–60; sexual images in, 47–48; as shallow, 26–27; as social cement, 23; as teaching device, 32; toxic version of, 3
pornography: business of, 42–44; on Internet, 84; propriety and, 44–45; "virtual" child, 2
Porter, Paul, 250
Postman, Neil, 55, 227–28
pregnancy, teen, 4, 76
premarital sex, attitudes toward, 76–77
presidential campaign of 2000, 214
Presley, Elvis, 129–31
Primedia Corporation, 31
privacy issues and Internet use, 85
proportion, loss of, 54–56
propriety, 44–45, 47
prosocial behavior and empathy, 174
protection of children and freedom of speech, 242–43, 246–47
prudophobia, 12
public interest, broadcasting and, 243–44, 252
public policy, 163–64
public school, 6–7
public *vs.* private experience, 45–48, 54
punk music, 132–34
Putnam, Robert, 9

Quayle, Dan, 29

radio, 243, 247–49
Radio Act (1927), 248
Radio Corporation of America, 247
Rainbow Six, 147
raising children: popular culture and, 40–42; problems in, 1–3; shift in attitudes toward, 219–23; social order and, 39; standard-setting and, 13–14
Raising PG Kids in an X-rated Society (Gore), 214
Ramboldi-Hnilo, Lynn, 216
randomized controlled trial, 195–96
rap music: alcohol in, 112–13; fans of, 115; "gangsta," 4–5, 98, 137, 141; lyrics of, 98, 109–10, 111; as transgressive, 136–37; videos, exposure to, 117
rating system: Motion Picture Association of America, 256; television, 216–17, 256; video games, 148–49, 163–64, 184
reality, perceived, and exposure to sexual content, 78
reducing media exposure: aggressive behavior, effects on, 200–204, *202*, *204*; conceptual model, *198*; consumeristic behavior, effects on, 205–7, *206*, *207*; curriculum for, 198–200; effects of, 200, *201*; implications of, 207–10; study of, 197–98; types of studies, 194–97
regulation. *See* government regulation; rating system
research: directions for, 164–65, 183–84; ecological study, 194; on effects of music, 140–41; epidemiological study, 194–95; on exposure to violence in media, 74, 149–52; field experiment, 196; laboratory experiment, 196; meta-analysis, 152–53; on music listening, 99; natural experiment, 195; on popular music, 119; prospective study, 195; randomized controlled trial, 195–96. *See also* reducing media exposure
rewards of media, 21–22, 25–26

on, 9–10, 68–69, 74–76; for young children, 256
terrorism, 85
textbook, dumbing down of, 32
third-person fighting game, 145
time of interaction: adult perception of, 97–98; age, class, and, 25; education and, 25; with electronic media, 9, 143–44, 215; with electronic vs. print media, 23–24; high-risk players and, 183; with music, 97, 98–100; with music videos, 107; reducing, 164, 193; with television, 66–67. See also reducing media exposure
Tinker v. Des Moines School District, 221
TIVO, 254
transgressive, music as, 126–28, 137–41

United Church of Christ, 251
U.S. Surgeon General, 75–76
utopian experiments, 59–60

values: community institutions and, 5, 6–7; crudeness, 28–29; of media, 27; norms and, 7–8; of parents, 1, 2; violence and, 27–28
V-chip, 12, 253–54
VCR, 67
victims of bullying, 178–81
video game players, number of in households, 23
video games: Conker's Bad Fur Day (Nintendo), 28–29; effects of violence in, 152–58, 162–64; history and content of, 143, 144–48; patterns of exposure to, 67, 144; realism of, 184; values, violence, and, 27–28; violence in, 11, 144–49, 162–64; violent, preference for, 176–77. See also high-risk players
videos. See music videos
violence: aggression and, 49–50, 74; in cartoons, 149; children involved with, 73–

76; "copycat," 49; definition of, 168; desensitization to, 49, 50, 74–75, 172–73, 175–76; fear and, 75; impact of by context factor, 69; in music, 111–12; negative effects of, 9–10, 149–52; preference for in video games, 176–77; in programs viewed by young children, 9; in rap music, 137; school shootings, 11, 65, 98, 149, 178; sexualized, 77–78, 147; sources of influence on behavior, 185; on television, 9–10, 68–69, 74–76; values and, 27–28; in video games, 11, 144–49, 152–58, 162–64. See also aggression
vulnerability: to transgressive music, 140; to violent video games. See high-risk players

Wagner, Robert, 249
Warshow, Robert, 233
West, Cornel, 48–49, 53
Westinghouse, 247, 248
White, E. B., 250
Williams, Rose Ann, 116
Wilson, Barbara J., 68
The Window (Dorris), 225
Winn, Marie, 224
Wolfenstein, Martha, 29–30
Wolfenstein 3D, 144, 145–46
women: as objects, 52–53; perception of African American based on rap videos, 118. See also gender
workforce, children in, 6
World Wrestling Entertainment, 241–42

Yang, Edward, 22
Yi Yi (A One and a Two), 22
Yo-Yo, 118

ZapMe!, 32
Zillman, Dolph, 102, 103, 117–18